T0099803

Running Away From Me

By

David Allan Reeves

Order this book online at www.trafford.com
or email orders@trafford.com

Most Trafford titles are also available at major online book retailers.

Note for Librarians: A cataloguing record for this book is available from Library and Archives Canada at www.collectionscanada.ca/amicus/index-e.html

Printed in Victoria, BC, Canada.

ISBN: 978-1-4269-0986-3

We at Trafford believe that it is the responsibility of us all, as both individuals and corporations, to make choices that are environmentally and socially sound. You, in turn, are supporting this responsible conduct each time you purchase a Trafford book, or make use of our publishing services. To find out how you are helping, please visit www.trafford.com/responsiblepublishing.html

Our mission is to efficiently provide the world's finest, most comprehensive book publishing service, enabling every author to experience success. To find out how to publish your book, your way, and have it available worldwide, visit us online at www.trafford.com

Trafford rev. 08/26/09

www.trafford.com

North America & international
toll-free: 1 888 232 4444 (USA & Canada)
phone: 250 383 6864 • fax: 812 355 4082

Endorsement

"Running Away From Me is a must read book for anyone suffering from addiction or has a loved one suffering from this disease. David's depiction of his constant struggles is all too familiar of those that have started down this road of destruction. It is my belief that nobody starts using drugs with the expectation of becoming an addict. The progression from having a good time to using to survive is a slippery slope that most people have difficulty in comprehending. I am fortunate to work with addicts. Those that are able to rehabilitate become productive members of our society. Because of the stigma associated with addiction most people don't get the help that they or a loved one needs. The field of addiction has always encouraged those in recovery to protect their anonymity. Unfortunately by doing so our successes have been minimized and failures magnified. If you see yourself or someone you love heading down the same path as David don't believe that it "won't happen to you". The consequences of addiction are all too real. I commend David for being brutally honest and hope that others may learn from his experiences."

George Crisco, Executive Director of The Friary.

The Friary celebrates over 30 years of helping people overcome life's challenges

The Friary, a service of Lakeview Center, Inc., is a center for the treatment of alcohol and drug dependencies and related problems. The Friary's residential treatment center is located outside of Gulf Breeze, Florida, on beautiful Pensacola Bay. The site was once a retreat for retired Franciscan friars, and since 1977, the tranquil, serene setting has proven to be ideal for those beginning the recovery process. In addition to residential The Friary offers detox and intensive out patient services. In 1996, the Friary became a service of Lakeview Center, Inc., which is an affiliate of Baptist Health Care, a regional network of hospitals and other health care facilities.

4400 Hickory Shores Blvd. • Gulf Breeze, Florida 32563 • Local: (850) 932-9375
Toll Free: 1-800-332-2271 • Fax: (850) 934-1281
TheFriary@bhcpns.org • Pensacola, FL

In Loving Memory

Of Brian, may all your pain have not been in vain.

Also to my beloved grandmother, Vera.

Acknowledgements

I would like to thank my mom for retyping my illegible manuscript, finding my editor, Barbara Ardinger, cover designer Sundara Fawn and a publisher, and telling me that I can do anything I want to, and many other things besides being my mom.

And thank you to Misty for making the right suggestion at the right time.

I also want to thank the following for taking the time to read my rough draft and giving me words of encouragement: Juan "Bruce" Garcia, Anthony Patrick El, Billy Turner, Morris Gullet, Derrick West, Eddie Wynn, Pat Schwartz, and Kevin Kirkpatrick.

Disclaimer

The events related in this book are based on actual events; however, every effort has been taken to hide the identity of some individuals. As the saying goes—but for our own, "the names have been changed to protect the innocent." In some instances names and other information has been changed to protect all parties concerned. Any similarity to existing names (other than those of the authors) is purely coincidental.

Contents

Introduction

I started writing this book when I was thirty-seven years old, had been in prison for seven years, and clean for barely three years. When I started writing, it wasn't my intention to publish a book. It didn't cross my mind until I started letting other people read what I had written and they encouraged me to continue writing. Once I started, I couldn't stop. It gave purpose to what felt like an otherwise meaningless existence.

I went back to the beginning of my life and wrote until I reached the present. By then, I had turned thirty-nine and had close to five years of uninterrupted sobriety. I learned a lot about my addiction while writing this book, much more than I would have learned otherwise. The act of sitting down and writing for many hours each day made me think long and hard about my inexplicable behavior. After I finished writing my first rough draft, I continued to learn more about addiction by reading everything about the subject I could get my hands on. The urge to keep adding what I was continuing to learn was strong, but at that rate, I would never have finished. Life is a work in progress.

It may seem falsely conceited and egocentric to write a book about one's life and expect others to want to read it. But I feel as if it is something I had to do. The alternative would have been to do nothing, and in prison, there is not a whole lot one can do anyway. If I'm expecting anything from the readers of this book, I'm expecting to scare the hell out of anyone who is using drugs or is even thinking of using. Not everyone who uses will go to the extremes I went to, but why take the chance? Why play Russian roulette.

My story is not unique. I've heard these same war stories over and over again in prison. Just different places and different faces. I just happened to put my story down on paper.

I've said all that to say this: most of what I've written, I wrote while blindly groping for answers to my problem. A lot of my opinions are just that - opinions. If I offend anyone, I apologize for not being wholly enlightened or politically correct. I once read that we do not see the world as it really is, but we see the world as we are. This book reflects how I was and what I thought of my past at this brief window in time.

Right now the thought of publishing this book feels similar to thinking of standing naked in front of a crowd. Here are all my flaws and imperfections on display. Ugly, but human. No excuses.

And finally, some names and identifying characteristics have been changed.

Chapter 1
From Sunrise to Sunset

How can you expect a man who's warm to understand a man who is cold?

-ALEXANDER SOLZHENITSYN
A DAY IN THE LIFE OF IVAN DENISOVICH

The drug incubus is still harassing me, even though I've stayed clean for more than three years. In my dream, I'm sitting in a hotel room with pill bottles, crack stems, and other assorted paraphernalia scattered about. I crush a morphine tablet and put the powder in a spoon, add water, stir, and add a piece of cotton to the mixture. As I stick the needle into the cotton, I accidentally knock the spoon to the floor, spilling the liquid. I try again. This time I add too much water and dilute the drug. I'm getting frustrated, so now I crush five pills and put the powder in a cup. Now I've got a huge ten cc syringe, which I fill up with water from the sink. But the water is brown and dirty when I squirt it into the cup.

I have to start all over again. Before I can begin, there's a knock on the door. Is it the police? I just got out of prison and I've already robbed a drug store. What the hell am I doing? I was going to stay straight. If I go to prison again, it will be for the rest of my life. I don't want to do drugs anymore. I don't want to break the law anymore. I don't want to go to prison anymore.

Suddenly I hear my Timex Iron man watch beeping. It wakes me up from another recurring nightmare. It's five a.m. and a relief to know that I am actually in prison and clean instead of free and doing drugs. The latter is a worse prison than the former.

I fix a cup of instant coffee with the lukewarm water from my sink and sit in the dark, listening to my Walkman radio as I wait for the CO (correctional officer) to unlock my cell door at five-thirty.

I'm in the United States Penitentiary in Pollock, Louisiana. Pollock houses fifteen hundred violent offenders of federal law, mostly big-time drug dealers, bank robbers, murderers, and gun law violators. I'm serving fourteen and a half years for three counts of bank robbery and one count of brandishing a firearm during a crime of violence. There are twelve housing units here at Pollock. I live in the "program" unit, so called because to live in this unit we are required to participate in the CODE program, which is a behavior modification curriculum designed to show us criminals the error of our ways. I decided to take the program because of two incentives—I've got a single man cell and my own guitar so that I can participate in the music therapy class.

As soon as my door is unlocked, I head straight to the exercise room and get on the treadmill. If I exercise in the morning, I feel energized all day, and I've been doing this routine for so long now that I feel sluggish if I don't. I run for thirty minutes, enough to work up a good sweat. I'll do a longer run in the evening when I have time. I take a quick shower. Contrary to what you see on TV and in the movies, federal prisons don't have group showers. The showers are in stalls that look like closets, but with a shower curtain instead of a door. Thanks to Hollywood, the public has a lot of misconceptions about prison...

After my shower I head to breakfast. I step outside the unit into the cool morning air. The sunrise has the sky lit up in an array of pinks and blues, the clouds making a beautiful pattern of textures stretching across the eastern horizon behind and above the guard towers.

I meet my friend, Bruce, coming out of his unit and heading in my direction. Bruce is a third generation Mexican-American. I speak more Spanish than he does. We both play in a prison heavy metal band. We've found that it's the best outlet for our anger and frustration at being tossed into this human garbage can for years on end.

"What's up?" I ask him.

"I hope you got plenty of food in your locker."

"Why? What's going on?"

"The Crips and DCs are beefing again," he says.

"Again? I guess I better try to make it to the commissary today. Maybe I can make it before the shit hits the fan. If not, I'll have to go to the store man."

The store man is a guy who lives in the unit (there's one or more in every unit) and buys an excess of commissary items, which he sells at fifty percent interest to guys like me who, for some reason or another, can't make it to the commissary. We're only allowed to shop once a week on a scheduled day, and even then we are only allowed to spend a certain amount.

"If they go at it again," Bruce says, "we're gonna be locked down for a while."

All I can do is shrug my shoulders. "Well, man, they gotta play their prison games. That's all they live for, anyway."

He nods. "Part of doing time, buddy."

Pollock is infested with prison gangs: Crips, Bloods, DCs, Gangster Disciples, Texas syndicate, Aztecas, Mexican mafia, skinheads, dirty white boys, and the AB (Aryan Brotherhood). They clique up according to race and geographic origin. Guys join gangs for all kinds of reasons: peer pressure (which can be as bad as or worse here than in any high school), protection, or just because they're young and impressionable and just want to fit in. More than once, I've seen a new guy come in with the look of fear etched all over his face. You see him two months later, and he's got a permanent scowl and fresh tattoos and he's emboldened by the sometimes false belief that his new brothers will back him up if he steps into shit.

After breakfast, I go to work at the UNICOR factory, where we make fitness trunks for the army. I work in the business office, where I am paid one dollar and thirty cents an hour to prepare the payroll for the two hundred and fifty or so inmates who are employed in the factory. The majority of them sew, which is where I started out. Then I became a sewing machine mechanic until I graduated to my present job.

The day goes smoothly. There are seven of us that work in the business office. Bruce works at the desk next to mine. We all cut up and laugh and joke all day. It's pathetic that when I was free, I couldn't relax and enjoy myself without being drunk or high, but in the end, even that wasn't fun anymore. Now, I'm not free, and there isn't a day goes by that one of these idiots in here doesn't have me laughing until tears are streaming down my face. I have often read how people in the most horrible situations can find humor in it. Besides, if I weren't laughing I would be crying for real.

At two o'clock I sneak out of work and head to the commissary. If we get locked down and I don't have any food in my locker, I'll have a hard time surviving weeks on nothing but the bologna sandwiches and pieces of fruit they give us in a paper bag for every meal. I buy plenty of peanut butter, oatmeal, ramen noodles, and instant coffee. Then I go back to my unit, where we are locked in our cells for one hour every day so the COs can count us. We are let out at four thirty when we have mail call. I get a *Time* magazine, but not any letters. The only people I keep in touch with are my mom and dad, who I call every other Sunday. After being locked up for more than seven years, I don't seem to exist anymore to the rest of my family and friends. Out of sight, out of mind, I guess.

As I'm waiting for the CO to let our unit out for chow, my "homeboy," Billy, walks up.

"What are you doing tonight?' he asks.

"I'm gonna run as soon as they let us out."

"How far you gonna run?'

"As long as I can," I tell him. "Which will probably be three hours before they close the yard."

"You better be careful out there. You know what's supposed to go down."

"Yeah, I know. That's all everybody's talking about today. But they never mess with me. Besides, if I get stabbed, then I get stabbed. I'm not gonna do my time scared. What are you gonna do?" I ask him.

"I gotta cut Ricky's hair, but I don't want to. He's hard to satisfy. The last time I cut it, he came back two or three times wanting me to fix it, but I didn't see anything wrong with it."

"Well," I say, "have fun. They just called chow. See ya later," I add as I head for the door with a towel and my water bottle.

It's dark and humid out now, about an hour past sunset. I've been running for almost three hours. Running is a drug and I'm a junky. I feel euphoric as I circle the quarter-mile dirt track around alpha yard. I hear a train in the distance, traveling down the tracks. The other inmates are clustered in groups around three different recreation yards that are divided by high chain link fences topped with razor wire. Some are sitting on the bleachers of the soccer field watching the dusty game as it winds down. There are several others walking around the asphalt track talking about their pathetic memories of the streets, embellishing and exaggerating, trying to impress their peers. The pious Muslims are answering their call to prayer, bowing their heads to the ground in the hope that Allah will answer their supplications. Other convicts are seated at picnic tables playing poker, and still others are making deals, trading postal stamps, which we use as currency for things like food, porno pictures, cigarettes, alcohol, and gambling. I am exhilaratingly oblivious to it all as I pass the twenty-mile point in my run.

The PA system announces "yard recall," signifying that we must return to our housing units for the night. The guard towers that circle the compound switch on their searchlights. I keep running because I only need five more minutes to make my run a solid three hours. There is the sound of a helicopter hovering above, probably from the nearby airport. The scene is surreal. The other inmates slowly make their way to their housing units.

Suddenly the sound of an air horn emanates from tower eight in the middle of the compound. I hear the sounds of jangling keys as COs come running from all directions. There is a fight in bravo yard. Actually, "fight" might not be a strong enough word. The Crips and DCs are at war. Some of them have steel shanks; others have belts with padlocks on the end. A recording is repeated over and over on the PA system: THERE

IS AN INSTUTIONAL EMERGENCY. ALL INMATES GET ON THE GROUND OR YOU MAY BE SHOT. A concussion grenade is shot from tower eight and the sky lights up like the Fourth of July. Anyone who wasn't flat on the ground before is now. Warning shots are fired from the tower, but the fighting continues. The COs do nothing but shout, "Get on the ground! Get on the ground *now*!" More shots are fired from the tower. Dust flies into the air where the bullets hit the earth just inches away from one of the gangsters.

Eventually the warriors tire out, lie down on the ground, and are handcuffed. Two nurses come running across the yard with a stretcher. I head back to my unit as quickly as possible so I can get a shower before they lock us down. I have the thought that living in a war zone in a real war wouldn't be much different from this. How in the hell did I end up here?

Chapter 2
Swallowing the Bait

Childhood shows the man, as morning shows the day.

-JOHN MILTON
PARADISE REGAINED

I had a pretty normal childhood. I can remember nothing that I can pinpoint as causing me to become such a drug-addled derelict, unable to fit into society. No abuse, no trauma, no divorced parents, just your average, small-town, middle-class upbringing near Mobile, Alabama. I had three brothers, both of my parents worked, and I attended a private school from the sixth grade until I graduated from high school. I made good enough grades to get by, even though I never studied or hardly did any homework. If I had tried at all, I know I could have made straight As, but like most kids, I hated school. I had a few friends in the neighborhood we lived in. We played football, basketball, or baseball, depending on the season. We also built forts in the woods, played army, and rode our bikes and skateboards.

Sports were what I loved, but my talents were in other domains. When I was in the fifth grade, I joined the beginner's band at school and learned to play the trumpet. I picked the trumpet because my older brother, Brian, played the trumpet in the high school marching band, and I wanted to be just like him.

In the band room, the director had hung a chart on the wall to track our progress through the book we were learning from. The fifty or so of us students were allowed to learn at our own pace, and the goal was to finish the book by the end of the year. Without any sense of competiveness or ambition, I blazed through the book. It just came naturally to me. Every time I completed the music on a page, the teacher wrote an X on the chart next to my name. One other student, a fat, nerdy, black kid named Nimoy who played the flute, and I finished the book before the second semester was half over. Our two rows of Xs were more than twice as long as the next kid's. The band director tried to have Nimoy and I placed in the marching and concert band before the school year was over, but our class schedules were incompatible with his plan.

I became obsessed with music that year. Music was magical to me, and I got caught up in all kinds of dreams and fantasies when I listened to it. The members of the band Styx were gods to me. Their music transformed the mundane world into a beautiful, sonic landscape in which I found a wonderful place to retreat. My fixation on Styx was one of the first signs of my addictive behavior. When all the other kids were still playing with toys, I was obsessed with obtaining every Styx album ever recorded.

When I was ten years old, I also discovered that I had the ability to run long distances without becoming tired. One day my dad decided he needed to get in shape, so he plotted out a mile-long course through the hilly subdivision we lived in. The two of us set off at an easy pace down the hill in front of our house. After a couple of blocks, my dad ran out of steam, but I kept running. For reasons that were not obvious to me, this amazed my mom and dad. Then my mom registered me for the Azalea Trail run 10K in Mobile. The race was 6.2 miles, beginning downtown and winding under the majestic oaks through the old historic neighborhoods before ending close to where it started.

My two older brothers, Renny and Brian, drove me to the race on an early Saturday morning in March. When the hundreds of runners began lining up in front of the *Mobile Press Register* building, I made my way to the starting line, right up front. One of the race officials came up to me and told me to get in the back or I was going to be run over. I had no idea what I was doing and couldn't figure out why a bunch of grown-ups would run over a little kid like me, but I backed up a little anyway. All the excitement and energy of a road race was a novel experience for me and I enjoyed every minute of it. When the gunshot started the race, I quickly saw what the official had been warning me about. Everyone was elbowing and pushing forward, and when I picked up one foot, there was hardly any room to put it back down. After a couple of blocks, I was running much faster than I should have been, but the pack finally started thinning out.

People were lined up all along the route, clapping and waving and shouting. There were rock bands and jazz bands playing on the corners, and every mile there were aid stations handing out cups of Gatorade and water. All the other older runners were encouraging me on and telling me I was doing great. I know of no other sporting event where there is such camaraderie.

After forty minutes of jogging, when I was within sight of the finish line, I got so excited that I sprinted the final distance. After the race I eventually located my brothers among the crowd of spectators and sweaty runners and we headed home. On the way, when we stopped at a convenience store to buy something to drink, I suddenly became nauseated and stuck my head out the car window to puke. When my stomach clenched up to expel its contents, I simultaneously crapped in my pants. My brothers had been complaining about how I smelled *before* this happened.

It was around the time, when I was twelve years old, that I started going to Jackson Academy. I soon started feeling that I was somehow different from other kids that I didn't quite fit in, that something was wrong with me. I had several of what I call "esteem killers." I tried out twice for a Little League baseball team and was not picked. A girl in my class had a birthday party and invited everyone but me. One time the cheerleaders in my class put up a big sign at pep rally that had everyone's name on it, except mine. They had forgotten me.

I always seemed to be falling through the cracks. I played on the basketball and football teams in junior high, but ended up sitting on the bench during games, even when we won by a large margin. I loved football at that age. I wanted to grow up and play for the Alabama Crimson Tide and then for the Dallas Cowboys. The so-called sports coaches at my school didn't teach me how to play sports, though; what they did was destroy what little confidence I had in myself. The message I got from them was that I was not good enough. The only sport I was any good at in school was running long distance on the track team. It also happens to be the only sport that doesn't require any athletic talent. You don't need coordination or the ability to manipulate a ball; you just run. Track season was my favorite time of year. I was invisible to the girls most of the year, but they suddenly took notice of me in the spring. The track meets were a blast and I developed friendships with some of the competitors from the other schools. I had a girlfriend from Wilcox Academy named Melanie, who I only saw at the meets.

At home I was a middle child. As an adult, I've taken a few classes in psychology and read a lot of articles in magazines relating to birth order. Middle children typically fall through the cracks, don't receive enough attention, and are usually described as "lost souls." I feel like I fit this description. But to blame my problems on these circumstances only serves to make me look weak and pathetic, which maybe I was, but I'm just trying to point out why I didn't feel good about myself. Some people just seem to handle life's troubles successfully, but some don't. Unfortunately, I fell into the latter category. I've met several people in prison with horrible, nightmarish childhoods that make mine look like I grew up in fairy tale land.

When I was fourteen, I began sneaking out of the house at night with some of my friends from the neighborhood. I had a sliding glass door in my room for easy exits, but my friends had to crawl out of their windows when I came around knocking. We would roll all the neighbor's yards with toilet paper and egg their cars. When I discovered an ice chest full of beer on the back of one of their trucks, the harmless pranks turned into juvenile criminality. I was the capo of this little crew and it was my idea to steal cassette tapes from some of the cars in the neighborhood. We went back to my house and listened to "*Hungry like a Wolf*" by *Duran Duran* while guzzling down the beer.

There was a baseball park located beside our neighborhood. When I proposed we break into the concession stand, there weren't any objections from my minions. It wasn't hard for me to figure out how to take the vent in the door off with a screwdriver. In a psychopathological way I was proud of my criminal ingenuity. If there is such a thing as a criminal mind, I had it at fourteen years of age.

We loaded up on bubble gum and candy. When we had filled our pockets I proceeded to destroy the place. Pent up rage, which I was unaware of, exploded from me like a time bomb. Gallon sized jugs of ketchup, mayonnaise and mustard exploded against the side of the building creating my own imitation of a Jackson Pollock painting. My friends just followed along and mimicked me. I don't know what was in their heads, but I was thinking, *take that you motherfuckers. You won't let me play little league, but I'll fuckin' show you.* Splattt!!! Red ketchup dripping down the walls. *You'll deal with me whether you like it or not.* This was the perfect outlet for my angst, which spilled over in this manner like an erupting volcano over and over again as I grew up.

It didn't take long for us to get caught. Someone recognized one of my gang as we were gallivanting down the street. Our parents were told to take us to the police station to be questioned by an officer. We were all so scared that we confessed to everything, even to the fact that it was my idea. I was the mastermind, the instigator, and the ringleader. We weren't prosecuted or anything, but I became acquainted with the term restitution, and I had to clean up the public display of my artwork and apologize to the neighbors.

For whatever reason, I jumped at the chance to experiment with drugs. When I was first offered pot, I didn't think twice about it. I was curious and already had a dare-devilish personality. I liked the way pot made me feel. It opened up a whole new world to me, it was like magic, and it was like a trip to *Disney World*. Pot made me look at the world from a new perspective, one I thought was better than the old one. It magnified and amplified my enjoyment of *everything*. I remember one time I was smoking with two of my brothers. We started laughing at each other. Then we started laughing at the laughter, and we started laughing harder and louder until our laughing muscles cramped up and tears streamed from our eyes and our whole bodies convulsed with fits of hilarity. Finally someone knocked a glass of water on the floor and we had to clean up the mess. This is how drugs seduced me. I was infatuated with them. I could see nothing wrong with smoking a little pot once in a while; I was blind to any negative effects. It was all pleasure and no pain.

When I was fifteen or sixteen, my brother Brian started using the needle. He was shooting Dilaudid, a synthetic opiate that is several times stronger than heroin. It scared the hell out of me, and I told myself that I would never ever do that. I would *never* stick a needle in my arm to get high! I was afraid of needles, for one thing, and Brian was paying about fifty dollars for just one pill. Just give me some weed. I didn't need anything more than that. Besides, I couldn't imagine anything making me feel higher than a nice, big, fat joint.

Over the next few years, Brian, whom I idolized, continued his romance with the needle. It would usually make him puke, and I couldn't understand how that could be a good feeling. But I was becoming less and less scared, desensitized. The needle didn't seem that big a deal anymore. I continued to smoke pot occasionally and drink beer with my friends from school every weekend. When I smoked weed, it was usually with my brothers and my uncle Tommy. No one at school did drugs. They hardly even drank. But I had such a bad reputation for drinking that the caption under my senior portrait in the yearbook said, "Always ready for a party." It was around this time that I started dating Rhonda, my future wife. Pretty soon we were inseparable, and I put my drinking and pot smoking on hold for a while.

I eventually graduated from high school and in the fall of 1988 started attending the University of South Alabama. I was living in a dorm room on campus, so of course I started back drinking. One night I got so drunk at a frat party that I went back to my dorm room (I have no idea how I got back) started filling the bathtub and passed out without turning off the water. I woke up about three a.m. I was lying on the floor in about two inches of water, and the resident advisor was beating on my door. I had completely flooded my room and the room below me. The next day I had to clean up the mess while experiencing one of the worst hangovers I remember having.

During Christmas break, I went to a party with Brian where everyone was doing ecstasy. It is not my intention to glorify or glamorize drug use with this story, but I have to tell the truth. I have to explain how I became hooked. Most of my story is about how I struggled after becoming addicted, but here I am just describing how I swallowed the bait. The only way to describe how ecstasy made me feel is *heavenly*, like I had arrived in paradise. Actually, there are no words to describe how it felt. This is the point in my life when I became irreversibly hooked.

And if one little pill could make me feel like this, I was willing to try them all.

I was now ruined, corrupted, infected. Drugs became an obsession. I didn't see anything wrong with doing them. I had watched my brother stick a needle in his arm for several years, and it didn't seem to be causing him any problems. Yes, I was completely ignorant of what drugs could do to people. I didn't know anyone who was farther along the road of addiction than my brother. Not that it would have mattered. I've always been one to find things out the hard way.

After Christmas, 1988, Brian asked me to come live with him. We smoked pot every day and did ecstasy every weekend. He was dealing it at this time. He threw a party at his house every weekend, and everyone that came would buy tabs from him for twenty-five dollars each. I bought fifty tabs at fifteen dollars, using my Pell grant for school and sold them all for twenty-five dollars. In about two hours, I made a profit of five hundred dollars. The hook was digging deeper into my flesh. It goes without saying that I wasn't studying. Hell, I was hardly ever going to class. Every day that I was supposed to be in class, I just stayed in my dorm room, smoked pot, listened to music, and watched TV. I ended up dropping all my classes at the last possible day so that I wouldn't receive any Fs. Little did I realize that since I was paying for school with Pell grants, I wouldn't receive any money for the next semester because I'd dropped all my of classes. My short-lived college career was over by March.

I was nineteen years old and had reached a fork in the road. One path led to a life of drug addiction and misery. The other led to a degree and a life free of drugs. Like driving at night, I could only see as far as my headlights shone, so I had no idea what was in store for me in the darkness further ahead. But what I could see looked exciting. The drugs colored days that would otherwise be drab and mundane. While I was living with Brian I experimented with other pills: Valium, Xanax, and Percodan. I also tried LSD for the first time. If ecstasy was a trip to paradise for me, then LSD was a journey into outer space, both scary and exciting. It can also be like a trip to an insane asylum, and it gets frightening to start to think you might not leave. It all depends on your mood and the environment you're in when you take it.

When I flunked out of school, I moved back home with my parents. I'm sure they were shocked at my metamorphosis. The transformation in my head manifested in my physical appearance—I had lost a lot of weight, my eye sockets and cheeks were sunken in, I was listless and lethargic, and my hair had grown long and shaggy. The look on my dad's face was one of dismay and disappointment.

Dropping out of college was one of the worst things that ever happened to me. What would I do now? I had no plans for the future, no ambitions except to get stoned. I got a job as a carpet installer helper and spent all of my money getting high and having a good time. I had to get high, because without I would have been forced to look at what I was, which was useless and worthless, a failure. But the thing I remember most is extreme boredom when I wasn't loaded. I wanted my drugs. I wanted to go to *Disney World*. I wanted to go to outer space. I wanted to go to paradise. Anything less was depressing.

I went to spend another weekend with Brian. All of our get-togethers now were for the purpose of getting high, and he usually had better connections than I did. On this occasion, though, there was nothing to be found. No weed, nothing. It was dry. But we could drive to Birmingham, which was about five hours away, and score some Dilaudid. What the hell? I was bored to death. After watching my brother shoot up for five years, I didn't see anything wrong with it anymore. I had done so many other drugs by now, in fact, that I was curious about this needle thing.

So we got up at three a.m. The drive was interstate all the way, and there were hardly any cars on the road. We drove the whole distance at 120 miles per hour. We were drug crazed. We were willing to risk our lives to get high. It's what we lived for. We blast into Birmingham at six a.m. on a Sunday and drove to a rundown neighborhood called Center City, were Dilaudids were served 24/7. Just drive through, place your order, pay, and drive to the nearest drug store to buy rigs (syringes).

I was apprehensive. I was used to dealing with dubious characters to score some dope, but this was scarier than usual. As soon as we pulled into the neighborhood, we were flagged down by a skinny, shady-looking figure that looked like he had been wearing the same clothes for a week. He already knew what we wanted. All he needed to know was how many.

Brian rolled his window down. "Give me five for two hundred."

"Can't give you but fo' fo' two hundred."

"Then give me five for two-twenty."

You have to haggle with these guys. They're users themselves, and they have to get as much of a cut as they can.

The guy glanced up and down the road, shook out five florescent yellow pills out of a vial. They were the smallest pills I'd ever seen. They're called K-4 on the street because K-4 is what is etched on the pill.

"Here you go." He reached for Brian's money with one hand while he held the pills in his other fist, waiting at the edge of the window. When he got his hand on the money, he finally gave up the pills. It was a square deal on both sides with no subterfuge involved. But it was a very tense situation, at least from where I sat. I wasn't desperate enough yet to go to such lengths on my own, but I trusted Brian and believed he knew what he was doing since he'd been doing this sort of thing for several years now.

I was relieved to be leaving the Birmingham ghetto. It was one of those places most people are scared to death to drive through. If they do, they roll up their windows and lock their doors. Anyway, we proceeded to the nearest drug store for the rigs. I went in and asked for a ten-pack of U-100s, just like I'd done it a hundred times before. Most pharmacies want some sort of proof that you are a diabetic, but not this one. They would probably lose half of their business if they did.

It was in this parking lot that I was indoctrinated into the art of mainlining. Brian took a business card and creased it in half. Then he took one pill and folded it up into the card, then crushed it with the handle of a screwdriver. Next he took the plunger out of the syringe and emptied the contents of the card into the barrel of the rig. He replaced the plunger, and then drew forty units of water (we had a plastic bottle) into the needle. All he had to do now was shake the mixture to completely dissolve the powder.

The reason K-4 is etched onto the pill is because it contains four milligrams of hydromorphone, which is a synthetic morphine. Four milligrams of this drug was four times too strong for me, so he took another syringe, removed the plunger and squirted ten units into it for me. Three milligrams for him and one for me. At that time, if I had been shooting morphine, I would have had to use twenty milligrams to get the same effect as one milligram of Dilaudid. According to my experience, Dilaudid is twenty times stronger than morphine.

Now it was time for the final phase of my initiation. I took off my belt and wrapped it around my upper arm to cut off the circulation to my lower arm. I extended my arm to my brother and turned my head the other way. I was still afraid of needles ... but apparently not afraid enough. He grabbed my arm. I was still waiting for the pinprick when he said, "Alright." I loosened my belt. What was going to happen? After a few seconds I was beginning to think nothing was going to happen.

"I don't feel anytheeeeeeeaaauuuggggghhh."

A huge wave of warm euphoric ecstasy washed over my whole being. Every muscle in my body seemed to tense and cramp up. It took my breath away. I fell off the edge of a cliff into a pool of red warm rapture. This rush lasted probably for thirty seconds. As it subsided, a feeling of well being moved in and took its place. It is not unlike an orgasm, only in reverse. In sex, you build up for a period of time, climax, and then return to a normal state. With the dope rush, the explosion is at the beginning, and then you slide back to a normal state. But you usually get sick on the way down. It's not a bad feeling at all. Your stomach just seems to feel the need to purge itself, as if to say, "I want to feel this, too, but I can't with this food in the way!"

If I was hooked before, I swallowed the hook even deeper that weekend. I was consumed. I became obsessed with getting high. I had crossed the line from casual user to bona fide addict. The courtship was over. I was now married to drugs. In sickness and health, till death do you part? If you had asked me at that time, "What is the single most important thing in your life?" I don't know what I would have answered. I was incapable of honestly looking at the situation. I never would have said drugs were, *but they were.* They were all that I lived for. Instead of giving up my life to follow Jesus, I had given up my life to follow drugs wherever they would lead me. And they would take me on one helluva roller coaster ride. The highs were up in space; the lows were down in hell. With drugs, you can't have one without the other.

Shortly after my initiation, while I was still living with my parents, I had another chance to ride that roller coaster through hell. We lived out in the country, surrounded by acres and acres of cow pastures, and usually where there is cow manure there are psilocybin mushrooms, hallucinogenic "shrooms." As you can guess, I became an expert 'shroom picker and cook. This one particular time, while 'shroom picking, I found the mother lode—huge mushrooms with caps as big as Frisbees, just waiting for me to come along and pick them. I could tell they were going to be strong because when I put them in the frying pan with a little water and mashed them with a spatula, thick purple juice oozed out and bubbled into a violet froth. I mixed the extract with some Gatorade and set off for Rhonda's house. She was still in high school and still living with her mother, so I spent most of my free time hanging out there. It wasn't the ideal environment in which to trip on mushrooms, but I didn't care. I wanted to get high, no matter where I was or whom I was with.

I knew this 'shroom mixture was going to be potent, so I took a couple of sips to test it out. I knew I was in for a ride when only ten minutes later the walls began to breathe in and out and the ceiling began to ripple like the ocean. It was time to put on my seat belt. The colors of everything began to change. I saw kaleidoscope patterns on Rhonda's face. I tried to play Nintendo, but the characters kept running off the screen. Same thing with a Clive Barker book I tried to read: the words drifted off the page and floated in the air. Then I started to get paranoid. Rhonda's sister was talking on the phone to her boyfriend, and I thought they were talking about me. I thought I heard her mother in the next room say, "What is wrong with David? I'm going to call the police." I started freaking out for real. The mushrooms in the cow pasture kept popping up before my eyes.

I remembered when a police officer came to our school when I was about twelve. He was trying to educate us about drugs and told a story about a guy in the state mental hospital who thought he was a mushroom. *That's gonna happen to me*, I thought. *I'm not ever going to come down. I'll be stuck like this for the rest of my life.* I remembered smoking a joint earlier in the day with some of my buddies, and one of them said there was arsenic in mushroom stems. Now I couldn't remember—had I cooked the stems or not? *Oh, shit! Now I am going to die.*

All of a sudden everything turned red. I saw flames shoot up the walls. *I'm gonna die and I'm going to hell.* I was petrified. I sat in a chair for what must have been hours and pretended I was reading a book. I was afraid to look at anyone. I was afraid to move. There was a window beside the chair. The curtains looked like they were being blown by a hurricane. The potted houseplants in the room looked alive. They had faces. They were laughing at me. I had to urinate, but I was afraid to get up. Rhonda's mother finally went into her bedroom, so I made a break for the bathroom. I shut the door and looked at my reflection in the mirror. My pupils were so huge there were no irises, just black and white eyeballs. The pores in my face were huge gaping craters. My long hair was alive and swirling around my head like snakes, making me look like Medusa. Then all of a sudden I saw Jesus staring back at me in the mirror. *I saw Jesus.*

My brother, Chris, finally came to pick me up because I didn't have a car at the time. But I was afraid to step outside the door. I thought the cops were outside the door waiting to arrest me. Finally, I went out anyway, saying goodbye to Rhonda, who had a worried look on her face. (I bet I was fun company that night.) There was a full moon, and the sky looked like a painting. It was too bad I couldn't enjoy it. I still thought I was about to die. I sat in the car, trying to decide what to do when I got home. I was planning on just walking into the woods and lying down and waiting for death. I told Chris I was gonna die.

"What the hell are you talking about?"

"I'm gonna die."

"Chill out, man. You're not going to die."

As soon as I got home, I went straight to my parents' bedroom, knocked on the door, and told them I was dying, I did not want to die, and I wanted to live.

"What did you take?" my dad asked.

I wanted to lie. I didn't want to tell them it was mushrooms, but in my convoluted mind, I thought he had extra-sensory perception. There would be no use lying.

"Mushrooms."

"Shit!" My dad hustled me out to the car, got me in, and we took off toward the ER.

For some reason, I started thinking about my step grandfather, Clayton, who used to always tell me I was going to grow up to be a preacher. He was a Mason, so I thought he had some kind of secret knowledge. He had passed away several years earlier.

"Clayton was right," I blurted out.

My dad didn't know what I was talking about. "What?"

"Clayton was right. I'm gonna be a preacher."

He must have figured out by now that I was just having a bad trip. "What are your symptoms?" he asked.

"I don't know. I think there was arsenic in the mushrooms."

He stopped the car, turned around, and headed back home. I'm sure he didn't want to go through the embarrassment of bringing his drugged-out kid to this small town hospital, where everybody would gossip about it for weeks. I was forever embarrassing my parents. My hair was long, and all my friends and I did was smoke pot and terrorize our little Mayberry town. I didn't fit in here, never had, and didn't want to.

I was going through teenage rebellion at nineteen years old. I was always a late bloomer.

When we got back home, they made me drink a glass of milk. I don't know how they knew this was a cure for a bad mushroom trip. I didn't think they knew anything about drugs. Then they started interrogating me about everything I had been doing. Still thinking they had ESP, I answered honestly, getting other people in trouble in the process. It didn't matter to me that I was snitching. I was still convinced that I was going to die. I lay down on the couch and, thanks to the milk; within ten minutes I was back to normal. I was ashamed of what I had done, but I was more relieved than anything. I was going to live!

The next day I decided to turn over a new leaf. No more drugs (although I wasn't about to give up alcohol). I had my mom cut my hair. I decided I would join the Coast Guard. It was what my dad wanted me to do, and I felt so guilty that I would have done anything he asked me to. Besides, I was beginning to get really depressed at the fact that my life didn't seem to be going anywhere.

First, I went through the process of joining the Coast Guard. I talked to the recruiter and signed up. I took the ASFAB test and scored pretty well. All that was left was the physical. Brian called me the weekend before I was to go to Montgomery for the examination and asked if I wanted to go to Birmingham with him. It had only been a month since I swore off of drugs, but the guilt was gone, and with it went my motivation to stay clean. We stayed with a friend of his and shot dope all weekend. I got so high one time that I bumped my head on a doorjamb and passed out for a few moments. It scared the hell out of Brian. I just lay on the floor in a pleasant dream state for several hours without moving.

The next Tuesday I went to take my physical. If they had drug tested me, I would have failed, but they didn't test Coast Guard recruits because it would be several months before we had to go to basic training. It didn't matter, though, because I wasn't going to make it that far. At the end of the physical, the doctor asked me a few questions.

"Are you allergic to anything?"

"Just yellow jackets," I said, thinking it was no big deal.

"You're allergic to yellow jackets?"

"Yeah, I had a reaction to a sting when I was fourteen. I had to be taken to the emergency room."

"Then you're disqualified from all military service. We can't be responsible for you if you get stung out in the field."

I was relieved. I didn't really want to join the Coast Guard. I was only doing it because my parents wanted me to and I didn't know what else to do with my life. Looking back now, I wish I had gotten in. My life would probably have turned out a lot different. But I can't be sure of that. I would probably have screwed it up one way or another. I was already addicted, corrupted, and infected by drugs.

When I called my mom to tell her they wouldn't let me join, I had a hard time convincing her that I hadn't failed a drug test. The yellow jacket story just wasn't very believable, not even to me, but it was the truth.

Around the same time this was going on, Rhonda moved to Mobile to live with her aunt and attend the University of South Alabama. I knew I couldn't go on living with my parents for the rest of my life, so I decided to find a job in Mobile and get my own apartment. It was pretty easy to do. I don't know why I didn't do it sooner. I found a job at a carpet store, and Rhonda's aunt and uncle were kind enough to let me live with them until I found an apartment a couple of weeks later. The apartment was in an old house close to downtown in the historic district.

For the first time in my life I was totally self-sufficient, which means I quickly became absolutely drug dependant. I smoked weed as soon as I woke up in the morning, at work, where I became the warehouse manager and was unsupervised for most of the day, and I smoked and drank beer all night every night. I stayed stoned. Every chance I got, I dropped acid and ecstasy and whatever assortment of pills I could get my hands on. When I turned twenty-one on November 12, 1990, my friend Randy and I were in a grocery store at midnight so I could legally buy beer for the first time. I lived to get high and got high to live. I was about to take another step off in the deep end.

I had a friend named Josh who lived down the street and used to come over and party with us. One day he came over when I was by myself. He asked me if I wanted to smoke some crack. Actually, he was just looking for someone with money to buy some because he didn't have any. I didn't have to think twice about it. I would have drunk piss if you could have convinced me that I would get high. We walked to the crack dealer's house, which was only about four blocks from my apartment. There were four black dudes hanging out on the porch of their shotgun house, drinking beer and smoking. Josh knew them and introduced me to a tall, slim, dark-skinned cat named Duke. I bought a twenty-dollar rock that was about the size and color of a peanut.

Then we went back to my apartment, where Josh showed me how to smoke it. He took a beer can and put a dent in the side, then poked four or five tiny holes in it with a sewing needle. Next, he put cigarette ashes over the holes and placed the whole rock on top of the ashes.He put the can to his mouth, then sucked a lighter flame over the rock, through the ashes, and into the holes. Now it was my turn. As I was inhaling, I felt my mouth go numb and my heart began pounding so hard I could hear it in my ears. I could feel it vibrating my entire body, as if my torso were one huge bass drum. The rush was so powerful, it scared me. I thought I was going to have a heart attack. Instead of holding my breath, I exhaled quickly as I felt my eyes roll back in my head. I blasted into a state of extreme bliss. I did not ever want to lose this feeling, but it was over before I knew it. We hit the can several more times, but it was gone. I had just spent twenty dollars for five minutes of extreme euphoria. I can't say that I was instantly hooked, because it seemed like it was a huge waste of money, but that feeling was recorded in my brain and I would try to recapture it in the future.

Soon all the drug use and partying were starting to put a strain on my finances. I got paid on Friday and was broke on Sunday. Sometimes I would go three or four days without eating. Several times my power was cut off because I neglected to pay the bill. When faced with the choice of paying a bill or buying dope, I bought the dope every time. I soon learned how to take the electric meter out of its box and remove the plastic tabs that prevented the electricity from running to my apartment. I never got in trouble for it. They just added it to my bill, which I would eventually get around to paying.

My addiction progressed over the next few years. I was doing way more drugs than my friends. The only person I knew that did more drugs was Brian. He stole prescription pads from doctors' offices and forged them for whatever he wanted. A lot of times I went in and passed the forgeries. The deal was that he would pay and I would go in and get the prescription filled, then we would split the pills in half. I never got caught doing this. It worked like a charm every time.

I could see that I was taking bigger and more dangerous risks to get high. It scared me. I wanted to quit. I did not want to continue living my life like this. I made a decision to quit, but to succeed; I would have to get out of the environment I was living in. I was living with my youngest brother and two other friends, and every night was a party. Everyone was always drinking, and the water bong was continuously being passed around. I called my mom and told her most of everything that I had been doing and asked if I could stay with them for a month to dry out and get my head screwed back on straight. She was all for it. So was my dad. They could see that I sincerely wanted to quit and were more than willing to help me. I also told my boss what was going on. He wanted to help me, too. He could tell I was strung out on something, so he agreed to give me a leave of absence.

The day before I left, I decided to get blitzed one last time. I decided to take the company van on my lunch break down to the hood to cop some Ts and blues off the street. I parked the van down the street from the corner, and walked up with head down and hands in pockets, to a dude I recognized from previous deals.

"I need a set, dawg."

"It's too hot. Come back later." He should know better than this. I wasn't not leaving until I got a fix.

"C'mon, man, I'm dying here."

He glanced up and down the street. One look in my eyes was all he needed to see to realize I wasn't budging. I was past the point of no return. By telling me to come back, he'd already let me know that he was holding.

"Wait for me in there," he finally said, nodding toward the rundown green house we were standing in front of. There was a trash-strewn path, which led to the back through the weeds and shrubs. I wouldn't have been surprised to see a dead and decomposing body with flies buzzing around it in the hot, humid, July heat. I stepped into the dark house, walking over used syringes. This place was obviously a shooting gallery, but there wasn't anyone in sight, at least not in this room, and I wasn't about to go any farther to find out.

As I was standing there waiting, a touch of sanity finally registered in my drug-besotted brain—*what in the hell am I doing down here in this drug-infested jungle of rot and decay?* My naiveté was going to be the death of me.

Before I knew it, the dude walked in with a couple of pills wrapped in aluminum foil. I handed him a sweaty wad of fifteen one-dollar bills. As I turned to walk out, the dude said, "Watch out. The task force is out there."

I just nodded and burned off. As I was walking back down the sidewalk, I spotted a Chevy Lumina with tinted windows on the other side of the street. *Shit, that's gotta be cops.*

As I was pulling the van away from the curb, I watched for the Lumina in my rear view mirror. Sure enough, it made a U-turn in the street. Too late (*God, I hate to throw away perfectly good drugs*), I tossed the foil lump out the passenger side window. The Lumina pulled up behind me with its blue lights flashing. *I'm about to see the inside of a jail cell for the first time.* I pull over to the curb.

There are two plain-clothes detectives, one black and one white, in the car. White jumped out and started looking for the foil.

"Turn off the ignition, and step out," Black yelled from behind the open driver's door of the Chevy. He motioned me to the back of the van and told me to assume the position. Then he started patting me down.

"What are you doing down here?" he asked as he slapped my thighs.

"Just working. I'm delivering carpet."

"Oh, yeah? Then why is your van empty?"

"Uh ... I already delivered it."

"Bullshit. You were buying crack."

"I wasn't buying crack!" At least I could say that with some conviction of truth.

"We were watching you. We watched you park, walk up the street, and talk to the dealer. We watched you go in the house and walk back down here. And we saw you throw it out the window. Take your shoes off."

I complied. By now I was sweating buckets. Sweat was dripping off my forehead in torrents. *Damn, it's hot.* White finally walked over with the foil and pills in his hand. He placed them in a zip lock bag. Now I was fucking fucked. "It's Ts and blues," he said.

As Black copied information from my driver's license in his notebook, White asked, "Where do you live?"

"Providence Place Apartments."

"Over by the university?"

"Yeah."

"Oh, yeah?" Black said. "Then you're gonna work for us. You're gonna make an ecstasy buy for us. Or acid. If you don't, then this possession charge could get you ten years."

"I don't know anybody that sells ecstasy or acid."

"Bullshit. We know what goes on at Providence Place."

White gave me a big smile. "You either help us or you go to jail right now," he said.

What could I do? "Okay," I said. I was staring down at the cracked asphalt where my drops of sweat were making puddles. I'd say anything to keep from going to jail, but what I'd actually do was another matter.

They got my phone number and told me they'd be in touch. Black did call me a couple of times after my month of attempted recovery, but I hemmed and hawed. He wanted me to make a buy while wearing a wire. I told him I would do it, but I never went through with it.

I never heard from them again.

August 1993 was the first time I attended a Narcotics Anonymous meeting. They told me that I would have to rely on God and pray for him to help me with my problem.

Well, I wanted no part of that. I didn't believe in God, and I couldn't force myself to. My spiritual development was nonexistent. I had my own ideas about how to quit and was determined to try it my way.

In the back of my mind, I didn't really want to quit. I was so bored after a couple of days at my parents' house that all I could think about was a nice, big, fat joint. Yeah, that would be the perfect cure for my boredom. Needless to say, as soon as I got back to my apartment after that clean, dull, dreary month, the first thing I proceeded to do was get stoned. It didn't take long for me to become worse than before. I tried to resist it at first, but I was on a slippery slope with nothing to hang onto. I was powerless over the desire. The cravings were little thoughts in my head that I could not ignore. They grew and grew until I could think about nothing else.

Everything I did revolved around dope. If I went to the beach or to see a movie or anything, I had to get stoned first. If I couldn't get high, then I wouldn't go. Even the few books I read were about drugs. I read William S. Burroughs' *Junky*, in which he vividly describes the first time he shot morphine. After reading that, I wanted to try it, too. A few days later, by some evil kind of coincidence, a dude I knew from work offered me some morphine. It felt just like Dilaudid, but it lasted a lot longer. I was instantly hooked, and it wasn't long before I had to have it every day.

Now I found out the true meaning of addiction. If I tried to go more than a day without morphine, I got sick. My back would start hurting, my nose would run, I wouldn't have any energy. I didn't want to talk to anyone. All I could think about was getting more. When I finally scored again, I had to fix while sitting on the toilet because my bowels would loosen up in anticipation of the rush. I started embezzling money from work to pay for my habit. This went on for a year. I knew I was out of control, but I couldn't stop.

The next thing I found was methadone. I found out about it from Brian. My brother was always one step ahead of me in the addiction process, and I followed him right along. If there is such a thing as a bad influence, then Brian was definitely a bad influence on me. But I take responsibility for my actions. He didn't have to stick a gun to my head. I went along willingly. If he hadn't been there to influence me, I still would have become a drug addict, but at a slower pace, and I would likely have never stuck a needle in my arm.

I went to the methadone clinic, told them I was a drug addict, filled out some paperwork, paid fifty dollars, and got my first dose, right there on the spot. That easy—a perfectly legal high that was supposed to stop me from getting high. Just ten dollars a day and I stay blitzed 24/7. In a matter of months, I was taking the highest dose allowed, which was a hundred milligrams.

About this time, I started a new job at a rug manufacturer. I had to be at the methadone clinic at five thirty every morning get my dose for the day, and then be at work by six. But methadone can be a more dangerous drug than heroin and other opiates. It stays active for a full twenty-four hours. That's why it's used to treat heroin and other opiate addictions. The logic behind giving this powerful drug to junkies is that it is supposed to keep them off the streets and out of the danger that usually accompanies purchasing illegal drugs, and ten dollars a day is much easier to obtain legally than a hundred dollars a day.

But it didn't work that way with me. It was like trying to put out a fire with gasoline.

Drug addiction is a progressive illness. If you are feeding the addiction, it only wants more, and eventually the cravings cannot be satisfied. Methadone speeds up the process with me. As soon as my body got used to being fed methadone every day, the need to become obliterated returned, stronger than ever. The opiates were no longer doing it for me.

Enter crack cocaine. It would be more appropriate to say I get low when I smoke crack instead of getting high. As I write this and look back, I cannot see why I (or anyone) would ever use this drug. Whoever said crack is cheap is an idiot. If I have a thousand dollars and decide I'm going to smoke a little crack, the next day I will be broke and more than likely trying to figure out where to get some more money, legally or not. You do that with heroin or any other drug and you are dead from a massive overdose.

After one particularly hard day at work, I just wanted to get high. I believed that crack was the only thing that would get the job done. Here's the really dangerous part about crack and me. I had a hard time paying for it, even if I had the money. Every time I smoked it, I was thoroughly convinced that would be the last time I would ever do so. So I figured, why pay these dudes that hung out on the street corners of certain shady neighborhoods? They ripped me off plenty of times, selling me a twenty dollar piece of soap or wax.

I knew this was a dangerous thing to do, but I was young, dumb, and full of desperation. I pulled over to the side of the street and rolled my window down. They knew what I wanted. A drug buy was the only reason a young, white male would enter one of these neighborhoods. I held a wad of bills in my right hand, away from the window, because if the cash was close enough, they would just reach in snatch it from me and take off running. I told them I wanted a twenty or fifty piece. Usually, if they really had some, they were eager to make a sale, and they stuck their hand, palm up, in the window to show me what they had. At this point, I slapped their wrist and put the pedal to the metal, burning rubber down the street and around the corner, with the rock rolling around on the floorboard. As I said before, I knew this was extremely stupid and dangerous behavior … but now it gets even more insane. I still can't figure out why or what I was thinking, but it goes to show how out of my mind I was. For some reason, I went back into the same neighborhood where I had already done my slap and burn routine.

On this day, that's what I did. As I drove slowly down the street after getting off from work, I noticed there wasn't anyone hanging out. I circled around the block one time, and then drove down the deserted street one more time. Still no one was out. I decided to try a different spot, so I turned down the next street. As I turned the corner, I looked in my rearview mirror to see if maybe someone had finally come out of the dilapidated shotgun houses. Someone came out, all right. He came running out into the street right behind my truck. He stopped running, spread his feet in a wide stance, held his gun in both hands, and aimed right at my head. My gut reaction was to duck. It probably saved my life.

There was an explosion of glass over my head, then another. I felt something hit my head. I put my hand up to the side of my head. At the same time, I was trying to drive while keeping my head down. I was driving as fast as I possibly could. I had to get the hell out of there. My hand felt something warm and wet. I pulled it away from my head and looked at it. It was covered with blood. Now I was really freaking out. What should I do?

My first thought was to drive to the hospital. But how could I make it all the way to the hospital with a gunshot wound to the head? I reached up again and tried to find the wound, but I couldn't feel a hole or a cut or anything. I looked in my rearview mirror. There was a bullet hole right through the mirror and through the windshield. There was also a bullet hole through the windshield right in front of my face. If I hadn't ducked, my brain matter would have been splattered all over the inside of my windshield. I was still driving like a maniac, still trying to find the bullet hole in my head. I finally found a cut on the back of my right ear. Glass exploding from the back window must have nicked me.

That is only one of many times I have risked my life to get high. I knew I was cheating death, but I was too insane to stop. The times I barely escaped serious harm only reinforced my feelings of invincibility. As I look back, I see that it's possible that I was as addicted to the thrill and adrenaline rush of buying the drugs as I was to the drugs themselves. Just pulling into one of these neighborhoods and driving past the hoodlums and thugs sent my heart racing and my adrenaline flowing. But my craving and desire to get high was so strong and overwhelming that it blotted out any other feelings, desires, and concerns. The drive to get high was so strong that it was the only thing I was living for. I would rather have died than lived without drugs. Life without drugs was dull, drab, monotonous, boring, and unbearable.

There was another neighborhood in the city where Ts and blues were sold. Ts and blues are two different pills. The T is Talwin, a painkiller, and the blue is an antihistamine. You crush them together and mix them with water in a spoon, draw up the elixir through cotton, and inject. It's a poor substitute for heroin and morphine, but it can get the job done.

Anyway, I pulled into the neighborhood and drove down a side street where I knew someone would be serving. A skinny, malnourished crack head with fire-scarred arms and hands came up to the passenger window, I rolled it down halfway and told him I wanted a "set." I showed him a few rolled-up one-dollar bills. He took a nervous glance up and down the street, and then looked in the window again.

"You ain't tha po-lice, is you?" he asked in a tense voice.

"Come on, man. I'm straight."

I used to get this all the time. I'm a clean-cut, white male. He had to gamble on whether or not I was a cop. This guy was so desperate to make a sale that he went for it. He stuck his hand in the window with the pills wrapped in aluminum foil. I'd paid for rocks wrapped in foil before, but not this time.

I slapped his wrist and popped the clutch at the same time. The pills went bouncing around and the engine stalled. I looked at him. He looked at me. I turned the key, he grabbed the window with both hands, and I gunned the motor and popped the clutch. I burned rubber down the street with this crack head holding on for dear life. I went faster and faster, but he held on. I was scared, he was scared, and I turned a corner with the tires screaming. I headed out of the neighborhood, and this dude was still hanging on. I was going about thirty-five miles per hour, and just when I thought he was not going to give up, the window shattered and he dropped out of my sight. When I looked in the rearview mirror, I saw him rolling on the pavement. It had to have skinned him up pretty bad, could possibly have broken a bone or two, but it didn't kill him. I feel bad about it now, but at the time I was just scared to death and glad to get away.

Chapter 3
Into the Pit

Sow an act, and you reap a habit. Sow a habit and you reap a character. Sow a character, and you reap a destiny.

-ATTRIBUTED TO CHARLES READE

I eventually got fired from the rug manufacturing company, officially for being late so many times, but unofficially for being an all around screw-up. The methadone had me nodding out at work and pretty much being a hazard to myself and everyone else.

A year before, Brian had gone to rehab and gotten clean, sober, and self-righteous. When he found out I'd lost my job, he convinced our mom and dad to perform an intervention on me to get me into rehab. But they didn't have to go to such drastic lengths. I was ready to quit, though I couldn't do it without becoming deathly ill. Brian had a friend named Mark, who was a drug counselor at a treatment center. Mark was able to get me a free stay for twenty-eight days at the Bowling Green Institute outside of Philadelphia, but I had to wean myself down to twenty milligrams of methadone (down from 100) before they would take me. It took me a month to do it, a month of doing nothing but lying on the couch watching TV all day because I had no energy to do anything else.

I accomplished very little in the twenty-eight days I was in rehab. That's because I was sick the whole time from drug withdrawal. My stomach was tied up in knots, I couldn't eat, and I had skull-crushing headaches. Also, I hardly bothered to participate in the group therapy sessions. For one reason, I was too immature to talk about my feelings, emotions, and needs, and for another, I couldn't see what any of it had to do with my drug addiction. I did drugs because I liked the way they made me feel. I didn't know there was a reason they made me feel so good. What I remember now is thinking the only way I could quit would be to erase my memory of how good the dope felt. For sure, it was causing me a lot of grief, but at the time the pleasure far outweighed the pain.

I met some interesting characters in rehab. My first roommate was named Frank. He was Italian, from Philly, about thirty-five years old and supposedly connected to the mafia in some way. He had been drinking a fifth of vodka every day for years.

"Where are you from?" he asked when we met.

"Alabama." I was almost afraid to admit it.

"Jeez. They don't have fuckin' rehabs in Alabama?"

"Yeah, but my brother knows a guy, who used to work here, and he got me in for free, since I don't have insurance."

Frank was the only person I met who was sicker than I was, at first, anyway. He puked his guts out those first three days. After one particularly violent purging, he came out of the bathroom shaking and sweating and talking incoherently. I hit the button on the intercom and told the nurse she needed to help my roommate. When she came in, Frank was writhing and moaning on the floor outside the bathroom. She gave him some medication and got him to his bed. When his head finally cleared, his cynical and bitter personality revealed its ugly self.

"I had to see the fuckin' psychiatrist today," he said. "He tells me I'm fuckin' depressed. The fuckin' cocksucker asks me two fuckin' questions, and says he's putting me on Prozac. Two fuckin' questions! I ain't taking no fuckin' Prozac. Fuckin' cocksuckers."

The F-word poured out of his mouth like diarrhea. "My fuckin' dog eats better fuckin' food than this." A little later: "These fuckin' assholes want me to go to fuckin' Alcoholics Anonymous. I ain't no fuckin' alcoholic, and I ain't tellin' a buncha cocksuckin' losers my fuckin' life story." The next day: "These fuckin' cocksuckers want me to fuckin' pick up fuckin' cigarette butts. They're out of their fuckin' minds. I ain't pickin' up no fuckin' cigarette butts. Fuckin' cocksuckin' assholes…."

As with school, work and other social situations, cliques formed. I hung around with Frank and Patricia, who was a fifty-year-old Irish lush whose wit and Dublin accent fascinated me. And there was Christine, too. She was the same age as me, but life had really been really rough for her. She was a stripper, and the insides of her arms, from elbow to wrist, were nothing but scar tissue from shooting coke. She was ditzy as hell, and I assumed every man in her life had used her up for whatever she was worth and discarded her like a piece of trash.

We had a meditation period every day in one of the group rooms. We were supposed to just lie there and be still, but trying to get a bunch of alcoholics and addicts fresh from the war zones of their lives to be quiet and meditate was an exercise in futility.

One day Christine, who was lying on her mat next to me, said, "I can sing like Stevie Nicks."

That made me open, my eyes. "Oh, yeah? Then sing 'Rhiannon.'"

She did. And she sounded so much like Stevie Nicks that, for some reason, I found it was absurdly hilarious. I couldn't control my laughter. She stopped singing, so I said, "Keep going." When she started singing again, and I cracked up again. Then I said, "Sing 'Landslide,'" and when she did, I laughed until my head hurt, which quickly reminded me how sick I was.

Every day I asked her to sing a different Fleetwood Mac song and for two or three minutes, the hurt was gone. As long as she was singing, she was all right with me, but I couldn't hold a conversation with her to save my life.

One day, with all sincerity, she asked me, "Do you guys have electricity in Alabama?"

All I could do was roll my eyes. "Yes, we have electricity in Alabama."

Then she said, "You don't dress like you're from Alabama."

"What am I supposed to wear? Cutoff jeans and no shoes?"

I finally gave up and let her believe I lived on a plantation and used a horse and buggy for transportation.

Another guy I met in rehab was John, a computer programmer who had been using heroin every day for thirty years. He looked and acted completely normal, like a forty-seven-year-old businessman or something. I talked to him the day after he came in and asked him how he was feeling.

"I feel pretty good," he said. "I haven't had any withdrawal symptoms or anything."

"You're lucky," I said. "I'm coming off of methadone and haven't been able to eat or sleep for two weeks."

"Oh, man, that's horrible."

I talked to him again later that night just before it was time for us to go to bed.

"What kind of music do you like?" he asked.

"Mostly alternative," I said. "I like a little jazz, too."

"Oh yeah? There's a new alternative band I like a lot, called Counting Crows. Have you heard them?"

"Yeah. They're alright." I didn't think of them as alternative. They were too poppy for my taste.

We were all given little menial jobs, I guess to give a sense of responsibility. I had to mop the dining area for a week, and then I became a greeter. In my third week, I was given the job of helping one of the counselors do room inspections every morning.

The morning after my conversation with John, we were almost through inspecting all of the quarters when we came to John's room. When we walked in, all the beds were made and it looked clean. But there was a set of wet footprints leading from the bathroom to the intercom and back. The counselor knocked on the bathroom door. Nobody answered.

"Is there anybody in there?"

Still no answer.

I was right behind him when he opened the door. John was lying naked in the bathtub full of water. It took one glance at his eyes to tell he was dead. He'd had a heart attack. His roommate said he'd been up all night because his withdrawal pains had started. He kept begging the nurse for something to ease his discomfort, but whatever she gave him, it wasn't enough. All she could do was advise him to take a hot bath. That obviously hadn't helped, either.

This was my first encounter with death from drug addiction. Yes, addiction kills, and it kills indiscriminately. With a drug like heroin, you reach a point where you literally can't live with it, nor can you live without it.

The only good thing that came out of my twenty-eight days in rehab was that I was now clean and the withdrawal pains were finally over. The bad thing was that rehab convinced me that I had a disease, a progressive illness. In my sick mind, this fact absolved me from facing responsibility for my actions. How could I be to blame if I went out and got high again? *I've got a disease.*

When I got out, I tried to stay clean. I went to a few NA meetings, but I didn't participate, didn't say a word, and left as soon as they were over. I thought just the act of being physically present was all I had to do. All I was thinking about was getting high. A shot of morphine would feel *so good*, and every second of my existence was *so boring* without it.

For two weeks, I sat around doing nothing but watching TV again, and then a friend of mine got me a job with his father, who had a powder-coating business. It was dull, monotonous, hot, dirty work, but I had to have a job and I was ill equipped to do anything else. So naturally, I said to myself, if I spend forty hours a week doing something I really don't enjoy, I'm going to need some relief. Right? All I could think about was getting high, but I was using sheer will power to abstain. That's what AA and NA call "white-knuckling it." It was like I was hanging over a pit, gripping a bar suspended above a black abyss. Eventually I'd become exhausted and my strength would fail. There were people on the edges who would have helped me if I'd asked, but I didn't know how to ask. Or I was too prideful or just plain afraid to ask. Besides, there was something in that pit that was very seductive, something that kept calling my name. The voices were getting louder and more frequent. Pretty soon, I couldn't go five minutes without thinking about getting high.

But I was afraid to get back on methadone. The withdrawal pains were too horrible. At the same time, I also didn't want to go back to buying dope off of the street and then have to keep going back every day. I knew it wouldn't be just one time. If I were craving it bad now, the desire would be multiplied after just one hit, toke, or shot. I wanted a big supply so I wouldn't have to worry about obtaining more for a long time. There was only one problem: I didn't have any money.

These are the thoughts that were going round and round in my head all day, every day, for several days. There wasn't enough room in my head for anything else. Images and smells and sensations flashed through my mind. A needle sinking into my vein. The sickly sweet smell of crack. Pills of all shapes, sizes, and colors. Fluorescent chemicals mingling with my crimson plasma, surging through my limbs, pulsing in and out of my heart, exploding in stars behind my eyes.

Rhonda and I were living in an apartment at that time, but we weren't married because neither of us thought it was that big of a deal. She wanted me to stay clean, but she didn't put a lot of pressure on me. I think she certainly saw that I was screwing up more and more because of the drugs. I was keeping a job for the most part and not getting into trouble with the law. While I was in rehab, her aunt had given her a small .25 caliber handgun because she was scared to stay in the apartment by herself. A few weeks after returning from rehab, a plan began to take shape in my mind, a plan involving this gun.

When I look back, I can see that all I really wanted was a little peace of mind. I wanted to get rid of all those voices in my head. They must have been a form of mental opiate withdrawal from the methadone. My body had recovered, but my head was still extremely screwed up.

Here's what I was thinking. I was thinking about taking the gun into a drug store and getting all the pills I could get my hands on. The thought turned into a fantasy, and the fantasy turned into a plan, and my plan turned into action. One night, I put on a cap and sunglasses for a disguise and set out on my mission. I found a drug store in a shopping center. It was approaching closing time, so there weren't many customers in the store. I found an aisle that led straight to the pharmacy in back. There weren't any customers at the counter, either, and I could see the pharmacist behind his computer. My heart was thumping in my ears, and my legs felt like lead as panic overtook my body. I knew I was falling down into that pit, but I was powerless to stop. The evil spirit of drug addiction had hijacked my flesh and bones. As I reached the counter I felt like I separated from my body and watched myself in horror from a distance.

The pharmacist came out from behind his computer. I had intended to make away with enough dope to last a year at least, a whole drug store with all the Valium, Lortab, Xanax, Morphine, Demerol, Ritalin, Dilaudin, Vicodin, Percodan, Adderall, Merpergan, Ativan, Dexedrine, and Oxycontin I could carry. Yes, I wanted it all. But when I pulled the gun out, all that came out of my mouth was, "Give me a bottle of morphine."

The pharmacist didn't say anything, but the look in his eyes said, *I'll get you whatever you want. You won't have to use that gun.* He turned around and brought back what I asked for, a bottle of a hundred pills called MS Contin (morphine sulfate).

Then I went into my escape plan. I grabbed the bottle off the counter and walked swiftly out of the store and around the corner. I jumped into my truck, which I had backed into a parking space with the motor left running, and pulled out of the parking lot. I looked in my rear view mirror, but no one came running out of the store and there were no cop cars in sight. I drove a few miles, found another drug store, and bought some rigs and a bottle of water. I couldn't wait to get home to fix, so I sat in my truck in the parking lot of the second drug store. My hands were shaking so badly I could hardly use them. The adrenaline rush from the robbery had my eyes bugging out and my kidneys aching. I tied off with my belt, gripping the end with my teeth, and found a good vein. I released the belt and pulled the needle out … *relief at last.* No more screaming voices in my head. No more debating about whether to do it or not. No more hanging over the pit.

In the days that followed, I remained high from the moment I got up in the morning until my head hit the pillow at night. Getting up was the best part of my day if I knew I had some dope to face the next twenty-four hours with. But it didn't take long before my tolerance reached an all-time high, and I required more and more dope to achieve the desired effect. And it didn't take long for the pills to run out. A couple of week later, I was back where I started, except now I was worse off because now I was going to get sick without it. The drug store robbery had been too easy, so I didn't have to debate very long about whether or not to do it again. I repeated the same plan as before.

Meanwhile, I was getting all of my friends high, too. A couple of them had never shot up before, so I initiated them. I was never a victim of peer pressure because I was always the one doing the pressuring. I was every parent's worst nightmare. I had one acquaintance named Amy, who had never done any hard drugs that I knew of. We were at a friend's house and three or four of us were shooting up, and she wanted to try it, too. I was more than willing to oblige because I was ashamed to do it around someone who didn't, for fear they might look down on me. If I could get them to do it, too, then I wouldn't feel so bad about myself. So I fixed Amy a small dose, and she gave me her arm. After I finished, her skin flushed all over and she became glassy-eyed. She had to lie down. It didn't take long for her to start puking. The dose was too much for her. I saw her later that night, and she was still sick. I didn't feel too bad about it at the time, of course; I didn't feel too much of *anything*. I haven't seen Amy since that night, but I've often thought about her since I've gotten clean. I think about how horrible it was to do such a thing to her. I need and want to make amends to everyone I've harmed, so she's definitely on my list, and hopefully by the time I finish writing this story, I will have contacted her and made my apologies.

Eventually, I ran out of pills again. It was too easy, so my robbery spree continued. I was out of control. I was drug crazed. One of the times, I got a bottle of Fiorinal, which is a compound of codeine and Phenobarbital. My tolerance was so high now that I required a massive dose to get a buzz. I was getting fucked-up for sure, but I wasn't getting the euphoric sense of well being I craved, so one night I took what must have been fifteen pills. The Phenobarbital had me stumbling for days. I could barely stand up. I couldn't see straight.

I was also constantly fighting with Rhonda by now. She had found my stash and wanted to know where I got so many pills, so I made up some story about having bought them real cheap from a drug dealer. Of course she didn't believe me. She was at her wits' end.

I was staying out all night, smoking crack, not going to work. One night I robbed a crack dealer in one of the crack hoods and then drove to the nearest convenience store to buy a lighter. As I was backing out of the parking space, the dealer came around the corner and saw me. He threw a beer bottle at my truck. It shattered my windshield. As I sped off, he jumped in his car and gave chase, following me in and out of neighborhoods and up and down side streets. He was right on my tailgate as I slid around corners and ran stop signs and red lights. Smoke, burning rubber, and headlights were all I could smell, hear, or see. All the contents of the cab of my truck were bouncing off the seat, sliding from door to door under my feet and ricocheting off the dash, including the small rocks and the aluminum can I was using for a pipe.

I eventually shook him off and got away, but the inside of my truck was a mess. I stopped in an Applebee's parking lot so I could find the rocks. I found some rocks all right, but not crack rocks. Wearing only shorts and no shoes, I got out and got down on my knees on the pavement and dug around in my floorboard. Every time I thought I found a piece, I would put it in the can and try to smoke it, but it kept turning out to be a pebble or a peanut. I thought maybe some had fallen when I opened the door. I'm sure I was a sight to the diners in the restaurant. There I was, half-dressed, on my hands and knees, my face six inches off the ground, picking rocks up off the asphalt and trying to smoke them. When I finally gave up this insanity, my knees and the tops of my feet were scratched and bleeding. To this day, I still have a scar on the middle toe of my left foot from this experience.

Then I ran out of pills again. Reality began to take hold. I knew I couldn't keep this up. The law of averages was bound to catch up with me. I tried to put on the brakes, but it was hard to go through the withdrawal pains when I knew I could have relief in as little as fifteen minutes if I wanted it. But I was not about to go to a dealer and pay for what I could get for free.

It was a long, agonizing, boring Sunday. I couldn't take it anymore. I grabbed my disguise and the gun and told Rhonda I was going to buy some beer. I drove to a shopping center with a drug store that was only a mile away. I parked in the back, just around the corner of the building, got out, and walked around to the front entrance of the store. As I was walking down the aisle toward the pharmacy counter, the druggist looked up and saw me coming. I noticed him reaching for the phone. He was still watching me. This spooked me, so I turned around and walked out. I figured I would just try somewhere else. As I got into my truck and started pulling out, however, I glanced in my rearview mirror and saw an old Volvo come speeding around the corner. When he got right on my tail, it dawned on me that this must be the pharmacist. I drove out of the parking lot and into the traffic on a congested boulevard, where I swerved in and out of traffic with this guy still right on my bumper. I noticed a side street coming up, slammed on brakes, and slid around the corner. In my rearview mirror, I saw the Volvo skid into the stop sign at the end of the street. I shook him loose there, but most likely not before he got my tag number. I didn't think it would matter. I hadn't robbed his store, but it scared me enough to just go on back home and suffer some more.

In fact, I was scared enough to go ahead and suffer through the withdrawal. It wasn't as bad as the methadone, anyway. After suffering for a more than a month coming off of methadone, I could go through a few more days of agony.

I became clear-headed again after a couple of weeks and started to believe that I had gotten away with the drug store robberies. The fear and guilt had gone away. What was left was a dull desire for more drugs. Up to this point, every time I quit using, it was not with the intent to stay clean forever. I couldn't imagine life without alcohol and drugs. I'd lost interest in everything else. The only thing I could get excited about was some new drug or a new connection. Quitting just meant slamming on the brakes when the car started going too fast. But I still had a destination to reach. I just didn't have a clue where or what that destination was.

It was a Friday, and I was sitting at home because I didn't have a job, having quit the powder-coating job because I was too fucked up to work. I was watching TV when I heard a cop radio outside my apartment, then a knock on the door. Of course there was no way I was going to answer it. I hardly ever answered the door or the phone anymore, even when I didn't think it was the cops. I snuck upstairs and peaked out through a crack in the curtains. They were leaving. It looked like a detective and two uniformed officers. I didn't know what to do, so I didn't do anything. I didn't know what they would or could do. Would they come back again? How many times would they come back if I just didn't answer the door? Would they get a search warrant? Would they go to the media to ask the public's help to find me? That was the last thing I wanted to happen. I didn't want to embarrass my mom and dad or Rhonda.

As it turned out, the cops did something I didn't expect. When Rhonda came home from work, she asked me where my truck was. I'm sure I looked like I'd seen a ghost. My hands and feet turned icy cold. I had the sensation of the blood leaving my body through my feet, going straight down into the ground. I ran outside and looked in the parking lot where I usually parked my truck. It wasn't there. It wasn't anywhere else. They had me.

I went back inside. I was too scared to tell Rhonda what I knew had happened. I realized that I would have to face the consequences sooner or later, so I called 9-1-1 and reported my truck stolen and continued to play the charade with Rhonda. They showed up fifteen minutes later with a knock on the door. Rhonda was standing right behind me when I opened it.

It was a different plain-clothes detective and another officer. "Are you David Reeves?" the detective asked.

"Yes."

"Mr. Reeves, you're under arrest for first-degree armed robbery."

I hadn't even stopped to consider what crime I could be charged with. Armed robbery sounded serious. I heard Rhonda inhale and in my peripheral vision saw her hand go to her mouth; I couldn't look her in the eye. I hung my head.

The detective wasn't done. "Would you turn around so I can handcuff you? You have the right to remain silent. You have the right...."

While the uniformed officer was leading me out the door, I heard the detective ask Rhonda if there was a gun in the apartment. She was not one to be dishonest or deceitful in any way, especially to an officer of the law.

My mind wouldn't let me believe this was happening to me. It was surreal, as if I were underwater or in a dream. My worst nightmare had become reality. As I walked from my apartment to the police car, I kept my eyes on the ground in front of me. My fear was so great that I wished I could shut off all sensory perception. I felt like I was jumping off a high dive. All I could do was brace myself and hope I survived the fall.

I was taken to police headquarters, where I was questioned by the detective about only one of the robberies. I was scared out of my wits, so I answered truthfully. I was still very young, very naïve, and I still felt invincible. *Nothing this horrible could happen to me.* I thought maybe if I answered honestly, he'd let me go. Maybe he'd feel sorry for me and just sweep this thing under the rug.

But my case didn't belong to the detective that was questioning me. It belonged to the one who had come to my apartment earlier in the day. So when the questioning detective suddenly found two more arrest warrants for me, I suddenly decided I didn't want to answer any more questions.

Being arrested and put in jail is an assault on the senses and emotions—the fear and stench, the disgust, the embarrassment. The deafening uproar of loud voices, the hateful eyes directed upon you. Anxiety, tight, tense muscles. Confusion. I was put in a cellblock with the most violent offenders—rapists, robbers, and murderers.

My first time in jail, and I went straight to the top. I skipped all the misdemeanors and property crimes. Call me an overachiever.

There is a smell in these places, a mix of sweat, piss, and disinfectant that gets in your skin and stays there. If you get a whiff of it years later, all those feelings and emotions come back and slap you in the face. It's the smell of condemnation.

My bond was set really low because this was my first offense and because I had confessed to the charges. I spent the weekend in jail, was arraigned on Monday, and my parents bailed me out on Tuesday on the condition that I stay with them until the matter was settled. They didn't want me to be where I could get in more trouble or skip bail. They wanted to be able to keep an eye on me.

My mom picked me up. My memory of what we said escapes me. What I remember is going to a bail bondsman across the street from the jail so I could sign some papers and he could let me know what was expected of me. Then my Mom and I went to my apartment so I could take a shower and get some clothes. Rhonda was there. I could see the hurt in her eyes. She didn't have much to say, and for the first time I feared she would leave me. Up until that point, I had always taken her for granted. I had always done what I wanted with no concern for her or her feelings. I was very selfish in our relationship, and she put up with a lot of idiocy. But now, with one look at her eyes, I realized she couldn't take anymore.

We had been together for eight years at this point, and all of a sudden she was the most important thing in the world to me. She sat down in a chair in our bedroom. I got on my knees and begged her to please not leave me now. I couldn't face this without her. When she gave me a painful smile and said she would stay with me, I immediately felt much better. The thought of losing her was worse than the thought of going to prison. I didn't want to have to go through two punishments at once.

I finished gathering my things and said goodbye to Rhonda. She was afraid to stay in the apartment by herself, so she was going to stay with her aunt for a while. She was afraid that I had made too many enemies that might want to exact revenge. It was true that I had made some enemies, but none that even knew my name, much less where I lived. But I couldn't blame her for being scared. Besides, I'd just turned her whole world upside down and hurt her more than I knew. She didn't need to be alone.

I was out on bond for ten months, ten long, excruciatingly boring, and dreadful months. The weight hanging over my head was too much to bear. My guilt and shame kept me clean for about one month, but when the cravings and the desire came back, they came back with a vengeance, amplified, multiplied, and magnified. The guilt and shame escalated to self-disgust and humiliation, feelings that had to be exterminated and annihilated. I completely blotted out the thought that I could be going to prison, even if it was just for thirty days. It would kill me. The twenty-eight days I'd spent in rehab had been like living in hell, and I couldn't even fathom how horrible prison would be. I was spineless and pitiful. I was tough enough to take a gun and stick it in people's faces to get what I wanted, but the thought of even a few days in prison had me whimpering and whining.

I needed relief from the gravity of my predicament, which was crushing what little soul I had left. When I got a few odd jobs like installing carpet and hanging wallpaper, I didn't waste any time in the houses where I worked. I went right to the medicine cabinets. Just about every house I worked in had something: Xanax, Lortab, Ritalin, or at least some cough syrup to catch a buzz with. I'm sure some of my customers realized what I was doing, but they never confronted me. This was just one more thing that made me feel like a low-life scoundrel, one more guilty feeling to kill. I would have to become a bigger scoundrel to kill that feeling, over and over again, *ad nauseam*. I even broke into my brother's house (he lived next door to my parents) to see if they had any pills. They did. I scored a bottle of codeine and some Tussinex cough syrup. The Tussinex had me itching all over and nodding out, the sublime opiate high.

One weekend when I went to the beach with some of my friends, I stayed so high and drunk that it was all a big blur. I was at the stage now where getting high on one drug just made me crave some other drug that I didn't have, so I was constantly seeking more. On the Sunday I came back from the beach, I was supposed to spend the night with Rhonda, who I had left alone all weekend in the apartment. But instead of going to our apartment, I got in my truck to go find some crack. I was high on Xanax and Tylenol 3s, and I was broke. Xanax turns me into a complete and total idiot—I'm afraid of nothing and no one. I wanted to smoke some rock, and nothing was going to stop me.

I decided to do what crack heads do best—steal. But, as with all of my criminal endeavors, I had to take it one step further. I broke into a church and stole some PA equipment. I didn't believe in God, so a church was an easy target. I put the equipment in the bed of my truck and went looking for a pawnshop, but none were open because it was late on a Sunday night. When I finally found an open pawnshop, the guy behind the counter didn't want anything to do with it. "I can't help you," he said. "I've got a bad feeling about this stuff."

I wasn't about to give up, so I found a crack hood and decided to trade the equipment for whatever I could get. The equipment was probably worth five hundred to a thousand dollars, new, but if it came down to it, I'd give it all away for a twenty-dollar rock.

As I drove around the streets, I noticed a few black dudes hanging out on a corner and sitting on the porch steps of a house. One of them flagged me down and came up to the passenger window. I rolled it down told him I wanted a fifty. He jumped in the truck before I could stop him. This was against one of my basic rules when dealing with these street thugs: never let them in the vehicle. But the Xanax had me where I didn't give a rip. I was beyond desperate. As I started to pull off, I noticed in the rear window, that several other dudes were grabbing the swag out of the bed of my truck. By the time I stopped, they were gone. There was nothing I could have done, anyway, especially with this guy already in my truck.

"If you get out," he said, "they gon' kill you."

I was way over my head. I didn't care. I was in a fight I couldn't win, but I kept swinging. The dude guided me down a maze of streets that I had never been through before and into a housing project. The parking lot was full of hoodlums drinking forty-ounce beers and bobbing their heads to the deep bass rumble of the hip-hop coming from a car stereo. As I pulled in, they swarmed my truck. Sheer insanity is the only explanation for what happened next.

My passenger opened the door and one of the dealers handed him a rock, which he gave to me. Earlier, I had stuck a pebble between my fingers, so when I tasted the crack rock to test it, I handed the pebble back to the dealer instead, saying I didn't want it. This might have worked had I not started pulling off before the passenger door was shut. There was a lot of shouting and yelling, inside and outside my truck, and my passenger put his hand on the gear stick and wouldn't let me shift out of first gear. Suddenly other dudes were hanging onto the open door, running along beside us. As we were wrestling over the gear stick, the first dude started grabbing the steering wheel. I had the gas pedal to the floor and the engine was sounding like it was about to explode. That's when I heard a loud *BOOOOM* and saw a flash of fire to my left.

I eventually got control of the steering wheel and finally shifted into second gear and shook off my pursuers. I managed to keep all four tires on the street and made a few turns, but there was a constant barrage of blows to the side of my head and arm from my passenger. I was trying to fend him off and shift gears with my right arm and steer with my left. He had a crack pipe in his fist, and started digging it into my scalp. I could feel my skin tearing. I swung as hard as I could but it wasn't doing any good. My backhand needed some work. I couldn't get him off me. I was losing control. I finally stopped the truck, but it was too late. I was dizzy from the blows and he was still gouging away at my scalp with his pipe. He reached over me, opened my door and pushed me to the pavement. I collapsed on the asphalt in dazed astonishment as he drove off. Now what was I going to do?

I didn't have time to contemplate alternatives of action because as the sound of my truck faded, the sound of police sirens grew. I jumped up and started running. *If the police catch me walking around in this neighborhood*, I was thinking, *and they run a check on me, they'll see I'm on bond, and then they'll take me to jail.* I saw the blue lights out of the corner of my eye as I leapt over fences and ran through back yards. Dogs were barking, adding to the noise of the cackle of a police radio, but the sounds of my panting and the pounding of my heart muffled it all. I ran till my legs burned and I felt like I was going to hyperventilate.

Despite all of the drug use, I was in pretty good shape. I had been doing a lot of jogging while staying at my parents' house. So I kept running in the general direction of where I thought the interstate should be. I finally made it there, but not without some comments from the night urchins, "That white boy must be lost."

I was about six miles from my apartment, so I set off jogging down the beltline. A trucker pulled over to ask directions to a business that was on the very exit I was headed for, so I got in with him and we drove there. I got out and walked to a gas station. I told the attendant that I needed to call the police and report my truck stolen. As with most of my dealings with authority figures up to this point, I thought a lie would be better than the truth, so when the cop arrived, I told him my truck had been stolen after I scuffled with the thief in the gas station parking lot. Of course he didn't believe me. It was around midnight. I'm sure I was quite a sight. I was high, sweating profusely, and had just been in a fight and had scalp wounds.

So I called Rhonda and asked her to come pick me up. She was beside herself with anger and refused to come get me. My lies made absolutely no sense. The apartment was only a mile away, so I could have walked, but the cop offered me a ride, along with a warning that I could be arrested for filing a false police report.

Rhonda let me in, but then she stormed off without a word and slammed the bedroom door. The police called me about an hour later. They'd found my truck on a dead-end street. It was stripped of the tires and the battery, and there was a bullet hole in the driver's door. They'd had it impounded. I slept on the couch that night and woke up the next morning with blood all over the pillow from my scalp wounds, plus a black eye and bruises all up and down my right arm.

No one believed my story, but I stuck to it. My truck stayed impounded for more than a month because I didn't have enough money for new tires, rims, a battery, and the impound fee. When I finally did reclaim it, I found the crack rock stuck between the weather seal of the driver's door and the floorboard. I'd paid a huge price for such a pitiful, small piece of dope. I didn't even get a good blast from it.

Another highlight of my ten months on bond was a drunken fight Rhonda and I got into one night. We were at my friend Randy's house, drinking with a bunch of other friends. Randy kept pouring all different kinds of alcohol into a glass and daring me to drink it. Was he crazy? Beer and whiskey? *Gulp*. Vodka and wine? *Gulp*. It was all the same to me. It wasn't long before I was making an ass of myself. Rhonda and I left the party and went to her mother's house, where we were spending the weekend. We were in the bedroom, and I was lying on the bed. I don't remember what we were talking about or what I said, but the next thing I knew, she was on top of me, swinging. I think she was just fed up with all of my crap in general and it boiled over that night, with a little help from the alcohol. I pushed her off and left the room.

I don't remember the exact order of events because I was more than a little drunk, but the next thing I knew, we were both outside, still arguing. I was pissed because I didn't think she had any reason to jump on me like she did. She wasn't explaining herself. She started swinging at me again, pounding me on the chest. I tried to defend myself by pushing her off me, but my open palm went right into her eye, and the blow knocked her on her butt. I didn't intend to hurt her. It was the only way I could get her to stop hitting me.

The next day she had a black eye. Not a huge, swollen, multicolored shiner, but it was bruised enough to make me feel like a real piece of shit. I hate physical violence. I was appalled at what had happened. The drugs and alcohol were eroding my moral principles in more ways than one.

Meanwhile, my case was proceeding through the courts. I was looking at twenty years to life. The thought crossed my mind more than once to jump bail and take off to Mexico or somewhere, but I couldn't do that to my family or Rhonda. I had already put them through enough. The weight hanging over me was unbearable. I was incapacitated by dread. I didn't even bother with trying to get a job.

My lawyer had me take a mental evaluation. After discussing the results with the state psychologist, he told me that I was going to have to do at least a couple of years in prison. This wasn't something I wanted to hear, but it did help me accept the truth of what was going to happen to me after trying for so long to deny it. My lawyer cut a deal for me to plead guilty to third degree robbery, which carried a sentence of one to ten years.

I moved back in with Rhonda and waited to be sentenced. My situation was a little bit easier to deal with now that the uncertainty was over and I could accept my fate. My days were long and boring. I usually just watched TV or read a book. I jogged in the afternoon to kill the restlessness and anxiety of the day, and at night I tried to relax with a six-pack of beer.

Chapter 4
Consequences and Repercussions

Junk is the ideal product ..... the ultimate merchandise. No sales talk necessary. The client will crawl through a sewer and beg to buy.

-WILLIAM S. BURROUGHS
THE NAKED LUNCH

March 8, 1996, was the day of my sentencing. My mom and dad, Rhonda, and her mother and aunt were all there to support me. Before I went before the judge, my lawyer told me I would be getting ten years, but would probably be in prison for just one year. I hugged everyone then and said my goodbyes. I remember Rhonda's mother crying. She always was an uncontrollable weeper.

When the judge sentenced me, he recommended that I go through the prison drug treatment program. As the deputy escorted me to the holding cell in back, I waved goodbye to everyone again. My belt, tie, and shoelaces were taken from me and I was locked in a cell by myself. Instantly, a wave of anguish and depression swept over me. Being in there was the loneliest feeling in the world. I cried and whimpered like a little girl, but it was over before I knew it. I never shed another tear for the rest of my sentence.

Next, I was taken to the county jail and processed in. There was that smell again, the smell of condemnation. For twenty-one days I sat around, bored out of my mind. I played a few games of chess and cards, but there was nothing else to do but watch soap operas and talk shows on TV. There weren't any books to read. The cellblock was designed to hold sixteen inmates, but there were usually twenty or more, and most of the cells had two guys in the bunks and one with a mattress on the floor. The floor is where I lived with two Colombians until I graduated to a bunk.

The guy who took my place with the two Colombians was a short, unshaven white dude with long, dirty, strawberry blonde hair. He was going through opiate withdrawals. For three days, he lay there on the piss-splattered floor by the toilet bowl, puking constantly. The other inmates thought he was dying. They kept trying to get the guards to do something about it but the guards didn't care; I saw right then that this was not the place to get sick in. You could die in here before you got any help. People often did die, and it seldom made the news. The public has absolutely no idea what goes on in these places. The people who think criminals are coddled should spend a week in Mobile County Metro Jail. Then they'd shut up. But people are always spouting off their opinions about things they know absolutely nothing about.

The day came when I was awakened at four a.m., shackled up with leg irons and belly chains, loaded up on a bus with about thirty other inmates, and driven to Kilby Correctional Facility to be processed into the state prison system. I was run through a battery of physical, educational, and psychological tests to see where I should be placed in the prison system. One of the guys with us from Mobile was a white guy about the same age as me. He had gotten into a drunken argument with his girlfriend and beat her head against some bricks outside their trailer. Then he put her dead body in his car and drove around for hours until he ended up in New Orleans. He called his family from there, and they convinced him to turn himself in. He was serving twenty years for manslaughter.

I was at Kilby for seven days, and then I was shackled up again, loaded into another van, and driven to the Ventress Correctional Facility in southeast Alabama. Ventress is a medium-security prison, which mostly holds inmates going through the substance abuse program that was just getting started there at the time. The prison had a large recreation yard that included a softball field, volleyball and basketball courts, and a weight pile. The metal warehouse-like buildings that consisted of dorms, the chapel, and buildings housing the education, administration, and medical services surrounded the yard. Except for the fences topped with razor wire and the guard towers, Ventress didn't look like what I thought a prison should look like.

While I was still in receiving and discharge, being processed in, a few of us "fish" were standing at the fence that separated us from the recreation yard. Streams of hundreds of white uniforms flowed out of the dorms and settled into a sea of convicted humanity on the large plot of dead earth before us. It was an intimidating sight, and one that will probably be imprinted on my brain until I die. To say that I was scared would be an understatement, but as I was to find out, there was nothing to be afraid of here.

These people were not only society's rejects, but also they were the State of Alabama's rejects - guys with bad tattoos, bad teeth, no social skills, and no education. That's how I judged them at first because that's what I saw. A lot of them deserved to be removed from society, though a lot of them didn't. They were *human beings*. Beautiful souls in corrupted flesh.

I've had more convicts tell me they never had a chance. They were born into crime. Their fathers, uncles, brothers, and sometimes even their mothers were criminals. I believe children are like unprogramed computers. Whatever their parents or their environment teaches them, that becomes the programs they will run on for the rest of their lives. Eventually these faulty programs reveal themselves to be incompatible with society's rules and regulations.

My stay at Ventress was short, only eight months. I spent my time running, playing volleyball, and reading. And I became addicted to weight lifting. In their quest for self-improvement, a lot of convicts become unbalanced by focusing only on the physical part of themselves. But I think it's such a huge waste of time to spend months or years doing nothing but lifting weights, when they are just going back to their old habits once they are released. Everything they gained during the time they were locked up is gone in a matter of weeks, since very few will continue working out once they are released. That was a mistake I made. I spent up to eight hours a day working out, but I was neglecting the spiritual and emotional facets of my being. These two atrophied aspects of my life were probably the main cause of my drug addiction. Even though I attended the drug program, gave what I thought was one hundred percent, and graduated, it wasn't enough. Either there was no substance to the program or I was lying to myself and everyone else. I still wanted to get high. Thank God there were no drugs, at least none were offered to me at Ventress. I wanted to stay clean, but I still had reservations to use.

During my stay at Ventress, I got word from my mother that Brian had been arrested after falling through the roof of a drug store and breaking his leg. I felt horrible for my mom and dad because now they had two sons incarcerated. When I say I felt horrible for someone else, that's saying a lot, because at the time the only person I really felt horrible for was myself.

Rhonda came to visit me every two weeks, which is every time I was allowed to have a visit. We also stayed in touch through letters and the telephone. She had a hard time living by herself, and I worried about her a lot, especially when she drove the six-hour round trip to visit me, but she hung in there for me and I was very grateful. I felt very lucky to have someone visit me every chance I had. The majority of inmates weren't so fortunate.

I didn't form any close friendships while I was there. There were a couple of guys that I worked out with pretty regularly, but no one I thought I had anything in common with.

I was rewarded for staying out of trouble for eight months by being shipped to a farm camp. Again, I was awakened early in the morning and told to report to receiving and discharge with my property. I was taken to Elmore Correctional Facility for a couple of days, and then driven to Red Eagle. I was surprised when we pulled up in the dark to what looked like a large ranch house with Christmas lights strung up (it was December).

The camp did not have anything more than a barbed wire fence around it. I was glad to see that, because it meant I was that much closer to freedom.

Red Eagle was located just outside of Montgomery, and the inmates were given orderly jobs in a lot of the state government buildings in the city or in other government facilities, such as the National Guard armory. I was given a job changing oil in the state cars at the motor pool, which was located downtown. One inmate, who I worked with, got strung out on crack (I didn't know about it at the time, or I might have joined him) and absconded with one of the state's cars. He was caught about a week later in another state after his parents turned him in. All of us lost our jobs because of this incident. I was put in the kitchen for a few months, one of the worst jobs you can give a convict. But I bided my time and eventually was given a worse job at the county landfill. I had to walk around picking up trash on the side of the roads that snaked through and around the garbage pits. On the first day, I found a bottle with two or three pills still in it, but they were antibiotics. Nothing I could get high on. But that little bottle was enough to kick in my drug seeking behavior. It didn't take me long to start digging through trash looking for better pill bottles, though I never found anything. But I did find something in the office trailer where I was given a job as an orderly after a couple of weeks. One old lady that worked there brought a bag full of pills to work every day and left them in the kitchen area. Was this a setup? There must have been twenty bottles in there, and the bag was clear plastic. I spotted Xanax right away.

I told myself there was no way I was going to risk getting into more trouble and lose my good time. I wanted to go home as soon as possible. But I couldn't think straight. Every time I walked past the bag, my hands would start shaking and my heart would pound in my chest until it hurt.

I eventually fell for it. I grabbed the bottle of Xanax, shook out a handful, put the bottle back, and went straight to the restroom. By the time the buzz hit me, I didn't care whether they caught me or not. I didn't care about anything. That Xanax high was a brief respite from all my anxieties, worries, and concerns.

It wasn't a setup, and I didn't get into trouble because of my small criminal venture. But the worst thing that could happen, occurred anyway, and without my cognizance. I had ended up in prison because of my drug addiction and I had completed the substance abuse program, *and I still used the very first chance I got.* In my mind, I was doing well because no one knew about my slip but me. A lot of drug addicts think like this. They think it's all right to use if no one knows about it. But the person who does know is the one they should be the most concerned about finding out—themselves. If you had asked me at the time if I was using, I would have said no. Not only would I have been lying to you, but I would have been lying to myself as well.

As I look back now, I wish I had been caught. That was a time I should have been dealing with my addiction, but I wasn't. I skated through, and the road was paved for me to keep fucking up. The beast inside of me was still in control and driving down my path of destruction.

I spent five months at Red Eagle. After being in prison for just thirteen months of a ten-year sentence, I was put in work release in Mobile. When I found out about it the day before I left, I was so happy that tears of joy were streaming from my eyes. It was a fitting end to my time in prison, considering that it started with tears of anguish.

Rhonda visited me the day I arrived at the work release center. She brought some clothes for me. It felt good to wear street clothes after wearing prison whites for so long. It was good to be close to Rhonda again, too. The best thing about work release was I could get weekend passes to go home. Rhonda and I had talked about getting married before I went to prison, but I wanted to wait until I got out. As soon as I got to work release, it seemed like a good idea to go ahead and tie the knot because only spouses and immediate family were allowed to pick up inmates for passes. There was also a waiting period to be approved for furlough. It would be ninety days before I would be authorized, but since I was going to get married, I was given a one-day pass right away to go to the courthouse and take care of the legal aspects.

I couldn't restrain myself on the ride back to the apartment after Rhonda picked me up from the work release center. I had been physically removed from her for more than a year and I was about to explode. The next twenty-four hours were better than any drug could have made me feel. The feeling of being free after being locked up for more than a year is a high in itself. If I could have felt like that for the rest of my life, I would never have to touch another drink or another drug. But I was incapable of dealing with life on life's terms. Life is a series of ups and downs, and I reached for the highs and was unskilled to deal with the lows. There is no above without a below, no light without darkness, and no good without bad. I had to learn to accept it and deal with it.

Chapter 5
Flying Under the Radar

In this country, don't forget, a habit is no private hell. There's no solitary confinement outside of jail. A habit is hell for those you love.

-BILLIE HOLIDAY
LADY SINGS THE BLUES

There was another inmate at the work release center who had been at Ventress Correctional Facility when I was there. He caused a drunk-driving accident and killed a young girl in Alabama, was convicted of vehicular manslaughter, and was given a fifteen-year sentence.

I was leery of Greg at first because he was a real Bible thumper, what I would call an aggressive Christian. I had seen too many jail house converts who just wanted God to get their ass out of the sling they had gotten themselves into, to believe he was any different. But he was different. He was much more intelligent, always had a smile on his face, and had an easy, down-home way of conversing with anyone about anything. Greg helped me get a job with him at a Super-Lube, a chain of ten-minute oil change shops. I also learned at this time that I could go back to college and get the state to foot the bill. The Alabama Vocational Rehabilitation Services would pay my tuition if I filled out a questionnaire about my drug use that proved I was a drug addict and therefore disabled.

In August 1997, I started working at Super-Lube during the day and going to classes at the University of South Alabama in the evenings and on the weekends I went home on furlough. This was a good time for me. I was only at the center long enough to sleep and shower. I was staying clean, but that was only because the opportunity to get high never presented itself.

Several of the inmates were asked by one of the counselors at the center to speak at the juvenile detention center. We were supposed to scare the delinquents with stories about how horrible prison life is. One or two of the kids may have listened, but it was a joke to the rest of them, even though we were even dressed in our prison whites. There was nothing we could tell them. They either thought they would never end up in prison, or weren't afraid of it and thought it might make them appear tougher. Some of them had probably been expecting to go to prison because their fathers and brothers and other male relatives were already in jail.

I thought it would be a good idea to become a drug counselor after this experience, so I started taking psychology courses at the university. I suddenly found that I might have a purpose in life after all. I made the president's list with a 4.0 grade point average my first semester. At work, I was promoted to assistant manager and was given a lot of responsibility, considering the fact that I was a felon who was technically still incarcerated, and would be for a while because I wasn't due to come up for parole until the next year.

I broke a few rules while in work release that could result in my return to prison if I were caught. The center had only four vans that carried us to and from work, and the driver had a lot of stops to make. This meant I was dropped off at work at six a.m., even though the shop did not open until eight a.m. I started using this extra two hours to jog in the neighborhood. It didn't take long for the idea to dawn on me that I could jog the three or four miles to Rhonda's apartment to spend an hour with her, then have her drop me off at the shop on her way to work. She also came by and took me to lunch two or three times a week. Sometimes I also saw her in the evenings, too, when I had a break between classes.

We were given plenty of money each week to buy food and other necessities. The state took a third of our checks and the rest of the money went into an account that we would receive upon release. For some reason, I thrived in this environment. The rules I was breaking were minor compared to what some of the other inmates were doing. While I was there, there were guys who didn't return from work and were charged with escape. More of them got drunk or failed a piss test. Some got caught stealing from work, and there were also a few dealing drugs. My rule breaking wasn't criminal, just a disregard for authority, or so I told myself at the time. I worked hard and studied hard. While I gained a new confidence in myself that I had never had before, I was still ashamed of the fact that I was a criminal.

Yes, now I was thinking of myself as clean and no longer a drug addict, because, except for my slip at Red Eagle, I had been clean for more than a year. The twelve step programs assert that alcoholism and drug addiction is a disease that we will have for the rest of our lives, a progressive illness that we can only arrest, but not cure. That's one of the reasons they have us say in meetings, "My name is David and I'm an alcoholic." But I didn't agree with that. I thought if I wasn't currently using drugs or drinking alcohol, then I was not an addict or alcoholic. I felt like I had this addiction thing licked and would never use again if I didn't want to. We were coerced into attending AA and NA meetings if we wanted to stay in the work release program. If we didn't comply, then we would be sent back to prison. So when it became my turn to introduce myself at the meetings I said, "My name is David and I'm a recovered alcoholic." That got more than a few heads turning and stupid stares. My egotism and lack of humility would come back to bite me in the ass.

A decision to do something or not do something is just that—a decision. Decisions can be reversed just as easily as, and sometimes more easily than, they were made in the first place. I listened to people saying, "You don't need NA or AA to quit. You've just got to make up your mind." Well, *I had quit.* It was easy as long as it wasn't in my face, and if it wasn't in my face, then it wasn't on my mind. What's hard is to *stay quit.* What's opposite of this? In sight, in mind!

Drugs have a way of finding me. I knew all the pill heads at the center and they knew me. Pill heads always have their feelers out to find out who's got the dope and whom they can share with or sell to if they've got a surplus. So it was only a matter of time before I was offered the chance to get high. I didn't hesitate. If I had made any kind of change during my time clean, that first pill instantly wiped it out. Months and months of abstinence were canceled out by one second of indulgence.

I didn't care about that at the time, however, because I was reunited with a long lost lover and everything was great. The only thing I was worried about at the time was the urine test I had to take when I came back from weekend furloughs. Opiates can only be detected in your urine for three days after use, so I had to time it so I wouldn't fail. There were more than a few times that I sweated over those tests. I would drink as much water as I could hold a few hours before the test to flush out my system, and then just hope for the best. But pretty soon I began to suspect they only tested for alcohol, marijuana, and cocaine. That was all anyone ever failed for. I still took all the precautions I could short of abstinence.

I didn't get totally out of control with my first use. My connections never seemed to last longer than a week or two before running dry, so I didn't have enough time to develop a habit in which I would get sick when I ran out. Then one of my cohorts, a guy named Pat, hooked me up with some morphine and a syringe. I met him for lunch at the What-A-Burger next door to my shop. I went to the restroom and fixed after we ate. Now I was in trouble. I loved this feeling more than anything in the world and that is not an exaggeration. My desire to get high was increased tenfold. To make matters worse, Pat told me where he scored and said all I had to do was go there and tell them he sent me.

Before I left work that day, I went to the bathroom and fixed one more time. I was high as a satellite, lit up like a Christmas tree. When I got back to the center, I took a shower and layback on my bed in a sweet haze presided over by the god Morpheus. I was on top, looking down on everyone and everything that was going on around me. I was at the apogee. Any higher, and I would have drifted out of orbit. There was no more gravity to pull me back down to reality.

The connection Pat told me about was an old lady who lived off of MLK Avenue in a drug-infested neighborhood that I was more than a little familiar with. It was only about three miles away from where I worked. One morning I decided to jog there instead of jogging to Rhonda's apartment. I'm sure I looked a little out of place, a clean-cut, twenty-something, white boy jogging in the hood, but I didn't care. I would do anything to get high if I could convince myself that I wouldn't get caught. But the streets in this neighborhood were fairly deserted at six-thirty in the morning. I found the dilapidated dwelling easily. I went through a chain link fence and across a couple of boards that were laid across a mud puddle, and then stepped up onto the porch. I knocked on the door. No answer. I knocked again. Still no answer. I hadn't run all the way down here for no one to answer the door. I knew someone had to be home. It wasn't like these people actually had jobs to go to. After the third knock, I heard some shuffling coming from the other side of the door.

"Who is it?"

"David."

"Who?"

"Pat's friend. David."

She finally opened the door. It was an old back lady with disheveled gray hair, wearing glasses and a dirty, ill-fitting nightgown.

"What do you want?" she asked me.

"I want an orange sixty." Morphine comes in an orange colored sixty-milligram pill.

"I don't know you." She shut the door.

There I was, still standing there trying to figure out what to do next when the door opened again. This time it was a younger black woman who looked like walking death. Her hair was dirty, matted, and sticking out in every direction, and she had open sores all over her arms. Pat told me later that her name was Rose and she was dying from AIDS.

She was the daughter of the older woman and obviously didn't care about whether or not I was a cop.

"What'cha want?" Rose asked. She had a pill bottle in her hand.

"An orange sixty."

She told me to walk into the foyer, and then she closed the door behind me. She shook several pills into her hand and picked one out and gave it to me.

"How much?" I asked.

"Sixty." A dollar a milligram.

I paid her the money, took the pill, folded it up in a dollar bill, and put it in my pocket. I looked up and down the street cautiously as I stepped back out the door and onto the porch. This neighborhood was hot. If a cop saw a young white male coming out of one of these houses down here, he would know a drug deal had just taken place. But there were no cars in sight. I stepped out into the street and took off jogging again, energized by adrenaline.

I was back at the shop by seven a.m. Greg was sitting in the customers' waiting room like he did every morning.

"How far'd you run?" he asked me.

"Six miles."

"You better be careful. You're gonna get caught one day."

"Yeah, I know." I headed for the restroom.

Of course, I knew I would not be able to make a habit of this. Spending that sixty dollars left me broke for the rest of the week. But that one pill would keep me high all day because I could split it into thirds. But where would I be tomorrow? I'd be broke and wanting more than ever to get high. I'd already risked my freedom. I had to draw the line somewhere. Who knows why I pick certain times to put on the brakes and sometimes not. I'd already exhibited plenty of risk-taking behavior without much concern for the consequences. I guess it depends on how far strung out I am at the time.

I wasn't strung out very far at this time, but during the next few weeks I ran down to "Mama's house" every time I got sixty dollars in my pocket. It was time to put on the brakes, and that would call for drastic measures. If I continued on this path, I knew where it would lead: I would steal from work or commit some other criminal act to obtain money. I was already taking tremendous risks with my freedom. Now it was time to stop.

Mama had started serving me the last few times I had been down there. I knocked on the door and soon as I heard a response I walked on in. She was lying on a bed off to the left of the foyer, where Rose was sometimes asleep on a couch. Mama didn't even get out of bed when I went in. She had her pill bottle in her hand and I just walked up to her bed, handed her my money, and got my pill.

I decided the best way to stop myself from going down there would be to rip her off. So one morning I jogged to her house as usual. Rose was asleep on the couch and Mama was lying in bed with the pill bottle. I could have grabbed the whole bottle, but she kept it too close to her and I didn't want to get into a struggle with an old lady with Rose lying in my path of escape. I had a couple of ones and a five folded up like it was more than it actually was. I told Mama I wanted the usual, and as soon as the pill was in my hand, I spun on my heels and headed for the door. All she could manage was a weak "Hey!" but it was loud enough to alert Rose, who jumped up and started moving a lot swifter than a person dying from AIDS was supposed to. I made it to the front door just ahead of her. She was barely able to grab my T-shirt sleeve as I hit the door. I jerked free and ran out the house and up the street. I ran hard for a couple of blocks, but it wasn't necessary. I don't think they even came out of the house after me.

That was settled. I couldn't show my face at Mama's house again. It's ridiculous that I had to take such extreme measures to stop, but I had no control over the compulsion to stick a needle in my arm. A few days later, Pat out found about my escapade from Rose.

"Man," he said, "you're a lunatic."

I had to agree with him. "It was the only way I could stop myself from going down there every day."

"That's a new one on me, robbing a drug dealer on foot."

"That's what that shit does to me," I told him. "It turns me into an idiot."

"Yeah. I know what you're saying. I've done a lot of retarded shit myself."

Every time I saw Pat over the next few weeks, he burst out laughing and shook his head. He got out a few months later and was dead from an overdose within a year.

I did all right for the next few months. I continued to work full time and go to school full time. I had been in the work release for almost a year and was due to go before the parole board in six months. Rhonda continued to pick me up for my weekend passes and I got a three-day furlough every ninety days.

But my period of abstinence? It was short lived. I knew another guy at the center named Brasher. He was a skinny twenty-three-year-old with bad tattoos and a trailer park personality. I occasionally bought an assortment of pills from him, Xanax, Lortabs, Valiums, and Fastens. Fastens were phentermine, half of the ill-fated fen-phen diet fad. They were uppers, like amphetamines. I took ten of them at work one day. Even though I was high as a kite and zooming all over the place, no one there seemed to be able to tell I was on anything, but I was sick as a dog for the next three days.

One day I bought some Lortabs and Valiums from Brasher with a fifty-dollar bill that I'd received from the work release center for my food allowance. Brasher didn't have change for a fifty, so he asked his friend, Lance, who lived in the same room with Greg at the center, for change. That same day, Greg and I took turns running the cash register. At some point in the day, or so Greg said, someone paid their bill with two fifty-dollar bills. At the end of the day, when Greg was cashing out the register, he came up one hundred dollars short. And the two fifty dollar bills weren't there. I didn't think anything at the time because I figured Greg had just made a mistake and would discover it eventually. Greg, Lance, and I ate supper that night in the cafeteria at the center. Lance overheard what happened at work that day as Greg tried to figure out what happened to the money. Greg and I were in a very precarious situation now because we were both technically still incarcerated for breaking the law and we were working at a business where money had gone missing. We could be sent back to prison for a lot less than stealing.

Later that night, Lance told Greg about my buying pills from Brasher with a fifty-dollar bill, and the next day Greg told our manager, Tracy. As I worked that day, I was still ignorant of the fact that they suspected me, and I didn't worry about it too much because I had never really been accused of doing something that I hadn't done without it being cleared up eventually. I was still very naïve in this respect.

At the end of the day, the cash register came up about seventy-five dollars over. Now it was clear that Greg hadn't made a mistake. Someone had stolen the money, felt bad about it, and had tried to replace it. There were five of us working the day the money went missing. Four of us worked the next day, when most of it was put back. Tracy was the manager, so of course he didn't steal it. Greg was a self-righteous, Bible thumping Christian, so he couldn't have done it. Chris, another assistant manager who had worked for Super Lube for several years, was also above suspicion. That left me, a drug-addicted convict with a history of going to extreme means to obtain a little chemical bliss. Even I could see how this circumstantial evidence pointed its ugly gnarled finger at my shameful head. I knew I was under suspicion now.

Greg confronted me that night. "I heard you bought some pills with a fifty dollar bill," he said.

"Heard from who?" I asked, shocked that he knew about it.

"From Lance. He told me you bought some pills from Brasher."

"Yeah, I did. So what?" Now I was getting pissed because I'd been snitched on.

"So you need to own up to taking money from the cash register."

"I bought those pills," I said, "but I didn't take that money!"

"So you are confessing to the lesser of the two evils. You need to get honest."

"I didn't take that money! This is bullshit. You know they give us fifty dollar bills for food allowance all the time."

"Like I said," he insisted, "You need to get honest."

"I *am* being honest. I'm not so strung out that I have to steal. I wish I did take that money, because it would be easier to confess to it than to try to deny it, even when I can see that it looks like I did it, but I didn't."

But I was stoned out of my gourd the whole time this conversation was taking place, and I knew it was easy to see. My eyelids were droopy and my eyes were glassy and bloodshot. I was beside myself with anger, but there was no one to be mad at but myself. I don't blame Greg; I would have done the same thing. I don't blame Lance, either, because he was Greg's roommate and friend and he didn't want to see Greg take the fall for something he hadn't done when it looked like I'd done it.

The next day it was Tracy's turn to confront me.

"I'm going to ask you one time," he told me, "and whatever you say, I'll believe you and we won't talk about it again. Did you take that money?" I could see he believed I had done it and was trying to make it as easy as possible for me to confess.

"Tracy," I said, "I'm sorry for doing drugs while working in your shop, but I didn't take that money." I was so angry that all of this was falling on my head that I gritted my teeth as I answered him.

But he stuck to his word and never mentioned it again. I liked Tracy a lot. He was a hard worker, intelligent, and had plenty of integrity—something I knew nothing about. He was a very religious man and walked the walk. He acted a little cool towards me over the next few months, compared to before, but he had me continue to operate the cash register when it was needed. Even if he thought I'd taken the money, he trusted me to not do it again.

By this time, I had my own suspicions about who took the money, but I couldn't be sure. I used the process of elimination to identify the one guy I suspected, but my means of sleuthing were shakier than theirs. I mentioned my suspicion to Greg, whom I continued to argue with about it, but he was unwilling to consider that it could have been anyone other than me. The situation continued to eat at my nerves and peace of mind over the next several months. Even today, ten years later, it still pisses me off to think about it. Why? I've done things much worse before and since, things that make this little theft look like stealing bubble gum. I guess it was because I liked Tracy and Greg and would not have done anything to hurt them. It could have sent Greg back to prison, and Tracy, the manager, was ultimately responsible for the money. I saw there was a lesson to learn. I was fucking up, and if I wasn't paying the consequences directly, then I was paying them indirectly. I could have kept myself above suspicion if I had not been getting high. What I learned was that if I continued to do drugs after getting into so much trouble because of them, then I would become a lightning rod for blame if someone around me decided to transgress. I still think that whoever took the money knew that I would be blamed. I was the one who put myself in those shoes.

So now I was scared into abstinence once again. This shit was causing me problems, even when I wasn't doing anything wrong ... except for taking the pills. The whole matter was never brought up again at the Super-Lube unless I brought it up. Every four months or so for the next two and a half years, I reasserted my claim of innocence to Greg or Tracy, but neither one ever had anything to say about it. They just stared at me stupidly until I changed the subject.

It was now the summer of '98. It had been more than two years since I'd lost my freedom. I was coming up for parole in August, so I stayed clean and tried to fly under the radar of the staff at the work release center. My addiction had been pounding on me beating me up over the last year, so I was really lucky to be this close to freedom. I was planning on taking a furlough on the day of my parole hearing to ride to Montgomery with my family and Rhonda. A couple of days before the date, the staff did a room inspection, as they did every week, and I was written up for having an off-white pillow case, the same one I had had for the last sixteen months.

On the day of the hearing, Rhonda came to pick me up, but they wouldn't let me go because of the write-up. That is how petty and ridiculous these people could be. I had to chalk it up to the bad karma I had created for myself. My family went without me while I sat around the center all day, sulking and pissed off, but glad that all this was about to be over with. They had no reason to deny me parole. I had stayed out of trouble, at least as far as they knew, and proven that I could return to society by having held the same job the whole time I was in work release. That night I called home, and my mom told me that two of the three parole members had been there. They'd said my chances were good and that the absent member would probably vote with them for my release. A few days later, I was given a release date that would be in two weeks.

I had been working part-time as an assistant manager at another Super-Lube shop for the last six months. Our general manager, Clay, decided that I could manage my own store as soon as I was paroled. I was surprised that someone would put such trust and faith in me, even though I knew I had been working hard. Surprisingly, Tracy did not want to lose me from his store and tried to stop Clay from stealing me from him.

All of this was going on the day I was paroled. Rhonda came that morning to pick me up, and we had to sit and wait at the center for them to process my paperwork. I was so excited and agitated because it took more than a couple of hours to process me out that I was beginning to think they had found some reason not to release me. They finally let me go with a check for eighteen hundred dollars, the amount that had been deposited into my account.

Even though I'd had plenty of freedom while at the work release center, my feeling of relief now was immense. I felt high for weeks, just from the freedom alone. The fact that I could go home after work was wonderful. There were so many things I had to do, I felt like I couldn't get them done fast enough, even with few days off work. I had to get my driver's license renewed, I had to visit my parents, I had to see my parole officer, and I still had to go to school and study. I also planned to buy Rhonda an engagement ring. The only people who knew we were already married were our immediate families. She wanted to have a real wedding and was consumed with planning it.

Chapter 6
A Snake in the Grass

If the devil doesn't exist, but man has created him, he has created him in his own image and likeness.

-FYODOR DOSTOEVSKY
THE BROTHERS KARAMAZOV

I had to go see my parole officer the next day. My PO was a grandmotherly black woman. As it happened, her office was right across the street from my first apartment where I had learned how to smoke crack. She had me fill out some paperwork, and then she told me what was expected of me. She handed me a cup and told me to go to the bathroom to fill it up, then she tested it right in front of me. That was a mistake on her part. I saw that she only tested for alcohol, marijuana, and cocaine just like they did at work release. I kept this in mind during the next nine months I was on parole.

It felt so great to be free that at first I didn't feel the need to get high. It was the farthest thing from my mind at the time. I had been clean for the most part of five months, ever since the cash register incident, but that was mostly from guilt. I'd also seen that I couldn't use drugs in the work release center without everyone finding out about it. Besides, the dope just wasn't in my face right then, or I would have used, guilt or no. I just wasn't actively seeking it out.

The week I got out I was given my own Super-Lube store to manage. Tracy would be my general manager, so we were both happy with the situation. It was more responsibility for me, but also more money. When I was in prison I worried about what I would do for a job when I got out. I hadn't been able to hold down a job the last couple of years I was free, so I thought it would be even harder with a criminal record, but upon my release, my financial situation had never been better. I also found out that there are a lot of people out there who are more than willing to help an ex-convict who tries to help himself.

I had been doing a lot of running while I was in prison and work release, so when I got out I was in really good shape. I read in the newspaper about a triathlon in Gulf Shores, and I thought it would be a good idea to see if I could complete it. I had a mountain bike and our apartment complex had a swimming pool. I only had three weeks to train from the time I was released until the day of the event. The swimming was by far the hardest part. I figured that swimming some laps in the small pool would be enough to prepare me to swim the six tenths of a mile that was required for the race. I was wrong.

There was a steady drizzle the morning of the triathlon. Drizzle was a good thing, though, because September in south Alabama is still oppressively hot and humid. Rhonda, her aunt, and her cousin came to see me race. There were about five hundred contestants. The swim was first, then we had to bike for seventeen miles, then the triathlon finished with a five mile run. The swim was half the distance into a lagoon and back with buoys strung together with thick rope to separate the two sides. There were lifeguards in canoes to rescue anyone like me who was not adequately prepared to swim the distance. We started in two groups, a fast group followed by the slow group, based on how fast we told them we could swim. I should have been in the slow group, but my pride put me in the fast one. I made it a good hundred yards before I gave out and had to start dog paddling. Some of the faster guys were swimming right on top of me. I wasn't even a quarter into the swim and was already thinking I was going to drown as I accidentally gulped down a mouthful of salt water. By the time I turned around at the half way point I was worn out from dog paddling, so I had to turn over on my back and just try to float in the general direction of the shore. I started seeing a lot of the women in the slower group passing me. My feet finally touched bottom, but not before almost all of the other five hundred triathletes had passed me in the water. Glad that the hardest part was over, I finally made it to my bike. The bicycle leg of the event was out and back along a highway that runs parallel to the beach and is lined by high-rise condos on both sides. I made it halfway and was headed back to begin the run, when one of the other contestants passed me on his five-thousand-dollar bicycle. He took one look at my cheap mountain bike and said, "You are either real brave or real stupid." I passed him a few miles down the road, where he was nursing a leg cramp. Asshole.

By the time I got to the run, the steady drizzle turned into a light rain. It felt so great because it cooled me down. I was so far behind everyone else by the time I started running that I was able to blaze past a lot of the other competitors. That's because running was the only thing I was really in shape for.

I finished the triathlon in one hour and fifty-one minutes, but I didn't care about the time or what place I finished in. I just wanted to be able to say I'd done it. I felt a strong need to redeem myself. I wanted to prove to everyone that I wasn't a loser. I wanted to put as much distance as possible between my past and myself. It felt so good to complete the triathlon that I turned to something even bigger, a marathon.

I had a lot going on in my life. I was staying very busy with work, school, and training for a marathon. Rhonda was busy planning a wedding. Life was good.

One day at work, a few days after hurricane Georges flooded the oil change pit at my Super-Lube, I was in the storage room checking my inventory when I heard a loud "Shit!" followed by the sound of heavy feet pounding on the metal steps coming out of the oil pit. It was my pit guy - a big, fat, lazy slob named Jim. I'd never seen him move as fast as he was moving now.

"What's wrong?" I asked him.

"There's a snake!" He pointed at the sliding aluminum grates the covered the pit.

I went over to have a look. Sure enough, there was a small snake curled around the grate. Out of the corner of my eye, I saw Henry, a black dude who was my assistant manager, crawl up on top of the cash register counter on the other side of the shop, about thirty feet away from the snake. I walked over to the snake and looked at it more closely. It didn't look like any kind of snake I had ever seen, not in Alabama, anyway. It was black and brown with a little bit of off-white. I got the Igloo cooler I used for a lunch box and used a broomstick to coax it into the cooler. Then I told Henry he could come down now. He jumped off the counter and ran out the door, yelling back that he wasn't staying in the same building with a snake. I took it to a pet store after work to find out what sort of snake it was. As soon as I saw the ball pythons in the aquarium, I knew that's what it was. I decided to keep it. We never knew how it got there, because pythons are definitely not native to south Alabama, so I had to assume that it must have crawled out of a customer's car.

Our wedding day came in November. After eleven years together we finally made it official. My dad was my best man and Rhonda's sister, Jennifer, was her maid of honor. Everything went well. We had the rehearsal and the dinner afterward, and we went to Gulf Shores for our honeymoon. We didn't want to spend a lot of money because we were saving for a house.

Except for a six-pack of beer now and then, I was staying clean for the most part. But I was beginning to get burned out at school. I lost interest in my classes and wasn't as motivated as I was when I was in work release. I was always stressed out about a test coming up or a paper that was due. Rhonda's and my salaries together were enough for us to live comfortably, so school just didn't seem that important anymore.

Our credit was good enough to buy a house so we put a lot of energy into hunting for one. My mom, a real estate agent, seemed to be more enthusiastic than we were and quickly found one that was only five years old and within our price range. It would only take a couple of months to work the details out. It seemed too good to be true. I never thought I would be buying a house so soon after being released from prison and still on parole. It was scary because I was making a commitment that I would be bound to for thirty years, which made me think I might be trading one prison sentence for another one. Soon I was feeling like a time would come when this house would feel like a ball and chain clamped to my leg, and I already knew what that felt like.

In the meantime, I continued training for my first marathon. Every week, I pushed myself to run farther and farther than I had run before. Sometimes I went too far and wound up feeling sick for a few hours afterward, but the mileage it took to make me feel sick kept increasing. It was sort of like drug tolerance. I kept requiring more and more to achieve the same effect. I can see now that running is what I turn to when I am not using. It's a natural high, and I abuse the hell out of it. I've been bent over a toilet bowl puking my guts out more than a few times because I ran too much. A lot of times when I start back using, I'll continue to run, trying to hang on to it, but it doesn't last long. The two just don't mix. Yeah, I know I am one sick puppy.

The marathon I decided to run was the *Walt Disney World* Marathon in Kissimmee, Florida—twenty-six point two miles through the different theme parks. Rhonda, her sister, and Rhonda's niece went with me. We made a three-day vacation out of it so we could visit the theme parks.

The race started at five a.m. with approximately ten thousand runners. It was elbow to elbow the first half of the race until the field started thinning out. I ran at a comfortable pace because I wanted to finish. The temperature was cool when we started, but steadily dropped through the first couple of hours, which is great for long-distance running. The last couple of miles were exhilarating, and my pace increased as I approached the end. The running high is one of the best feelings in the world, much better than any drug high. I crossed the finish line with my arms raised, enjoying my little private victory. My time was three hours and fifteen minutes, which was good but not great.

Adrenaline alone fueled me the rest of the day as we visited the Magic Kingdom. No matter how many times I've been or how old I get (or how tired I may be), Disney World never fails to inspire awe in me. I wish I could live there, but I can't.

Back to reality. I woke up the next morning with legs as stiff as a couple of boards. The stairs in the hotel were pure torture as I carried our luggage down to the car for our drive home. The tenderness in my legs increased throughout the day, exacerbated by the eight-hour drive to Mobile. I could barely get out of the car the couple of times we stopped for gas, but I eventually made it home and to my couch. Ahhh, sweet relief.

Notwithstanding the sore muscles, my feeling of accomplishment was so grand that I couldn't wait to do it again. I registered to run the *Blue Angel* Marathon in Pensacola, Florida, a month later.

At the same time, we closed the deal on our house and moved in. I was at the apex of my sobriety, on a pink cloud, as AA members say. Although I was compelled by my PO to attend meetings, I wasn't working the program at all. I showed up for the meetings, didn't say anything or talk to anyone, got my parole slip signed to prove I had attended, and left. I wasn't using at the time. That was all that mattered.

But it didn't take me long to become disillusioned with my current situation. Material-wise, I had everything I needed. Every time I got what I wanted, my energy and attention would shift to something else I wanted to buy. It was as if I were being pulled along by the thrill of consuming. We acquired a lot of bills, and it started to seem as if the whole meaning of life was to buy, buy, and buy. In other words, I felt empty inside. Except for buying, life had no meaning.

A few months after moving into our new house, I was driving home from work one day when I stopped for a red light. I looked over at the car next to me and saw that it was Benjamin, a guy who used to work with me at Super-Lube. He rolled his window down and invited me to come over to his house. I knew why he was so eager to invite me over, though. It meant he had some pills he wanted to get rid of. The last few months we had worked together, he had sold me pills a couple of times. He knew I liked them a lot and would buy whatever he had.

Benjamin had been out of work with an injured back ever since the day he was eating his lunch in the storage room and a truck pulled into the parking lot and failed stop. It slammed into the wall where Benjamin was sitting. Greg, Tracy, and I ran over to see what had happened and found him lying on the floor under a pile of air filters, oil filters, and belts. He didn't seem to be hurt at the time, and the whole situation seemed really funny because we knew the guy driving the truck. He worked for the company that supplied and washed our uniforms. He had dropped his clipboard as he pulled into the parking lot and was trying to pick it up when he lost control of his truck.

So now I followed Benjamin over to his house, and, sure enough, he had some pills. I bought a few Ritalins and some Darvocets from him … and, without even realizing it; I had started down my path of destruction all over again. The cunning enemy of life would exert its influence upon me one more time. I had plenty of money now, and I felt I could control and hide my drug use a little better this time. Thanks to my many years of experience, I had become an expert. I was still on parole, of course, but I had never been tested after the first time. Besides, I knew what drugs they tested for.

But even though I thought I knew what my PO tested for, I still made sure I was clean on my monthly visits to her office. I finished my parole like this. I had it all under control. I could stop when I wanted to. Why stop at all?

Parole finished, and with no PO to watch over and restrict me anymore, I was now completely free. I never told myself, *As soon as I get off parole, I'm gonna start shooting dope again*, but that's what happened. It was more than a year since I'd ripped Mama off. I knew she would sell to me again if I went down there, because she was careless about how she sold and whom she sold to. As I headed to her house, therefore, the only thing I was concerned about was that she might no longer be in business. My fears were unfounded. She was there, she was selling, and she sold to me.

I went down there everyday for the next several weeks until Rhonda discovered what I was doing. I don't remember exactly how she found out; she probably found my hiding spot after she began suspecting what I was doing. I do remember her crying. First I tried to pathetically lie my way out of it, then I finally admitted it, but that made her cry even more. I somehow talked her into letting me get back on the methadone program and try to wean myself off what Mama was selling me. After only a few weeks, I was already too strung out to quit any other way. My will power was nonexistent. At the first sign of withdrawals, everything else could go to hell. I was gonna get some dope.

So I went back to methadone and actually worked the program the way it was supposed to be worked this time. I didn't increase my dose or do any other drugs while I was on the program. My life pretty much returned to normal during the next six months. I went to the clinic every morning at six, paid my ten dollars, drank my dose, and went to work.

Then I started to get an itch for a new truck. Nissan had just come out with a crew-cab Frontier, which was just my style. I had never owned a brand-new vehicle before and had always wanted to be able to drive one right off the lot. This was the perfect incentive to get me off the methadone. I was already spending three hundred dollars a month to stay on the program. If I quit, I would have enough for a car payment.

First thing, I weaned myself down to five milligrams from forty. It was pretty easy, and I was proud of myself for having the willpower to do it. I bought the truck I wanted, right off of the showroom floor. My materialistic wants and needs were met for the time being. What could I buy next? He who dies with the most toys wins, right?

Now I was becoming dissatisfied with my job. I did not want to be a Super-Lube manager for the rest of my life. It was pretty much a dead-end job. While reading the classified ads one day, I saw a position for a service writer at an automobile dealership. I had picked up enough experience for this type of job and knew I could start out earning what I already made at Super-Lube.

It was an import dealership that sold Porsches, Volkswagens, and Saabs. I got the job and gave Tracy my two-weeks' notice. He offered me a bigger salary to stay, but it wasn't about the money. I was ready for a change. My mind was made up. Besides, I was still harboring a pretty strong resentment against Tracy over the cash register incident.

Not long after I started my new job, I was back over at Benjamin's house to buy some Lortabs. *Here we go again*. I stay clean just long enough to buy my truck, a little detour before I get back on the highway to hell.

One night Rhonda went to spend the night with her mother. She was unaware of what I liked to do when she left me alone. I went on a crack binge. I drove my new truck around from crack hood to crack hood, spending twenty dollars here, fifty there. I pulled over in a parking lot, took a hit, and drove another block before pulling over for another blast. When I ran out of money, I became desperate for more. I couldn't stop if my life depended on it, but I wasn't about to let a little thing like an empty wallet stop me from getting some more.

I knew how to get into the Super-Lube building I used to manage. I didn't need a key. I could just pop the locks on the roll-up garage doors if I had the right tool, which I just happened to have. I figured if Tracy and Greg still considered me guilty of stealing that one hundred dollars, I might as well have done it anyway. All the Super-Lube cash registers kept at least one hundred dollars for change, and I knew where they hid the bank bag with the money in it. It was in the towel dispenser in the bathroom. I went straight for it. Then I locked the garage door and went out the side door that I could lock from the inside, but not deadbolt.

I spent the whole one hundred dollars and went back home to smoke it. I was paranoid as hell. I turned off all of the lights and went into the bathroom to take a hit. Before I could exhale, I ran back to the dining room to look out the window. I went back to the bathroom, but then I had to go to the window again before I could take another hit. I thought someone had driven up that quick. I tried to smoke on the back patio, but after a couple of hits I thought someone was watching me through the fence, so I went back inside. Now I thought someone had snuck inside while I was on the patio, so I grabbed a fire poker and went around and checked all the closets. I went back into the bathroom and put everything I had left on the soda can. I had to hurry up and get rid of this shit. It was driving me insane. I took a huge blast and immediately thought someone was beating on the bathroom door. I was freaking out. I flushed everything that was left down the commode and put the can under the sink. I thought I could still hear beating on the door, but there was so much blood rushing through my ears; I couldn't be sure what I was hearing. I braced myself with the fire poker and opened the door real quick, but of course there wasn't anyone there. As the rush passed, I realized that it had been my heart beating that loud. Now I was cursing myself for smoking up and flushing away what was left.

When I had it, I didn't want it. When I didn't have it, I wanted it. How insane is that? I downed a six-pack of beer as fast as I could. This was the worst feeling in the world, and I had to kill it as fast as I could. After the rush of the last hit is gone, all negative emotions are amplified—anxiety, fear, guilt, loneliness, self-disgust. All of this produces intense physical discomfort that lasts for several hours unless you've got a strong central nervous system depressant like alcohol or Valium. By the time I got to the sixth beer, the warm embrace of Bacchus was soothing my distress and massaging my tense muscles.

I was thirty years old. The drugs had such a strong hold on me that I couldn't think of anything else. I had a beautiful wife; we both had good jobs; we had a nice house in a good neighborhood, and I had a brand-new vehicle. I had everything I could want, material-wise, but I was empty inside. More than just hollow. I had a vacuum where my heart should be.

The only thing I wanted that I didn't have was more drugs.

I was reaching the peak of another of my using cycles. The cycles start with a period of sobriety, which is usually motivated by guilt from some kind of trouble I've gotten myself into. The trouble gets bigger with each successive cycle. This white-knuckle abstinence usually lasts less than thirty days. The guilt seems to dissipate over a short period of time, and my reasons for quitting are no longer very strong. This is where I convince myself that it would be all right to drink a few beers. I'm not realizing that this is only feeding the monster inside of me and making him stronger.

Eventually the demon monster is screaming, *I want more!* He must be fed now. I can think of little else but him. I can't concentrate on anything, and the only way to shut up the demon's voice is to feed it. If there's the voice of an angel in my life, this shuts it up. Now that I'm in a catch-22 dilemma, the two most dangerous words I can utter escape from my lips. *Fuck it.* Lortab, Darvocet, Percodan, Vicodin, Tylox ... I take a couple here, a few more there, I'm functioning well now, and life is a little bit easier. The pills don't cost a lot. They are relatively easy to find.

Obviously, my tolerance level increases. It increases faster and rises higher with each successive cycle. I started taking more and more pills, throwing Valium and Xanax into the mix. Still, the demon inside me is screaming, more, more, MORE! He cannot be sated. There's no reasoning with him. Only one thing calms him down, and the time he stays calm is getting shorter and shorter. Now it's time to bring out the big guns—morphine and the needle.

Back to Mama's house, she was always there and someone was always dealing. If she was out of morphine, then she always had something else injectable, like Oxycontin, Demerol, or Dilaudid. Any time, night or day, one of her kids or one of her grandkids would be on the front porch doing business. Every dope head in Mobile knew about Mama's house. Each time I returned to her house, I was instantly hooked again. I went back day, after day after day.

Since I was working at an auto dealership, now I fell into a pattern of taking a customer's car for a test drive to Mama's house. I purchased my pill and returned to work, heading straight to the restroom. At first, a sixty dollar pill would get me through the day if I divided it up, but as my tolerance increased, I ended up doing the whole pill in one shot.

Chapter 7
Belief in a Lower Power

Pardon me while I burst into flames.

-BRANDON BOYD
PARDON ME

All of this time, I was trying to hide my drug use from Rhonda. I was so ashamed of it that I tried to hide it from everyone. There were several obvious reasons why Rhonda didn't want me getting high, but I think what hurt her the most is that I tried to hide it from her. She told me several times that if I just told her the truth, she wouldn't get mad. I tried that a couple of times, but it didn't work. She just got even more upset. But I couldn't do anything about my drug use. I was out of control.

By this time, I was going to greater and greater lengths to get high. Anytime I went to someone else's house, whether it was family, a friend, or whatever, I went through their medicine cabinet looking for pills. One time, Rhonda caught me digging through her mother's purse. The more I did these things, the more I felt like a piece of shit. The more I felt like a piece of shit, the more I needed drugs. The more I needed drugs, the more I did these things. It was a self-perpetuating, vicious, downward spiral.

The next downward twist in this brutal cycle was the methadone clinic. My plan was to stay on the program for a month, then slowly wean myself off the methadone. Of course, like most of my well-laid plans, this one didn't work out. A drug addict's capacity to lie to himself is greater than any other human being's. In the back of my mind, I must have known that I would start at a low dose and then increase it as much as I could, as fast as I could. That's exactly what happened.

For the first couple of months, I was what the doctor at the clinic called, "stabilized." ("Immobilized" might have been more appropriate word.) Mostly because I was immobilized, I had no cravings for any other drugs. Every morning, I woke up thirty minutes before my alarm clock went off. My circadian rhythm while I was on methadone was the best alarm clock I ever had. I was at the clinic door every morning as it was being unlocked.

When I was on methadone, I seemed perfectly normal … well, unless I sat in one spot for too long, because then I would start nodding. If I was at home and eating or drinking, I would nod off and drop whatever was in my hands. My cravings for sweets were insatiable. I spilled a bowl of Blue Bell chocolate chip cookie dough ice cream on the floor every night like clockwork.

I started increasing my dose every couple of weeks as my tolerance increased until I maxed out at four or five months. I was taking a hundred milligrams a day and no longer getting high. This was the most dangerous part of the cycle. I couldn't go back to shooting morphine because I would have had to shoot an insane amount to feel it just a little bit, but that increased my chances of overdosing. I was now what you would call drug-crazed. This means that for the most part I could still function normally. I could work and be around people, and they would never know (unless they know what to look for) that I had an insane amount of drugs coursing through my veins. Eventually, of course, the cracks in my façade would start to show.

Next I started injecting Ritalin, which I bought from Benjamin, every day. I needed something to cut through the methadone. I still couldn't get enough. Whatever I was trying to escape from or whatever feelings I was trying to stamp out, they only got stronger. I'd already tried to kill it with a hammer, then a baseball bat, a stick of dynamite. Now I was going nuclear. I had methadone for breakfast, Ritalin for lunch, and crack for supper.

The monster inside of me was raging. He could not be quieted or sated. The more I fed him, the more he wanted, and he wasn't going to settle for less. I had already pawned all of my possessions I could without Rhonda finding out about it. So now I borrowed money from our credit cards. I borrowed from cash-till-payday businesses with my personal checks. I even took out a loan from Wells Fargo to finance my self-destruction. I was fast getting deeper and deeper into debt, and this cycle was coming to a head. I never expected the calamity that would result.

Not only was I trying to hide my use from Rhonda, I was now trying to conceal all this debt, too, but I knew it would inevitably come to the surface. I knew I had to stop. I wanted to go back into rehab. But Rhonda didn't want to be left alone for a long period of time again. She thought all I had to do was quit. Use a little will power.

Quitting drugs is as easy as pie. Not true. The very nature of addiction implies that quitting is *not* easily done. The definition of addiction is a habit that persists even in the face of negative consequences. I'd never be able to quit. Nothing could have been more difficult for me, especially after years of smoking, ingesting, snorting, and injecting the strongest chemicals I could get my hands on. I was way past the point of quitting on my own. I was past the point of no return. By now, I could go into rehab again and admit everything I had been doing, or I could continue on this path to hell until I crashed and all would be revealed, anyway.

So I concocted a dumb-ass plan to rob a bank. If I robbed a bank, I'd have the money to pay my debts, and maybe I would have enough left over to get really blitzed. I would guess more than ninety percent of bank robberies happen this way. Drug-crazed, desperate, dope fiends reach the end of their rope and decide to rob a bank without any forethought of the consequences. They fail to plan what to do if they actually do succeed. I've known a lot of bank robbers, and if any of them actually succeeded with the first one, they kept robbing banks until they were finally caught. But I didn't know any of this at the time. All I was thinking was that I needed some money and I needed it fast. The drugs had long ago completely corrupted any morals I may have had. The only thing that had prevented me from robbing a bank before now was fear. As I got more desperate, the fear faded away.

On Saturday morning, October 28, 2000, I found a bank I thought would be easy to rob. It was in the parking lot of a big shopping center on a very busy boulevard about a mile from my house. That was my first mistake—never rob a bank close to home. It would be better to go to another city. The reason I chose this one, however, was because it had a good escape route. I bought a few Valiums the day before so I'd have the courage (or the stupidity) to do what I planned to do.

I got up at five-thirty to go to the methadone clinic and get my dose for the day, then went back home and watched TV until nine o'clock. Rhonda was still asleep. I put on my disguise: a bicycle helmet, sunglasses, a T-shirt, and sweat pants. Then I got my mountain bike out of the tool shed behind our house and pedaled off to my destruction.

I had one small moment of clarity as I went down the street. It was the voice of the angel on my shoulder, though it was only a faint whisper compared to the roar of the demon voice. "You don't have to do this," the angel whispered. "You will get caught." But I shut it out of my mind and kept pedaling. I had made the decision and put the plan in motion. I wasn't about to change my mind now.

It may seem stupid to rob a bank on a mountain bike, but you've got to realize that I definitely was not operating at full mental capacity. One thing I've come to realize is that intelligent people (not that I am particularly intelligent) can act really stupid. A high intelligence quotient does not necessarily equal intelligent behavior. They are two different things. Well, at the time my plan made sense to me.

It happened like this. I pedaled up to the side of the bank and parked my bike against the wall. I had written a note before I left home that said *this is a robbery; give me all of the cash in your drawer. No dye packs and give me the note back.* I had heard about the dye packs that tellers slip into the bags of money. The dye pack blows up when the robber leaves the bank, spraying him and the money with some bright color, making the cash useless and marking the robber for easy identification. I also knew that tellers are trained to give the robber whatever he asks for, so as to not endanger her life or the lives of customers in the bank at the time of the robbery.

As I walked in the front door of the bank, I noticed there was only one customer and two tellers. I brought a backpack with me to put the money in. As I walked up to one of the tellers, I handed her the note and took off the backpack. She was a slender, black, twenty-something female. She read the note and never looked up again. As I laid the backpack on the counter, she reached into the drawer and started shoving money into it. Despite all of the drugs flowing through my system, I was still nervous. I knew I had to be in and out as quickly as possible, and I knew she probably had tripped a silent alarm. Ten seconds passed like ten minutes. My plan was to be in and out in sixty seconds. The teller was still stuffing money into my backpack when panic completely overtook me and I said, "That's enough."

I grabbed the backpack off of the counter and zipped it up as I turned around and started walking out of the bank. I stepped out the door, turned to the right, and went around the corner to my bike. No police cars in sight. I hopped on and started pedaling toward the side of the strip mall that was behind the bank. My heart was pounding in my ears and pumping so much adrenaline through my body that my legs were pumping the wheels of the bike as fast as possible. I knew I was getting away because I didn't hear any police sirens or any other kind of commotion behind me. I sped along behind the mall and came to the other end. There was an old church there with a parking lot on one end and a large subdivision on the other end. I cut through the parking lot behind the church and wheeled into the neighborhood. I cycled around two blocks and came to the wooden fence at the end of the street.

This is why it was to my advantage to use the mountain bike. When I reached that dead end, I lifted the bike and dropped it over the fence, and then I jumped over. There was a clearing on the other side for power lines, with a narrow trail that ran downhill for about a hundred yards. By the time I got to the other side of the fence, it was obvious that I was not being chased, so I coasted on down the hill. At the bottom I jumped off the bike, walked through the woods to the right of the trail, and came out in my own neighborhood. I rode the two blocks to my house, put the bike in the tool shed, and sat down and counted the money.

I was expecting at least five grand. What I found in my backpack were mostly one-dollar bills. I couldn't believe it. I counted again. It wasn't even two thousand dollars. What was worse than this was I suddenly realized that the note (which had my fingerprints on it) was not in the bag. Well, there was nothing to do but get high, which was what I proceeded to do.

The middle part of that day was pretty much a blur. I remember visiting Benjamin to purchase some Ritalin and whatever else he might happen to have. I paid him seventy-five dollars in one-dollar bills. He looked at me like I was crazy, which I was. When I got home, I washed my truck so I could have a pretext for getting the spare tire out to hide the money in, in case Rhonda asked me what I was doing. In the late afternoon, Rhonda and I went to run a couple of errands.

It was when we returned home that all hell broke loose.

Parked in my driveway were two unmarked police cars. This is where a switch in my head flipped. It turned on a determination to escape by all means necessary, at all cost, and it cut off all rational thought. This was more than a fight or flight response. It was an I AM NOT GOING TO PRISON response. From this point forward, there was no looking back. As soon as I saw the cars in my driveway, I knew who they were. My gas foot went to the floor. There were a couple of cops in my front yard. I read their lips as I sped past. "That's him!" The worst crime I ever committed, which I was not prosecuted for, was that Rhonda was in the passenger seat right beside me when I took flight. She screamed at me, "What did you do?"

I'll never forget how calm I felt as I said, "I robbed a bank."

As I sped down the street she continued to scream at me, "Oh God, no," and, "Let me out!" I was driving like a bat out of hell, squealing around corners, jumping the speed bumps in our neighborhood. All the while, her shouting "Let me out! David, *stop!*" was deafening my right ear. I came to the wide, busy boulevard at the end of the street and hardly slowed down as I went across and into the westbound lanes. The other cars were blowing their horns, swerving, and slamming on their brakes to avoid running into me or me running into them. Rhonda was still screaming at me and holding on for dear life, but all I could think was ESCAPE. By now, a few more police cars had joined the chase. I had no idea where I was going or what I was going to do when I got there. I was just going.

I was coming up to a traffic light and could see cars were stopped in all three lanes ahead, so I made a real quick turn down a side street I was familiar with. I suddenly realized this would be a good place to let Rhonda out, because the street made a ninety-degree turn to the left. "I'm going to let you out," I yelled at her. As soon as I made the turn, I slammed on the brakes and said, "Go!" and she jumped out. Out of my truck and out of my life forever.

It took a long time for me to realize what this experience must have been like for her. I was too wrapped up in my own self-inflicted pain and agony to even begin to think about how my actions affected the people close to me, especially my wife. No one should ever have to go through what she went through that day. I now realize how traumatic it was for her.

Even after what I had just put Rhonda through, the police (and there were at least three police cars chasing me at this point) didn't even stop to pick her up. She had to walk a mile or two back home. It must have been the longest walk of her life. I may never fully realize what I did to her that day. As I said before, I know that was the worst crime I ever committed. Maybe I'll be able to make it up to her somehow, some way, some day.

Before I start getting all-sentimental, let's get back to the chase. After Rhonda jumped out, the pedal went to the metal again. Tires spinning and squealing, running stop signs and red lights—you've seen it all a thousand times on cop shows and movies. A maniac behind the wheel, digging himself in deeper and deeper into trouble, all in vain.

With police sirens in my ears and flashing blue lights in my eyes, I cut through shopping center parking lots and corner gas station lots, flashing my lights and blowing my horn, forcing other drivers off the road. I was bound and determined to escape. There must have been at least ten police cars chasing me by now. A combination of methadone, Valium, Ritalin, and adrenaline had me in a very calm, focused state of mind. I just knew that I was going to get away. It was like some other kind of power was driving me, guiding me as I made all the right turns and moves.

As I came to another major intersection, I made a sudden right turn into another shopping center parking lot. If I'd been thinking rationally, I would never have turned there. It was a dead end. There was only one way in and one way out. I sped to the back and down the length of the mall. The cops probably thought they had me cornered, but then I did something that I didn't even expect. I drove straight to the edge of the pavement and off into a ditch.

Before my truck came to a full stop, I was out the door, on my feet, and into the woods. The sirens were deafening, so I didn't even hear anyone yell, "Freeze!" or anything else. I never looked back, so if they were on their feet behind me, I never saw or heard them. I was sprinting, ducking, and dodging through the thick woods as fast as I could, with tree limbs slapping me in the face and briars cutting my legs. I ran a hundred yards and came to a chain link fence and someone's back yard. I grabbed the top of the fence and hopped over, ignoring the metal digging into my palms. I could still hear the sirens of the police cars as I ran across the yard and leaped over another fence. I crossed the front yard and ran out into the street and came to a dry concrete culvert. I jumped in and kept running. My heart was about to pound out of my chest and my lungs were on fire, but I continued on, fueled by mind-numbing fear.

The culvert ran behind the back yards of several houses. I finally had to stop and catch my breath and my bearings, and that's when I saw the Ford pickup truck behind the house to my right. I climbed out of the culvert and over another chain link fence and dropped into the yard, squatting low and keeping the truck between the house and me. I looked in the driver's side window and saw the keys in the ignition. Jackpot!

As I said before, it was as if some other power (satanic?) was guiding me, pointing me in the right (or wrong) direction. These "lucky" breaks were just helping me dig myself deeper and deeper in the hole I was already in. If I had been caught right then, or had given up, I would have gotten only a three or four-year sentence. But I didn't know this at the time. I never stopped for a second to consider it. I let that power continue to drive me.

I jumped into the Ford and turned the key. The engine didn't quite turn over, so I tried again, and this time the motor fired up. I put it in gear and spun out. As I pounded down the driveway, the owner of the truck came running out of the house. He ran across the yard toward me, but he was too late. I accelerated down the street and out of the neighborhood and headed for the interstate.

I was safe for now, but I could still hear the sirens wailing in my head. I had to keep looking in my rearview mirror to make sure the sirens weren't real. After my heart rate and breathing returned to normal, I was calm enough to look around inside the cab. There was a box between the two front seats. I picked it up and almost dropped it because it was so heavy for such a small box. I set it on the passenger's seat and took the lid off. What I saw was the one thing I would need if I was going to live my life on the run. This evil power that was driving me gave me exactly what it wanted me to have—a .44 Magnum revolver.

Life as I knew it was over. Even though I was still very much alive and kicking, I had destroyed myself for good. The only things I owned now were the clothes on my back and my wallet, which contained my driver's license, three credit cards, and about seventy-five dollars. I would never be able to go home. In my mind, I had done enough to earn a life sentence. There was no turning back. The switch was on. I was now living outside the law. I was a real outlaw, and I felt a pathological sense of complete freedom in this knowledge. If I wanted something, I would take it. *I am invincible, the evil force, this satanic power thing is with me, and I can't possibly be caught with such a diabolic energy on my side. I will satisfy all my base desires, I will live like an animal, and I will act and exist on a primal plane. Going to prison would be worse than a thousand deaths.*

Prisons are built precisely for people who think and behave like this. A successful society cannot exist peacefully and harmoniously with people like me gallivanting about, seeking to fulfill every primitive desire with no regard for anyone else's rights.

I was on the interstate driving west into the setting sun. As I crossed the state line in Mississippi, I realized I was going to need a few things for my outlaw life. I needed clothes, a different vehicle, and (above all else) drugs. I was not about to go through methadone withdrawal when I had a gun and nothing to lose.

First I needed to get rid of this truck. I took the next exit and drove to the next town. I was going car shopping. As I drove past a Chevrolet dealership, a brand new Tahoe caught my eye. I made a plan. I was going to take a test drive and pull my gun on the salesman and make him jump out. Then I became conscious of the fact that I didn't look like someone who could afford to buy a Tahoe. I was dirty and sweaty and had scratches all over my arms and legs from running through the woods.

My first priority changed. I found a mall close by and went in and bought some respectable attire with one of my credit cards. I didn't care about the police tracking down my credit card purchases because I was just passing through this town. I wouldn't be here long enough for them to catch me. I found a bathroom in the mall, went in and changed, put my old clothes in a new backpack I'd also purchased.

Now, cleaned up and at least looking respectable, I drove back to the dealership, parked the stolen Ford, and walked around the lot and looked at a few of the other cars. I still liked the Tahoe. When a salesman approached me, I told him I wanted to take a test drive.

"I'll need to make a copy of your driver's license first," he said.

Now for an episode straight out of *America's Dumbest Criminals.* Fuck it, I thought. The person that I was was dead to me. What's one more crime added to the long list of offenses the authorities know I've committed? I didn't care. They couldn't catch me, and I was going to change my identity, anyway. David Reeves will be wanted for multiple charges, I said to myself, but I won't be David Reeves anymore.

I gave the salesman my license, and he went to make a copy and get the keys. I put the gun in my backpack. We hopped in the Tahoe and took off. The salesman tried to make salesman conversation by asking salesman questions.

"Where do you live?"

"Here."

"What do you do for a living?"

"Pharmaceutical sales rep." How I lied.

"How do you like it?

"It's a job."

I was vaguely familiar with this town. I turned north to get back on the interstate, telling the salesman that I was going to drive by my house to show the SUV to my wife. I found a small street that turned off to the right and looked deserted and came to a section with thick woods on both sides of the street. As I slowed down, I grabbed my backpack off the floor. Coming to a stop, I unzipped the bag and pulled the gun out.

"This is—"

Before I could get the words out of my mouth, he was out of the door and into the woods. All I could see was leaves falling and branches shaking where he dove in. Well, that was easy. I made a U-turn and headed back for the interstate. Now I only needed one more thing. Drugs.

It was dark now. I continued into the next county and to a bigger city where I knew there would be plenty of pharmacies still open. As I said before, I was not about to go through withdrawals when I had a gun and not a care in the world. I was just as afraid of opiate withdrawals as I was of going back to prison.

When the police were chasing me earlier, I still had seven or eight Ritalins and three Valiums left in a cigarette cellophane wrapper in my pocket. I had downed all of them, not because I didn't want a drug possession charge, but because I didn't want them taken from me. What was a drug possession charge when I already had a bank robbery charge? Just don't take my drugs away from me.

All those pills plus the adrenaline rush still flowing through me had me feeling powerful and invincible. I was extremely focused, with tremendous strength and remarkable mental clarity, but there were no emotions or feelings of regret over the fact that I had just annihilated my former life. What little moral consciousness I might have had before had been blotted out of existence. I was on a mission now and would not stop until it was completed.

I found a shopping center with a large grocery store that also had a pharmacy. I backed into a parking space beside the store and left the motor running. I put my gun into my backpack, zipped it up, and proceeded toward the entrance. Luckily, there were no customers waiting at the pharmacy counter. The pharmacist was a young, white guy, probably younger than I was, working behind the counter by himself. The counter had a low, swinging door, no higher than my waist, way back to the left. The druggist didn't even notice as I reached over the door and unlocked the sliding bolt from the inside. As

I walked in, I reached into my bag and pulled out the gun. He looked like a deer caught in headlights.

"You know what I want," I said. I held out my backpack.

He didn't say a word. He just took the backpack and unlocked a drawer where he was standing. Every pharmacy has one of these drawers, and it stays locked. It contains all of the Schedule II narcotics. These are the most addictive drugs that have medical value: morphine, Oxycontin, Demerol, Adderal, Dexedrine. Schedule I drugs are highly addictive or dangerous and have no medical value: heroin, crack, LSD, ecstasy, and so on.

The pharmacist began filling the backpack with Schedule II and III pill bottles, one after another until there was none left in the drawer. A customer, a little old white lady, walked up to the counter while all of this was going on. She never realized what was happening. He handed me the bag, and I zipped it up and walked out coolly and calmly. *Like taking candy from a baby.*

I jumped back into the Tahoe, and got on the interstate heading west. As I was driving, I opened the backpack and dumped the contents on the passenger seat. To a dope fiend like I was at the time, this was the most beautiful sight in the world. It's every addict's fantasy. This was what I lived for. Give me a place to stay, like a motel room or someplace no one will bother me, and I might not come out for days, weeks, or even months. Or so I thought at the time. Those were the last thoughts and the last thing I can remember of that long and eventful day. That was the day that will overshadow the rest of my days. Everything that had happened in all the years before led up to that day. Everything that has happened since has happened because of that day.

The next morning, I woke up in a cheap motel room in New Orleans that stank of stale cigarette smoke. I don't remember how I got there. The last thing I remember is heading west on I-10. I got out of bed and went to the bathroom, dazed, as if in a dream. As soon as I saw my reflection in the mirror, the realization of what I had done the day before hit me. It hit me hard. The reflection of my face in the mirror contorted into an expression of grotesque agony. My hot tears welled up and distorted my vision; my throat constricted, and from the bottom of my empty soul came a cry that I have never in my life heard before. *What have I done? How could I have done it?* I've never felt so alone before or since. Words can't begin to describe my anguish.

Yesterday seemed like a lifetime away. I had to mentally go back to the preceding morning and replay the events of the day until I got to the part where I robbed the drug store. That's when I became conscious of the fact that I had the best part of a pharmacy in my backpack.

I ran back into the motel room, still sobbing. Only one thing was going to kill this pain. I tore at the zipper on the backpack and the pill bottles spilled out onto the bed and on the floor, along with a pack of U-100 one cc syringes that I didn't remember acquiring. I grabbed a bottle of Xanax and shook out a handful and gulped them down without water. I continued picking through the bottles until I found the Dilaudid. This would be the quickest. It's a pill that junkies call "cold shake" because all you've got to do is crush it, put it in a syringe, and draw up some cold water and shake it. I could hardly see what I was doing through the tears, but relief was only seconds away.

This is the paradox of addiction. You use drugs to kill pain, but the things you have to do to obtain drugs only create more pain. At first, the pain is subconscious. You're not aware of any pain. You just know that this particular substance makes you feel good. It's such an improvement over your normal, negative emotional state that you want to feel it again and again. I believe this is why normal people don't become addicts or alcoholics. Their normal emotional state is not negative, so there's no huge improvement when they drink or use a drug.

I think if your constant state of being is one of anxiety, depression, anger, or boredom, or you just plain don't feel good about yourself, then you're going to do something to relieve that psychic pain, whether it's drugs, alcohol, food, gambling, sex, working, working out, or whatever it is that temporarily makes you feel good. All of these things eventually cause problems, some faster and worse than others. People who used to be normally good steal, rob, cheat, lie, and kill to obtain drugs. More pain equals more drugs equals more pain equals more drugs, *ad infinitum.*

From this moment forward, I would not look back. The rest of the day is still a complete blur. I had to anesthetize myself so those horrible feelings I had that morning wouldn't come back. I remember realizing that I was out of money, and I was still sane enough to know that I couldn't pay for the motel room with one of my credit cards. If I did, I would surely have the cops beating down my door within an hour.

So I went out and looked for a business to rob. It was late on a Sunday night, so there weren't too many places to choose from. I found a drug store that was still open and had a good escape route. I parked in the back because it was connected to a residential neighborhood that would allow for easy flight.

I walked in and strolled up and down a couple of aisles. It was nearly closing time, so there were hardly any customers in the store. I walked back toward the checkout register. There were two ladies behind the counter. One of them looked like she was counting money in the cash register. The other lady stood right next to her, jabbering on and on about something. I had written a note earlier, and now I handed it to the lady counting the money. I had my gun in my backpack, but I didn't pull it out; I didn't think it would be necessary. The lady read my note and started putting the money on the counter, saying, "Alice … Alice … ALICE!" But Alice was steadily running her mouth. She finally realized what was happening, but by then the cash register was empty and I was placing the money in the backpack.

I turned and started heading toward the door when Alice came running from behind the counter. She jumped between the door and me with her feet spread wide and her arms waving in the air. This woman was crazy. I could have just run right through her, but I didn't have to.

Let me explain something here. Up to this point, I had committed several robberies in my short criminal career. I would never shoot anyone, and if I did accidentally, I would probably turn the gun on myself, because that is one thing I would not be able to live with. Despite what I have been telling you, I do have a conscience. I would not be able to handle taking someone else's life. I've had a hard enough time dealing with the crimes I'm telling you about, anyway.

Even though I'm considered a violent criminal because of the crimes I committed, I'm a coward when it comes to violence. During one of my county jail stays, I saw a guy get knocked out in a fight. He fell headfirst on the cement floor and his head bounced up and down as the other guy continued to pound his skull. When he stood up, I could see the knots rising as his whole head swelled up and blood started streaming down his face. He didn't know what had happened, or who or where he was. I felt sick to my stomach. I've seen much worse violence since then, and it still always turns my stomach.

I used a gun because I thought the threat of physical violence would get me what I wanted. I looked it as a ticket. Show 'em my ticket, and I get what I want. But now I know that people react differently to having a gun pulled on them. The majority are scared shitless and will do anything you tell them, whereas some just freeze up and you can't get them to do anything. Others just simply can't believe what's happening and think it's a joke, and a few others know what's going on, but choose to act stupid. Then there are the few that are either stupid or extremely brave. I encountered all of these reactions while I was on my crime spree. If I saw I wasn't going to get cooperation, I just turned around and walked out. I guess I was lucky that none of them ever came after me and forced me to do what was necessary to escape.

I thought this was going to be one of those times. Alice jumped in front of me. I paused for one second, long enough to grab my gun out of my backpack and show her what I was working with. If you have ever seen a Smith and Wesson .44 Magnum, you knew without a doubt that it was no toy gun. This was Dirty Harry's weapon of choice. Alice's eyes got big as saucers. She jumped out of my way as quick as she'd jumped in my way.

I headed back to the motel and counted the money—four hundred and something dollars. It wasn't a lot, but it would buy me a couple of days to decide my next course of action. The first thing I had to do was ditch this ratty motel. Before I left, I noticed my wedding ring still on my finger. I knew my marriage was over. I could never go back. I loved Rhonda dearly, but, unfortunately, I loved drugs more. I took the ring off and put it in the drawer of the nightstand and left.

The following days are still a haze. I have vague memories of other robberies and other hotel rooms in other cities. I remember buying one hundred dollars worth of crack in a McDonald's parking lot in Galveston, Texas. I went back to my current motel room to smoke it, but instead of getting high, I got paranoid. I thought every car that pulled into the parking lot, every door I heard slam, and every voice I heard was the police.

I stood there, frozen at the peephole in the door, afraid to turn away long enough to hit the pipe one more time. I had the lights off and was so scared I was sure the cops outside the door could hear every breath I exhaled and every step I took to shift my weight. Crack did this to me, even when I was not running from the cops. Why did I expect it to be any different this time? I couldn't even light my lighter because I was afraid they could see the light through the peephole. I ran to the bathroom, but as soon as I shut the door, I had to run back and look through the peephole again. I must have repeated this little dance twenty or thirty times. The paranoia wouldn't let me smoke the stuff that was making me so paranoid in the first place. I finally gave up and flushed the crack down the toilet, grabbed my backpack, and left the motel without checking out, even though I had already paid and had only been there for a couple of hours.

On Monday, November 6, 2000, I was in Houston, Texas, and I was a walking, chemical cocktail-induced zombie. The pills in my possession had multiplied, and I had to let the back seat of the Tahoe down to make room for all the junk I had purchased. I had been to several malls and bought everything that caught my eye. I had guitars, amplifiers, stereos, TVs, camping gear, a bicycle, books, magazines, clothes, and shoes. The inside of the Tahoe was so full I had to buy a bicycle rack to mount the bike on the back.

My plan was to hit two more banks and obtain enough money to lay low for a while. I was using my same modus operandi as my previous robberies. I would find a large shopping center with a grocery store that had a bank branch in it. Then I would park on the other side of a building at the edge of the shopping center. When I was making my escape, I went around the corner of the building and the Tahoe was waiting with the motor running.

I don't remember the first robbery, and I only remember bits and pieces of the second one. I got really greedy on this one. Instead of hitting just one teller, I hit two. I had been adding the words "large bills" to my notes because if I didn't, I would get nothing but one-dollar bills. I also pulled the gun out because I thought that if I put a little extra fear into the tellers, I would get more money. What a plan.

Chapter 8
A Thousand Deaths

I beheld the wretch – the miserable monster whom I had created.

-MARY SHELLEY
FRANKENSTEIN

I was on Interstate 10 traveling back through Houston. It had been about forty-five minutes since I robbed the last bank on the west side of the city. I was now on the east side and feeling confident that I'd avoided detection by the blue meanies. I can't tell you exactly what I was thinking by that time because I was so jacked up and ripped out from all of the pills that my mind wasn't functioning. This brings me to the point that I must remember for the rest of my life.

Here I was. My drug addiction fantasy had come true. I had a super abundance of pills, plenty of cash, and an outlaw's sick sense of total freedom. But I had no feeling, no emotional affect, nothing that could be described as good or positive. I was not high or even slightly euphoric. On the contrary, I was low and dysphoric. The elation and sense of well being I'd been seeking from the pills were more elusive than ever. This is the end of the tape I still have to play out whenever I think about getting high or even taking a sip of beer. This is the inevitable conclusion, the dead end of the long road that this goose chase led to.

Now let's get back to the chase, the chase that, thanks to the tracking device in my backpack with the loot, I didn't even realize was a chase. Maybe if I had done a little more thorough research in robbing banks, I would have known that banks now hide tracking devices in the currency they give to bank robbers. I knew about the dye-packs and the bait money (bills with recorded serial numbers) that are used as evidence to connect the robber to the robbery, but I was ignorant of tracking devices.

Anyway, I was thinking I'd gotten away. It had been more than forty-five minutes since the robbery, but I was still in Houston because it's a huge city. Traffic is always congested.

So now we're back for another episode of *America's Dumbest Criminals*. I was hungry. I've got to eat sometime, right? Hey, there's a Jack in the Box. Man, I really like their hamburgers. It's lunch time anyway, so why not? *Why not?* You ask. *How about the fact that you just robbed a bank?*

C'mon, man, I reply in my drug-induced confidence. *There are no cops behind me, and it's been more than forty-five minutes. Besides I've done this several times now. I know what I am doing.*

How can you even think about food in a time like this? You ask.

Think? Who said I was thinking? My prefrontal cortex had started malfunctioning days, no, weeks ago. It obviously didn't like what I was doing and wanted no part of it.

See you later, it said. *I'm taking a sabbatical. Mr. Id will look out for you now.*

Well, Mr. Id was hungry, and he wanted what he wanted when he wanted it. Superego, where were you when I needed you? He must have been on hiatus, too.

Pull over, Mr. Id commanded. *I'm hungry. I got us everything we wanted—pills, cash, and gun, this brand new Tahoe. I've been working hard and I'm ready to eat. Let's go.*

So I pulled into the drive-thru, placed my order, and waited for my turn at the window. As I sat there, I wondered where I could go when I left Houston. Maybe I could go back to New Orleans and chill out there. New Orleans would be a good place to hide out. I'd fit right into all the dirt, crime, hedonism, and all-round freakishness of that city. New Orleans is a good place for miscreants, cretins, villains, and rogues. It's a real cesspool of humanity.

I was next in line at the pick-up window. Suddenly the parking lot was full of police cars with their sirens going. I must have had my attention on something inside the vehicle, because when I looked up I saw at least three police cars, and the cop in one of the cars was aiming a shotgun right at me.

And just when you think this tale can't get any more absurd and I can't act anymore idiotic, it does and I do. When I got back into the stolen Tahoe after the last robbery, for some reason I placed the Magnum between the driver's seat and the console. When I saw the shotgun pointing right at me, my gut reaction was to place my gun under my chin. When I tell this story now, I jokingly say I was trying to take myself hostage, but, well, I wasn't really thinking anything. My response was more of a muscle contraction than anything else. Or maybe it was a contingency plan Mr. Id concocted without consulting me. I don't know anymore. What I do know is that as soon as I raised my gun to my chin, at least three cops unloaded on me … right in the Jack in the Box drive-thru, where there was one car in front of me and several more behind me. Glass exploded all around me. The Tahoe shook as the tires blew out. Hot lead ripped through metal, plastic, fiberglass, leather, and my flesh. For some reason (divine intervention or whatever), I didn't blow my head off. I just fell forward, unconscious, onto the steering wheel. Then I heard a voice.

"He's dead."

I opened my eyes. I was laying on my back in the parking lot, looking up at a bright blue, cloudless sky.

"No, he's not. Call the paramedics."

The sweet waters of oblivion claimed my consciousness.

* * *

That was my version of the shooting as I remember it. The following is a police report of the events that I obtained from my attorney.

> *On Monday, November 6, 2000 at 1:27 pm, David Allen Reeves entered the Bank United located at 14344 Memorial Drive and robbed it at gunpoint. Employees of Bank United provided a good description of Reeves and the vehicle he was driving, a maroon colored SUV. This bank robbery is being investigated by the robbery division and is documented under HPD incident #146409800.*
>
> *Unknown to Reeves, an electronic transmitting device was included in the money he had taken from the bank. Immediately after the bank robbery a citywide alert was issued for all "RAT" units to switch to and operate on channel five and to attempt to locate the bank robbery suspect utilizing their tracking receivers. These units, along with a fox unit, were able to track the suspect and within a short period of time pinpointed his location to be at the SW corner of the Gulf Freeway feeder and S. Wayside.*
>
> *There is an Exxon station at the corner. Just west of and adjacent to the Exxon station there is a Jack in the Box restaurant. The drive through lane of the Jack in the Box is on the east side of the building so that the only thing separating the lane and the Exxon parking lot is a narrow grassy area with concrete curbs on the east and west sides.*
>
> *At approximately 2:00 pm, Officer R. E. Walker and his partner, Officer D. Thomas, pulled into the Exxon station still monitoring their RAT receiver. The receiver led them directly to the maroon GMC Yukon that was in the drive through*

lane of the Jack in the Box. The Yukon was northbound and was behind a car that was at the drive through window. There was another car in line behind the Yukon. Officer Walker, who was driving, stopped his marked unit at a point where it was separated from the suspect's vehicle only by the narrow grassy area that is between the drive through lane and the Exxon parking area. The front of their marked unit was just east of the passenger's side doors of the Yukon. Both officers could clearly see the suspect and the suspect clearly saw the officers.

Almost simultaneously, officers R. D. Rodriguez and W. R. Parker, both riding in units with RAT receivers, arrived in separate marked police vehicles. Rodriguez pulled up on the south side of the Jack in the Box property, exited his vehicle with his duty weapon, a Glock 40 caliber semi-automatic pistol, and took position in the drive through lane behind (south of) the suspect's vehicle.

Officer Parker was riding with Officer B. G. Gonzalez and Officer J. J. Esquivel. Officer Gonzalez parked their marked unit in the south most lane of the eastbound feeder, directly north of the drive through lane and across a wide grassy area. The drive through lane makes a mandatory turn to the west at the north side of the Jack in the Box building. The wide grassy area is between that portion of the drive through lane and the feeder street. Officer Parker exited the passenger's side of Gonzalez's vehicle armed with his duty weapon, a Sig Sauer 45 caliber semi-automatic pistol, and began to advance to the south toward the suspect's vehicle. Officer Walker exited his vehicle armed with a Remington 870 12 gauge pump shotgun. Officer Thomas exited with his service revolver. Both officers approached the suspect's vehicle from the passenger's side, concentrating their weapons on the suspect. The suspect's reaction was to place an S & W 44 Magnum revolver with an 8" barrel to his own head. Walker and Thomas both shouted verbal commands for the suspect to drop the gun, which the suspect ignored.

Right at that time the vehicle in front of the suspect's vehicle left the drive through lane. The suspect's vehicle started to roll forward and the suspect took the gun away from his own head and swung it toward Officer Thomas who had taken a position at the passenger's side front fender of the Yukon. Officer Thomas took evasive action to get out of the line of fire and to get out of the way of the now moving Yukon. Officer Walker, fearing for the life of his partner, did not feel he could fire directly at the suspect due to the fact he had seen an employee at the drive in window, which was in his line of fire. For this reason, Walker fired one round from the shotgun at the passenger side front tire of the suspect's Yukon, flattening the tire. This caused the suspect to stop the movement of the gun toward Officer Thomas for a moment, but he then continued driving forward and again raised his gun toward Officer Thomas. Walker, now fearing his shotgun blast could hit officer Thomas or other officers or civilians, fired again in a downward trajectory, flattening the rear passenger's side tire with two rounds.

Officer Rodriguez knew that the suspect had robbed Bank United with a handgun. As Rodriguez was advancing toward the suspect's Yukon from the south in the drive through lane, he noticed a uniformed officer (Walker) approaching the Yukon with a shotgun, yelling at the Yukon. Rodriguez heard Walker's first shot but he could not tell from his position that fired the shot. After the shot, the vehicle parked directly behind the Yukon started backing up, giving Rodriguez a clear view of the Yukon. Thinking the suspect had shot at the officer, Rodriguez fired two shots at the rear of the Yukon from his position in the drive through lane, directly behind the Yukon. The suspect continued north in the drive through and ran into the east curb at the point where the lane makes a 90 degree left turn to the west. Officer Parker, who was advancing to the north toward the Yukon, saw the vehicle coming towards him and saw the suspect with a gun in his hand. Parker shouted orders for the suspect to stop. When the suspect continued south, Parker, thinking the suspect was intentionally coming towards him, fired two rounds at the suspect from his position in the grassy area north of the Jack in the Box. The suspect turned to the left and continued to the west.

As the suspect went around the corner to the west, Officer Walker fired another round from his shotgun at the side rear tire of the Yukon, flattening the tire. The Yukon then had three flat tires.

Officer Thomas ran around the south side of the Jack in the Box, thinking the suspect would come in that direction. Officers Rodriguez and Walker ran to the north side, front, of the restaurant in the foot pursuit of the Yukon. Officer Parker ran west in the grassy area, north of the Yukon as the Yukon traveled west. The suspect continued pointing his gun toward Parker. As a result, Parker fired several more rounds at the suspect.

By this time officer Rodriguez had reached the north side of the restaurant and saw the suspect raise his gun toward someone (Officer Parker) and heard several more shots (Parker's shots).

The suspect continued west and was attempting to turn left again when he struck a parked car at the west side of the Jack in the Box parking lot. The collision was with such force, that the parked car was pushed into another parked vehicle. The suspect's vehicle also struck another parked vehicle, finally coming to a rest facing south on the west side of the parking lot.

Officer Rodriguez advanced to the west and took a position near the north

> *entrance doors of the Jack in the Box, east of the suspect's vehicle. He saw the suspect lean over toward the passenger's side of the vehicle, then sit back up and turn towards him with the gun in his hand. Rodriguez then fired two more rounds at the suspect from his position.*
>
> *Walker advanced west to a position near a light pole just east of the Yukon. Rodriguez moved to a position behind Walker and to his left. Parker was in a position behind Walker and to his right. Walker saw the suspect again lean toward the passenger's side of the Yukon, almost entirely out of Walker's sight, then immediately sat back up looking directly at Walker. Officer Walker ordered the suspect to stop. Ignoring the command, the suspect began to raise his right hand at which time Walker fired his shotgun one more time toward the suspect and the suspect fell to his right.*
>
> *Several officers approached the Yukon, including Walker, Thomas and Rodriguez. The suspect was removed from the vehicle and was found to have sustained several gunshot wounds. An ambulance was requested and the suspect was transferred to Ben Taub Hospital by HFD.*
>
> *A total of three officers discharged their weapons at the suspect during this incident. None of the officers sustained any injuries. Other RAT units arrived at the scene while the incident was unfolding, but did not get involved with the discharging of firearms.*
>
> *At Ben Taub, where the suspect was identified as David Allan Reeves, it was learned that he had sustained several gunshot wounds to the right abdomen, right back, left upper arm, and left shoulder and left upper back. Reeves underwent surgery and will survive his wounds.*

I find this version of events hard to believe. Not once did I fire my own gun. If I were shot so many times while holding a gun, surely I would have accidentally squeezed the trigger. But none of the police reports ever mention my gun being fired. From this version of events, it seems as if I was begging the officers to shoot me. I believe that after falling forward, unconscious, into the steering wheel, my foot accidentally pushed down on the accelerator and the vehicle moved forward, prompting the officers to repeatedly fire at me.

The following is a witness's version of events, taken from the same police report:

> *Saucedo, an employee of the Jack in the Box and was working in the drive up window at the time of the offense. She was interviewed at the scene by Sgt. Smith, as well as by A. D. A. Don Smyth who recorded his interview with her.*
>
> *Saucedo speaks broken English and seemed very nervous during the interview*

with Sgt Smith. She stated that she was working the drive through and noticed the suspect's truck next in line. The car she was working on left and the suspect pulled up and stopped to pay when the police started shooting at him. The truck took off and Saucedo went to the floor. She said she saw the suspect's truck hit her own truck in the parking lot. She then saw a police officer open the door to the suspect's truck then reach in and shoot the suspect in the shoulder.

Sgt. Smith questioned Saucedo in regards to the officer opening the door and shooting the suspect in the shoulder point blank. She then stated that she didn't actually see that but she saw the officer open the suspect's door, then she heard a shot. She didn't know who fired the shot but she saw the suspect move and she assumed it was because he had been shot. She said the suspect was sitting in his truck when this happened. During additional questioning Saucedo stated that actually there were no officers around the suspect when she heard the shot and she wasn't sure if the door was open.

A.D.A Smyth recorded Saucedo's statement before Sgt. Smith interviewed her, however, Sgt. Smith did not have knowledge of that interview when he interviewed her. In the recorded interview, Saucedo told Smyth that after she went to the floor she got up and ran outside and saw officer's open the suspect's door and shoot him. She said while the door was open, "They continued to shoot." When questioned by A.D.A. Smyth, Saucedo stated she did not know which officer was shooting and she couldn't remember how many times they shot the suspect. During this interview she had also repeated several times that the suspect did not have a gun. Upon additional questioning by Smyth, she stated she couldn't see his hands and she didn't know if he had a gun or not.

During the interview at the scene, Gaston Rangel had not arrived. When Saucedo arrived at homicide to make her written statement, it was decided to have a Chicano squad interview her in her own language since she had difficulty expressing herself in English. Investigator F. E. Martinez videotaped the interview with Saucedo. It should be noted that in this videotaped version, Saucedo stated that she did not go outside after she got up from the floor. She said once the shooting stopped, officers approached the truck and the suspect moved as if he wanted to get up. She then heard another shot from and unknown location. She said she did not remember if the driver's door was open or not when she heard the last shot.

I was shot in the upper left arm, the back of my left shoulder, the right side of my torso, and my stomach, and there was also a deep grazing wound across my back. I was unaware of all this at the time, of course. Thanks to my god, Morpheus, I never felt anything. The anesthesiologist in the emergency room had to do a blood test to see how much and how many drugs were in my system before they performed surgery. He later said I had enough morphine in my blood to kill a normal person. Ten to twenty milligrams is enough to make the average human sick as a dog. I was shooting one hundred and twenty milligrams at a time and popping Demerol, Xanax, and Dexedrine along with it.

Needless to say, I was lucky to be alive, although I didn't feel very lucky at the time. The drugs alone should have killed me. (They were almost the same pharmaceutical cocktail that killed my brother, Brian, less than two years later. I'll get to that eventually). The gunshot wounds from the cops should have killed me. I'm sure they were trying to kill me. I don't blame them. Although I know that was not their objective, they actually saved my life. At the time, I would rather have died than go to prison. That was the only half-ass contingency plan I ever had when I committed my crimes—if they caught me, I would just kill myself.

Game over. End of story, goodbye, cruel world. Easy to say, hard to do.

My world was now pitch black. Sensory deprived and comatose, I fell into blank, empty space. My heart was still beating and my lungs were still breathing, but I existed in a vacuum, in a blank, hollow, limitless void. I was aware of no one and nothing.

It could have been a day, a week, a month or a year. I didn't know. In reality, it was only a couple of days.

"Mr. Reeves? Mr. Reeves?"

A voice. I opened my eyes, slowly and heavily. A suit and tie, a detective.

"I need to ask you a few questions," the detective said.

"Yeah. Whatever." I didn't care.

"Did you point your gun at the police officers?"

He wasn't reading me my Miranda rights.

"No," I said, still groggy. "I pointed it at myself."

"Did you rob a bank?" he asked.

I was conscious enough to say, "I don't want to answer any more questions without a lawyer."

"All right. We need to take a picture of you." They raised the bed and took a photo of me, IV drips, oxygen hose in my nose, and all.

I fell back into the black pit of nothingness.

I was awakened again sometime later, by a doctor telling me they had to perform an angioplasty to make sure the surgery on the artery in my shoulder was successful. They will, he says, have to make a six-inch cut on the inside of my right thigh and insert a catheter into my femoral artery and run it up to my left arm to make sure the artery is open.

"Alright." Back to sweet oblivion.

When I resurfaced again, I was in a hospital room with three other patients. One was a Latino who had been shot when someone tried to steal his car. The other two were diabetics, one of whom was having his leg amputated, the other having complications from an amputation. A Harris County Sheriff's deputy was responsible for guarding me. One of my legs was shackled to the bed, and my left arm was completely numb and useless. I couldn't even twitch a finger. I was also hooked up to an intravenous morphine pump. All I had to do was push a button and morphine was injected into my bloodstream.

You really have to be careful about what you wish for. I've heard of people throwing themselves down a flight of stairs in order to obtain a prescription for painkillers, but I've never heard of someone getting into a shootout with the police with the object of obtaining a prescription for a morphine pump. But this still wasn't enough for me. I was in the midst of a nightmare from which I could not wake up. I could not physically escape, but maybe I could try to mentally escape. Yeah, I wore that button out. I pushed it, punched it, and held it down with all of the pressure and strength I could muster. I couldn't get enough morphine, not after all of the narcotics I'd been mainlining, ingesting, and smoking.

The only thing I accomplished was delaying the inevitable inferno of withdrawal.

After a couple of days, they took me off the morphine and put me on Darvocet. Darvocet wouldn't even cure a headache for me at that time, let alone the pain from gunshot wounds. I tried telling them that my tolerance level for opiates was very high and that I would soon start going into withdrawal. They didn't care. I was a criminal, and in Texas even the doctors jump at the chance to punish a crook. I was telling my doctor about this one day while he and several other doctors were making their rounds.

He said I could get on the methadone program when I was released from the hospital. "Oh, yeah," he said in mock comprehension. "You're going to the big house. Too bad." They all snickered.

Next I tried to wear out the nurse's button. I gave them such a hard time one night that they finally brought a syringe of morphine. I enthusiastically held out my arm, exposing the inside of my elbow.

"No, no, you bad boy," the nurse said. "This is for intramuscular injection only."

Oh, well, it's a lot better than Darvocet. That was the last night I slept for well for more than a month. The doctor said no more morphine.

My thirty-first birthday came and went with me screaming bloody murder. The deputy thought it was funny. He told me I was scaring the nurses and my roommates. I lay in my bed fantasizing about escaping. The deputy un-cuffed me, so I could go to the bathroom, but I was so dizzy I could barely stand up and hardly walk. I had staples in my right ankle where they'd removed a piece of artery to repair the one in my arm. I had staples on the inside of my thigh. I had staples all the way down the inside of my left arm. I had staples just above my belly button, where they'd removed shotgun pellets. My left thigh was deeply bruised and sore. I still don't know what happened between the time I was shot and when I was on my back in the parking lot, but I had all kinds of cuts, bruises, scrapes, and scratches on every part of my body. I had also lost a lot of blood. The doctor gave me a choice to be given a transfusion or just take some iron. The transfusion sounded scary, so I said I would take the iron. Needless to say, I was in no condition to escape.

During the next couple of days in the hospital, I started falling into a deep depression. I had to face the fact that I was going to prison for a very long time. I was about seven or eight stories up in the hospital, and I kept staring out the window. I remember thinking that if I could get un-cuffed and open that window I'd jump. Those cuffs were not protecting society from me. They were protecting me from myself. There was nothing left for me in this life. Nothing. I was estranged from my wife and my family. I was physically handicapped. The opiate withdrawal was gradually (and ominously) increasing. I was going to jail the next day.

Wearing nothing but a hospital gown, I was shackled up and loaded into a paddy wagon. We drove to the Harris County jail in downtown Houston and pulled up to a big garage door that slowly opened.

Why couldn't I wake up from this nightmare? It just kept getting worse and worse. I limped into a cavernous room with about ten rows of benches. The walls were painted black. About twenty pairs of scared eyes stared at me as I was un-cuffed and pushed into a space on the bench. One by one, we were photographed and fingerprinted. When it was my turn, the deputy said, "Aha, you're the one that got in a shootout with the police. We've been waiting for you."

"I didn't shoot at anybody." I said angrily. I had the impression that they'd have liked to kick my ass if I hadn't already been so obviously mangled.

"Well," the cop asked, "how does it feel to rob a bank and get caught?"

Did he seriously expect me to answer that question? I didn't say anything. I just wanted to get this part over with. I wanted to get everything over with. It was agonizing to stand for more than ten seconds.

It took more than twenty long, excruciating hours for them to process me. I went from one piss and sweat smelling holding tank to another. Bad breath and body odor from the other losers of the game of life mingled with the persistent stench of the cells. There was barely standing room. I felt like I was descending into the pit of hell as I traversed the subterranean tunnels that connected the four or five buildings that made up the jail.

At three a.m., I was finally in a cellblock. They gave me a mattress, a blanket, a towel, soap, a toothbrush and toothpaste, and a disposable razor … hey, that would come in handy for something other than shaving. There were no individual cells, only one long cell on each side of the dayroom. The room I was assigned to had about ten bunk beds lining the wall. All twenty beds were full, so I had to find a spot in the farthest corner. I threw my mattress down on the floor and vainly tried to get comfortable. That was impossible. It was as cold as a meat locker in there, so cold I could see my breath.

Then the withdrawal symptoms started kicking in in full force. The monkey was on my back and the ants were crawling all over my skin. I was briefly able to drift off into something that seemed vaguely like sleep. I dreamed that I was crawling through the sewer system of some unknown city. I kept waking up and going back into the same dream, on my hands and knees again, slithering down the pipes. Breakfast came around on a cart at about five a.m., but food was the last thing on my mind at that point. My stomach was beginning to cramp and knot up. Shortly after breakfast, a nurse came around with the medication. I was sure she had something for me. The doctor at the hospital had prescribed Darvocet for me, along with antibiotics and iron, but I needed the pain pills more than anything—more for the withdrawal symptoms, in fact, than for my wounds. This nurse was my only hope for something to put out the raging fire that was scorching my soul, boiling my blood, and burning my bones. I was woefully disappointed when she told me it would take a couple of days to fill my prescriptions and even then I wouldn't be given anything stronger than extra-strength Tylenol for the pain. That was the final straw.

There was nothing to do but go back and lie down. But I couldn't go through this. I was scared, I was sick and I was cold. I knew it wasn't going to get any better for a long time. I knew it would only get worse. I didn't want to talk to my wife or family, either. I was tired of disappointing them, and this time I'd hurt them far worse than I would know for a long time.

I remember thinking that if I just killed myself, it would hurt them one last time, but I wouldn't be able to hurt them ever again. To use the old AA cliché, I was sick and tired of being sick and tired, but I didn't feel like I had the option of getting better. I felt like I was in a chess game and I'd lost my queen, my most valuable piece. Now there was no hope of winning. What was the point of going on? I was ready to concede. Life as I knew it was completely over. As I was coming out of my drug-induced fog, I was appalled and dismayed at the thought of what I had done. If they had let me out of jail right then, I would have still felt hopeless. I had lost all confidence in myself and my ability to function normally, in society.

As these thoughts were running through my head, I was lying on a mattress in that cellblock, struggling with the physical misery that was beginning to reach its agonizing apex. I couldn't lie still for two seconds. My arms and legs were aching to the bones, my stomach was cramped into a tight knot, I was suffering from diarrhea, and my skin felt like it was on fire, like my whole body was severely sunburned. I was freezing to death and sweating at the same time. And I knew that this suffering was just the beginning. Methadone withdrawal lasts three to four times longer than heroin withdrawal.

I was at the end of my rope. My only hope now lay in the razor blade they gave me. My left arm was completely numb, so I knew I wouldn't feel any pain when I cut myself, at least not anything worse than the pain I was already experiencing. My biggest problem was getting the blade out of the plastic encasement. I had only one hand that worked. I tried and tried to get my fingernail in the plastic seam, and finally, with much concentration and effort, I managed to get a corner loose. Now I was using my teeth. So what if I cut my lips? I didn't plan on using them anymore, and the whole point of this endeavor was to draw blood, anyway. I eventually broke the plastic and exposed almost an inch of blade. I figured that was enough to do the job. I'd heard somewhere that it's more effective to cut down the length of your arm instead of across the wrist, where the tendons prevent the blade from going deep enough. So, without hesitation, I put the blade to my skin, took a deep breath, and yanked down fast and hard. All I felt was a sort of tugging pressure in my left arm. As the blood spilled out, a smile spread across my face. The feeling of relief was enormous. I pulled my blanket up all the way over my head and let the edge drape on the floor between the mattress and the wall. That's where the blood was draining. As I lay back and closed my eyes, an image of my dad suddenly appeared in my mind. I knew I was hurting him, my mother, my wife, and the rest of my family, but for some reason I felt particularly sorry for my dad. I felt like I was hurting him more than anyone else. But I shut those thoughts out of my mind. I was hoping I'd just fall asleep and not wake up.

It must have been an hour later when I looked at my wrist. The blood was barely dripping out because the wound was clotting. It was a coagulated, bloody pulp. So I took the blade and dug deeper into my wrist. That seemed to work. At least the blood was flowing freely again, running all down my arm and getting all over my orange jail uniform. What a sticky mess.

Eventually they brought lunch trays to our block. Someone asked me if I wanted mine. Without bothering to take the blanket off my head, I told him he could have it. A few minutes later, I heard a couple of loud voices, and then everyone else got quiet. Then came the scuffling sounds of a fight. They were fighting over my tray. That's exactly the kind of brutal savagery that I didn't want to deal with. It's the same behavior you see when you put dogs in a pen and throw in some food. Even if there's enough for everyone, they're going to fight over it.

I eventually dozed off. Maybe an hour or so later, I woke up. *Damn, I'm still alive.* And the cut was clotting up again, probably because it was so cold in there. I grabbed the razor blade and looked at it. It was so caked with dried blood that I didn't think it would cut anymore. Well, there was only one way to find out. I hacked and whacked and slit and sliced. The gash was now about four inches long and half an inch wide. Dark plasma was dribbling out again. This was obviously not a good way to commit suicide. I guess I'd been watching too much TV. I'd been lying there bleeding for six or seven hours, and I was still very much alive, even after having lost all that blood when I was shot. I was also thirsty as hell. I hoped the thirst was a sign that I was on my way out.

But I wasn't about to get up. The wound was still clotting up, so I tried to wipe away all of the clotted blood with my right hand, but it was clotted back up within five minutes.

I remember when I was a kid. Starting when I was ten years old, every Labor Day weekend for three years in a row I got into some sort of mishap or accident that required stitches. The first year I was bitten on the face by the neighbor's dog. The next year I cut my foot in a swimming pool. The third year my brother, Chris, kicked me in the mouth and split my lip while we were playing football at the neighbor's house. The next Labor Day weekend, my mother wouldn't let me leave the house. When I was a kid, I was scared to death of all of the blood I lost, but now I knew it's not easy to die from blood loss unless you cut a major artery. Lying in that cell, I reckoned that if I had to lie there bleeding for twenty-four hours that was just what I'd do.

If I'd known what would happen next, I would have gone ahead and cut my carotid artery.

It was four p.m. Count time. What I didn't know yet was that everyone was supposed to line up in the day room to be counted. I just lay on my mattress. The other guys started telling me I had to get up. I told them I was sick. The guard came into the day room, did his count, and realized he was one short. Someone told him I was still in the cell. He stomped in and kicked my mattress and told me to get up.

"I'm sick," I told him.

Again, "Get up!"

"I'm sick."

He snatched the blanket off of me. "*Shit!*" He took off running out of the cell, screaming at the other inmates to get into the cell on the other side of the day room. Other guards came running in. One of them grabbed me by the ankles and dragged me out of the cellblock.

"Fucking Christ! He's got staples everywhere."

"Looks like he cut himself," another guard said. He bent down over me. "Did you cut yourself?"

I shook my head and made incoherent noises.

A nurse arrived, took my blood pressure, and checked my pulse. "His blood pressure is high," she said.

"Wouldn't it be low if he's lost a lot of blood?" the guard asked.

"No. It would be high."

One of them bent down over me again. "Listen," he said, "we gotta take you to medical and we can't put you on a stretcher because the elevator is broke. Do you think you can walk?"

"I'll try," I muttered.

Two of them grabbed me under my arms and lifted me up. With their support, I limped down a couple of flights of stairs. By the time we got to medical, I had the impression that this was an everyday occurrence. The nurses treated me with indifference, though they did seem to be impressed by the nastiness of my wound. When I asked them if I could have some water, because I was on fire inside, they gave me a Styrofoam cup of water. I drank it in one gulp and asked for another one. I drank the second one and asked for another. I drank that one and it was the best water I ever drank I my life.

Now I was in a worse situation than before. I was already in hell, and I just kept digging in deeper and deeper. I wanted to die, but I couldn't. They were going to make sure I didn't have the means now. First they stitched me up, and then they took me to the psychiatric ward of the jail. When I saw the psychiatrist a little later, I told her I didn't want to live anymore. I'd screwed my life up beyond repair.

"I'll probably be locked up for at least twenty years because of everything I've done," I added. "I won't have a family or anything left after all that time."

She told me, "David, you don't know what the future holds. You never know. You might be one of those that get lucky and fall through the cracks." That was enough to give me a small sliver of hope.

At least I could wait and see what was going to happen next. For now, though, I was put on suicide watch. They gave me a paper jumpsuit, a blanket, and a different mattress, and took me to another cellblock with a day room and two four-man cells on each side.

Then they put me down on the floor of the day room. I wasn't allowed to get off of my mattress for five days, except to eat and use the bathroom. A guard was assigned to watch me at all times. There wasn't anyone in the day room when I was brought in, but gradually, one by one, zombies shuffled out of the cells and sat down at the tables. No one said anything. Well, that's not quite true. A few of them were laughing and talking to themselves. They seemed to be waiting for something. A few minutes later I found out.

"Medication!"

The nurse came in and everyone lined up. When it was my turn, the nurse still didn't have anything for me except a couple of Tylenol pills. When they finally did have something for me, it was a handful—antibiotics, antidepressants, anti-psychotics, iron, and some more Tylenol. It wasn't nearly enough to end the misery and agony, though it did somewhat dull the edge. I still couldn't sleep. I rolled around and tossed and turned.

After five days they finally put me in a bunk in one of the four-man cells. I was still in excruciating distress. The few times I managed to briefly fall asleep, I kept dreaming that I was in some kind of machine and I'm trying to make it work, but I can't figure it out, and I keep trying and trying, and it's frustrating. If only I could do it right, whatever it is that I'm trying to do. I can't get rid of the sense of frustration.

When I was awake (which was most of the time), I was also suffering from extreme boredom. There were no books, no playing cards, no TV, no chess. Nothing, nothing to do but stare into space. I couldn't talk to the other inmates. If they weren't full blown schizophrenics, they were drugged out of their minds. I'm sure I fit into the latter category myself. At night I heard a lot of laughing, plus the occasional blood-curdling scream. One of the other inmates was saving his piss in plastic soda bottles and collecting all sorts of trash in his cell. After our so-called meals, everyone dumped their leftovers in the garbage. One of the inmates was eating out of the garbage can. I also saw a guy drink out of his toilet. One young kid, about seventeen or eighteen, also cut his wrist. He kept pulling his stitches out, and then he walked around, pressing both hands to his neck, trying to put enough pressure on his carotid artery to pass out. Another one kept rapping into the telephone receiver and pounding on the buttons.

All of this lunacy just added to my sense of despair. The medication they were giving me was having an effect on me, but it wasn't a positive one. It was making me angry. A couple of times I became aggressive toward the other inmates. One night there was a crazy Mexican in my cell. He had a plastic spoon and was walking around, jabbing it at the wall like he was trying to dig a hole through the bricks. Pretty soon, I was feeling like he was poking that spoon straight into my brain. I asked him to stop a couple of times, but either he didn't hear me or he didn't comprehend, so finally I jumped up and got in his face and told him to lay the fuck down. That seemed to work, for at least a little while. All the laughter, talking, and screaming around me was making me as crazy as everyone else in there. One time I got up and stood by the door and screamed, "SHUT UP!" That had no effect whatsoever.

In spite of everything I was feeling, I was aware that eventually I would have to call home. So I finally called Rhonda. But when I heard her voice, I got so distraught that my throat constricted and I could hardly get a word out.

Here's what I finally managed to say. "You might as well divorce me and go on with your life."

She was silent for a long time. Finally, she said, "I thought I made you happy." At least that's what I remember her saying.

There's not much I could say then, or could say now. No amount of apologizing will ever be enough. I called my parents, too, and what could I say to them? For some reason, I thought the phone calls would make me feel a little better. My mom, dad and Rhonda told me they were planning to come see me in a few days. I wanted to see a familiar face so bad, but I dreaded it all the same. I didn't know if I could even look them in the face.

And when they came, the first thing my mom said was, "What do you have to say for yourself?"

How could I deal with that? "Please don't ask me any questions I can't answer," I answered.

It was pure torture to sit through those thirty-minute visits. There was nothing I could say. I just sat on my side of the glass. I couldn't even make eye contact with them. All I could do was look down. By that time, of course, I was also at the nadir of my withdrawal, and I wanted them to leave so I could go back to my cell and lie down and wallow in misery and self-pity. That's all I did for the next few weeks. I didn't shave or shower or brush my teeth. When the food trays came, all I could do was take one bite. Even though I was half starved, my stomach revolted.

At three-thirty one morning, one of the guards came in and told me to get ready to go to court. So I got ready. Then I had to wait almost eight hours in the stinking, standing-room-only holding cells with fifty other inmates. My public defender came to a window in the back of the cell to talk to me. My charge, he said, was assault on a public servant. I did not believe it! Of all the crimes I'd committed, and which they could easily prove, they charged me with something I didn't do. *I was the one who was assaulted.*

My lawyer told me I didn't have anything to worry about on this charge. There were three police reports. One said I pointed the gun at the officers, the second said I pointed the gun at myself, and the third said he did not see a gun. The police initially charged me with attempted capital murder, but the prosecutor dropped that charge down to assault on a public servant. They would eventually drop that charge, too. They figured the feds would give me enough time, anyway.

Thanks to the medicine, I caught a little sleep. The cellblock was infested with roaches. I lay on my bunk and watched them crawl up and down the walls. A couple of times one ran across my face while I was catnapping.

One morning about a month into this nightmare, a guard yelled, "Reeves, ATW!"

ATW means "all the way," It's what every county jail inmate wants to hear because it means you're getting out. In my case, though, it just meant I was going from one hellhole to another. The feds were coming to get me. The guards shackled me up and took me to the federal courthouse.

I'm sure I was quite a sight in my paper suicide jumpsuit, unshaven and unshowered for more than a month. I was arraigned and taken to the federal detention center in Houston. I looked so pathetic that one of the correctional officers asked me if I had been living on the streets. When they took me to medical for a physical exam and I stepped on the scales, it registered one hundred thirty-five pounds. My normal weight is one hundred-eighty-five, and I am sure this is what I weighted when I was shot. Even though I was doing a lot of drugs, I was still eating regularly. In fact, methadone usually made me gain weight because it made me crave sweets and slowed my metabolism rate. So when I stepped on the scales I thought they were broken.

"No," the nurse said. "They're not broken. *You* are broken."

I'm sure I looked like a skeleton at six-feet-two and one-thirty-five pounds. I had lost at least fifty pounds in one month. No wonder the CO thought I'd been living on the streets.

My arrival at the detention center coincided with the cessation of my serious physical symptoms. In fact, everything got a little better. The center was cleaner, the "clientele" was of a higher class, I was given a cell all to myself, and the food was edible. Speaking of which, I was suddenly ravenously hungry. My first meal there was pancakes for breakfast. I ate all of mine, which was more than enough for a normal meal, and the guy sitting next to me gave me his, which I proceeded to wolf down. And I was still hungry! Food became the only thing I had to look forward to. After each meal, I could hardly wait for the next one.

During this time the deepest depression I have ever experienced set in. I missed my wife more than anything in the world. Even though I knew I was about to lose her for good, I wanted to talk to her. But when I called, all she could do was cry. There was nothing I could say to her to help. After these calls I hid my face as I walked back to my cell. My hurt and pain were so overwhelming that I didn't want to talk to or see anyone. So I stayed in my cell, but all that did was exacerbate my loneliness. I remember thinking it was insane to make those phone calls when I knew I would just want to die afterwards. Finally, I decided I'd just wait a few weeks to call again. I knew Rhonda was struggling to pay all the bills I had accumulated, along with the house payments and everything else. I was so self-centered and wrapped up in my own misery and agony that I couldn't empathize with her. I just wanted someone to feel sorry for me because I was the one in jail. At that time, I was incapable of realizing what I was putting her and my parents through.

When I finally decided to call again, she didn't answer. Neither that time, nor any of the other times I tried. She had promised to visit me again, but she never did. I had a hard time dealing with this snub during the next few years, but I had done this to myself. After thirteen years together, I was cut out of her life like she had slammed a door in my face. Six months after I was arrested, I received divorce documents in the mail to sign. Of course, this was due to my own actions. But on the other hand, I thought she was leaving me when I needed her the most, but I was really the one who left. "For better or worse, in sickness and health, till death do us part"—those are words that didn't mean a thing to me anymore. You can bet that if I ever marry again, I'll pay closer attention to those vows.

If that sounds harsh, just let me say that I don't blame Rhonda at all. She did what any normal human being would have done. To have done otherwise, she would have had to been superhuman. People get divorced all of the time for much more trivial motives than drug use, bank robbery, and incarceration. But to say I had mixed feelings doesn't quite explain how I felt. Yes, the first time I phoned from jail, I told her to go ahead and get on with her life, but what I *said* and what I *felt* were two different things. I at least hoped she would do it slowly and easily, but I guess it was best for her to do it real quick, like jerking a Band-aid off real fast, so she could go ahead and begin to heal the wounds I inflicted on her. It took a long time for me to realize that I had ripped through her life, the lives of my family, and the lives of my victims like a human tornado.

When I received the divorce papers, I wrote her a letter and told her I would sign them with one stipulation, that she come to see me one more time. I just wanted to say good-bye face-to-face, not over the phone or in a letter. No response. No response to my phone calls, no response to my letters. Was it too much to ask? At that time, I didn't think so. I felt rejected, so it was easy for me to disregard the divorce documents. If she was going to ignore me, why should I give her what she wanted? I knew the right thing to do would be to go ahead and sign them and get it over with so she could get on with her life, but I was in a severely screwed up state of mind. I realize now that I had been sick for most of my life and the drug use was just a symptom of my sickness. Add to this the weight of a potential life incarceration and the possibility that I was going to be severely handicapped, and you basically have someone who thinks at the level of a six-year-old.

My depression at that time was so intense that I caught every little cold or flu virus I was exposed to. One of the infections got so bad that my eyes started swelling up and secreting thick mucus. Every morning for almost two weeks, I couldn't open my eyes when I woke up in the morning because my eyelashes were stuck together. My arm also started to hurt like hell. I kept having sharp, shooting, electric-white pains that made me jerk. Sometimes they were so intense that tears came into my eyes. Added to the physical pain was emotional pain: I dreamed the same dream every night that I was free, but then, still in the dream, I realized I was in jail, and I woke up.

I started reading the Bible at this time. I was groping, grasping at anything I could hold onto. As with most people who find themselves in my situation, the Bible offered some comfort, some hope that all was not lost. I became obsessed and consumed by the Bible. My addictive nature found something new to latch onto, and I found myself identifying with some of the people in the stories, especially King David, who had committed adultery and murder. He was crushed by guilt and remorse. In Psalms 51, he pleads for God's mercy and forgiveness. I could definitely relate.

My lawyer was visiting me pretty often during this time. At one point, he was telling me that I was looking at about seventeen years just for two bank robberies. I would still have to face another charge of bank robbery, the armed theft of a vehicle, vehicle theft, the armed robbery of a pharmacy, and whatever else they could pin on me.

That's when I started fantasizing about escaping. It was the only way I could cope. I told myself I would never be able to deal with anything more than ten years in prison. I wasn't going to try to kill myself again, although I wouldn't have cared if I fell asleep and never woke up. I wasn't afraid of death anymore. I'm still not. I've looked death in the face, begged and yearned for it, but it obviously hasn't been my time to go. In all of my escape fantasies, the first thing I wanted to do was rob a drug store. I needed something to kill this mental and physical agony. Yes, my escape dreams were more about obtaining drugs than obtaining freedom. I noticed my thought patterns running through a cycle. I would think about my lost life and Rhonda, how she was ignoring me. This created an intense psychic pain that only a shot of some narcotic (any narcotic) would cure. The only way to obtain that chemical relief was to escape and rob another drug store. But escape was all but impossible from this fortress I was living in, not to mention that I was too handicapped to even do a push-up. All I could do was indulge in my reveries.

Eventually, of course, I had to go back to court and plead guilty. They had caught me red-handed. My lawyer's advice was to just beg for mercy and hope and pray for the best. At the sentencing, the judge asked me if I had anything to say. I couldn't get more than a couple of sentences out before I choked up. I was so weak and pathetic; all I could do was hope to invoke a little pity from him. My lawyer went beyond the call of duty for me, even though his hands were tied because of the evidence against me. Compared to the other "public pretenders" I've had since then, he was a prince. He obviously tried everything he could to help me.

I ended up getting seven years for brandishing a firearm during a crime of violence, the mandatory minimum allowed by the U.S. sentencing guidelines. It cannot run concurrent with other federal sentences, so added to that I was given five years and eleven months for two bank robberies, for a total of twelve years and eleven months. The judge sentenced me to the maximum for the bank robberies and then, since I'd already received such a stiff sentence, recommended that the judges and prosecutors in my other cases give me concurrent sentences or drop the charges altogether. He said he intended this almost thirteen-year sentence to cover all of my crimes.

Chapter 9
On the County Jail Tour

There still remains to mortify a wit, the many headed monster of the pit.
-ALEXANDER POPE
IMITATIONS OF HORACE

In a way, I was relieved that I didn't get more time, but that was little consolation. In the federal prison system, I will have to serve eighty-five percent of my sentences, instead of the thirty-three percent that I had to do in the state system. I will only get fifteen percent off for good time if I manage to stay out of trouble. If I'm lucky, I'll have to serve eleven years with no parole and only six months in a halfway house.

I still had other very serious charges to face.

My mom, dad, and brother came to visit me the next day at the Houston Federal Detention Center after I was sentenced. I was thoroughly disappointed that Rhonda did not come with them. I was aching to see her more than anyone, but what did I expect? She wouldn't answer my phone calls or letters. When I walked into the visitation room, my mother burst into tears as she hugged me. All I could say was, "I'll be alright."

I don't remember ever seeing her cry before then, and it hurt me more than anything to know that she was crying now because of me. Some women seem to be able to cry at the drop of a hat, so their crying doesn't really mean anything, but not my mother. If she's crying, then something is horribly wrong.

Prison visits are such bittersweet reunions. I was glad to see my family, but the situation was extremely embarrassing. When they left and I had to return to my prison reality, I felt a deep hatred for every face my eyes fell upon. The faces of my family were so beautiful to me after being surrounded by strangers for so long that every other face was suddenly loathsome and repulsive.

I stayed at the Houston Federal Detention Center for a few more weeks, then one morning I was told to pack my property. I had no idea where I was going, but the last place I expected to be taken was back to the Harris County jail. Just being processed in was a nightmare, going from one stinking holding cell to another stinking holding cell for hours and hours. My charge was supposed to have been dropped. What did they want with me again? I found out a couple of days later when I was taken to court for an extradition hearing. Mississippi wanted to extradite me for a charge of armed robbery of a vehicle.

I waived extradition, and they were given two weeks to pick me up. On the fourteenth day they came for me. I was cuffed up and stuffed in a cage in the back of a windowless van with ten more inmates. It was the middle of July, and the van was not air-conditioned. I was thoroughly soaked in sweat within thirty minutes.

The two guards in charge of us worked for a private company. They were contracted by state governments to extradite charged suspects from state to state. I'm sure it's quite a lucrative business.

We spent ten hours that day traveling from county jail to county jail across the state of Texas, then stopped in Liberty County to spend the night in their fine establishment. I was half dehydrated, stinking, and stiff as I stumbled out of the back of the van. I reached my destination two days later and was processed into the Jackson County Adult Detention Center in Pascagoula, Mississippi. For once, I was relieved to be processed into a jail. It meant I was out of that hot van.

They put me in a cellblock with the most violent offenders. This was by far the worst county jail I've had the luxury of lodging in. The amenities were far from pleasant. I was basically tossed into the cellblock and left to fend for myself. There were at least three guys in there charged with capitol murder. There was no guardroom or control center to watch over the block, no cameras, and no emergency/panic buttons. This jail was a death trap, a place where only the strong survive. If you weren't up, standing at the door when they passed the food trays into the block, then you didn't eat. Four or five of the rowdier inmates had cliqued up and would target one individual and mercilessly torment him until he fought back. There was one young kid, for example, who had supposedly ripped off one of the guys in the clique while they were on the street. They were on him like white on rice. He could forget about eating. After his third day, my cellmate, a sixteen year old whom everyone called Juve (short for "juvenile") picked a fight with the kid in his cell. As Juve was walking out of the cell, the kid threw a boiled egg that hit Juve right in the back of the head and splattered on three or four guys that were standing outside the door.

Juve turned back around, and the kid jumped off his bunk and they went at it. Everyone crowded around to watch. It was a pretty even match, and when they were finished, they were both exhausted and panting for breath. When Juve walked out of the cell, one of his buddies, a big guy named Gip who looked like a silverback gorilla, stepped in and started pounding on the kid with both fists. By that time, the kid was too tired to do anything but crouch in the corner, balled up in a defensive position. When Gip finished, another one stepped in, and then another.

When they finally finished, and everyone went back to what they were doing, the kid eventually stumbled out. He had pissed on himself. His head, which he had just shaved the day before, was covered with red, purple, and blue knots. He staggered to the telephone and made a call, then stood by the door to the block. About thirty minutes later, a guard opened the door and the kid slipped out into the corridor, almost knocking the guard down.

"What's goin' on in here?" the guard asked.

"We just watching TV, boss," Gip said. "And playing cards."

The guard nodded. "So nobody's got nothing to say huh?"

If anybody were to say anything about what happened, they'd have to run out the door, too. If they stayed, they'd get a worse beating than the kid just got. The guard knew this.

Suddenly, Gip ran out the door and tried to attack the kid again. But as he stepped out, two more guards were coming down the corridor. They wrestle with this big ape for about five minutes before the door was shut and we could no longer see what was going on. I saw the kid a couple of months later. They had moved him to another cellblock. They took Gip to the hole.

It didn't take long for them to turn their attention to me. My left arm was still pretty much useless. It was still numb, and I couldn't even make a fist with my hand. I was like a bird with a broken wing in the midst of a pack of jackals. When I saw how they acted, I tried to stay cool and not attract attention to myself. I mostly lay on my bunk, reading every book I could get my hands on.

But I couldn't stay inconspicuous for long, not with Juve living in the same cell.

Juve had already been locked up for eighteen months. He had gotten into an argument at a skating rink and pulled a gun and tried to shoot the other guy, but he'd missed and hit a teenage girl instead. She didn't die, so he was only charged with attempted murder. Now he was waiting to go to trial. When we were locked in the cell, he was friendly to a degree, and he sometimes read his Bible. But out in the dayroom with his buddies, his whole demeanor changed. That's where he followed the thug code of conduct.

One night I was sitting on one of the benches watching a football game on TV. Juve came out of the cell.

"Who stole my candy bar?" he asked.

Nobody said anything, but a few of his buddies were laughing.

I looked up. "Not me. I've been watching football." I suspected it was just one of their games. They were always stealing from each other and trying to place the blame on whomever they were picking on at the time.

Juve walked away, and my mind went back to the game. Suddenly, it felt as if a bolt of lightning had struck me. Everything flashed bright white and my right ear started ringing. I jumped up off the bench and turned around. Juve was standing there breathing hard, his nostrils flared and his fist clenched, ready to fight.

"What the fuck did you hit me for?" I was instantly angry and wanted to beat his brains out without even thinking about it. I started walking toward him, and he started backing away from me toward an open area in the cellblock, away from the benches and everyone else. Out of the corner of my eye, I saw his buddies circling in. They smelled blood.

That's when it dawned on me that this would be no fair fight. There was no such thing as a fair fight in a jail or prison. I would have to fight Juve—and the rest of them—with only one good arm. This was not a win-lose situation, it wasn't even a lose-lose situation. I had already lost. The only thing left was for me to get the piss beat out of me and hope I didn't suffer any permanent damage like a busted ear drum or a broken nose or get my teeth knocked out.

"I can't fight all of y'all," I said as I came to the conclusion that I would rather be a coward with teeth than a crash-test dummy without teeth.

"We ain't gonna do nuttin'," said one of the thugs.

Even if I did fight Juve and win, I was twice his age. There wouldn't be any satisfaction in that. I turned around, walked back to my cell, and got up on my bunk. I didn't need this bullshit. I had already lost everything and hardly even had the will to live. All I could think about that night was that I wanted to escape or die.

Just a few days before this, I'd received a second set of divorce documents from Rhonda's lawyer. She still wouldn't answer the phone when I called. It was hard enough for me to deal with losing her without the weight of this present predicament.

That night, when we were locked in our cells, Juve's buddies started joking with him, yelling through the doors. "You better sleep with one eye open tonight, Juve." The thought did cross my mind several times that night to beat the brakes off him while the doors were locked, but that would be pointless. The whole episode was just one more brick added to the weight on my shoulders.

God does indeed work in mysterious ways. I was moved to another cellblock the very next day. The inmates at this jail were classified into two groups, those who have been convicted and sentenced and those who have not. The classification officer realized that since I was already serving a federal prison sentence, I should be in the latter group.

I couldn't believe my luck. I was glad to be getting away from this block and distanced from those retarded imbeciles. They were so stupid they thought that anyone who shaved hair off his face was a homosexual. If someone clean-shaven came into the block, they called him "booty lips," and he instantly became a target. My new cellblock was much more laid back. Even though there weren't any rocket scientists present, at least they didn't have that idiotic, juvenile, pack mentality.

There was one guy that actually was mentally retarded, though. His name was Sam. He was about forty-two years old, short, and had a speech impediment. He also had some kind of skin disorder that caused knots to pop up all over, like he had marbles under his skin. Sam had been sentenced to life for murdering his wife. He told us that she had cheated on him with his father. He shook with rage and cried as he recounted the events to us. I was embarrassed to listen and felt like I was eavesdropping or being a peeping Tom, but morbid fascination had me engrossed. After he killed her, he hid her body in the septic tank of their trailer.

A lot of the guys picked on Sam mercilessly, but if anyone tried to take advantage of him in any way, the same guys would defend him. I played cards with him a lot out of sheer boredom. I felt sorry for him and thought there should be some other way to punish him. He was going to be thrown in a human garbage can for the rest of his life. Maybe, I thought, some guys would look out for him like they did here when he got to where he was going.

The day after I moved to the new cellblock was September 11, 2001. Everyone remembers where he or she was when they heard the news. I was in hell. For four hours that morning I watched those jets slam into the Twin Towers over and over again. I was unable to fathom what I was seeing. After we'd watched the towers crumble for about the hundredth time, our TV was shut off. It stayed off for several days afterward. I'm a news junky, so this was especially irritating. I had to call home to find out what was going on, but you can only find out so much in a fifteen minute phone call that costs about a dollar a minute.

I finally went to court, made a plea of not guilty, and was assigned an attorney. The media always make a big deal out of what famous defendants plead when they're arraigned. I saw what happens when a defendant pleads guilty right away. This guy I saw was charged with some minor felony like burglary. He didn't have a lawyer present to represent him. When the judge asked him what his plea was, and he said "Guilty," the whole courtroom burst out laughing.

Even the judge was chuckling. "Son," he said, "you don't want to plead guilty because then the prosecutor is going to ask for the maximum sentence, and I'll have to go along with him."

So the confused defendant changed his plea to not guilty.

Is this is how these judges, lawyers, prosecutors, and court personnel feed off of the justice system, squeezing every little dime they can get out of the taxpayer? I may be wrong, but that's what it looks like from this perspective. This defendant would have to come back to court three or four more times before he had to plead guilty anyway. It's all a big game they play, and the criminal is forced to go along because, well, he's a criminal. I'm sure the prosecutor had all of the information and evidence he was ever going to get in this little, minor case. The defendant said he was guilty of the crime. So why not go ahead and convict him, and sentence him with a little mercy for his admitting guilt and taking responsibility? Why not save the games for the criminals that claim innocence and want to fight the system?

My brother, Brian, got out of prison in Florida around Thanksgiving of 2001. He said he was through with drugs. He just made up his mind, it was that simple. I know he wanted to quit. No one wants to live like that, but when you stick a needle in your arm for years and years, you don't just make up your mind to quit and that's it. There's a heavy price to pay, and when the debt collector shows up, you're going to pay one way or another. When Brian visited me that winter, it was the last time I saw him.

Unlike Brian, I wasn't even close to making a decision to quit using. I craved it more than ever. I felt like I had nothing to lose, anyway, and drugs were the only thing that would make my predicament bearable. I needed a way to purge the loneliness, anger, self-hatred, and boredom that was eating me alive from the inside out. I was still taking the antidepressants prescribed in the county jail in Houston, but they were no match for my desolation.

In a typical county jail or prison, the medical staff will not prescribe anything addictive or that has the potential to be abused. The strongest thing prescribed for pain is ibuprofen. But I wasn't in a typical county jail. One day, one of the guys in my cellblock approached me and asked if I liked Lortab.

"Hell, yeah, I do!"

We worked out a deal whereby I would give him a couple of dollars of my commissary goods for each pill. It was the first time I'd gotten high in almost a year. It was like a glass of ice-cold water after crossing the Sahara.

Next I complained to the nurse about my nerve pain, hoping to score something good for pain. I really was having quite a lot of discomfort, and if I'd been on the street, I'd have had no problem getting a prescription for some kind of opiate. But it was the psychic pain that I was trying to obliterate. The jail doctor prescribed Neurontin for me. I'd never heard of it, and it didn't do anything for me. But there was an old man in my block that was getting Valiums. He liked Neurontin, so I struck up a deal with him, too. Even hell is a little more tolerable with a little medicinal relief.

When I went back to court for my pre-trial hearing, the witness in my case, the car salesman, could not be located. He had moved out of town, and the prosecutor could not find his new address. Without this witness, they had no evidence. Here's an example where the criminal justice system lost, strictly because of the game they were forcing me to play. Because the standard procedure is for the defendant to plead not guilty at the arraignment, I was able to avoid being convicted of this crime. But I didn't get away. When the federal judge in Texas sentenced me to the high end of the guidelines because of all the other charges against me, this was one case he mentioned specifically. The State of Mississippi had dropped the ball, but the feds were backing them up.

All I'm saying is that there should be a way for a criminal defendant to accept responsibility and plead guilty right away. That way, he can be sentenced to a length of time within the range that he is notified of before he enters his plea, and everyone can thus skip all the bullshit and free up the court system. I know all of this bullshit was put in place to protect the defendant, but it seems that the only person who doesn't know this at the time is the defendant. Unfortunately, I've had the privilege of going through this process more than a couple of times. Each time, I've had to play this game to the end, only to stand before the judge to say, "Your honor, I'm guilty. Please have mercy on me." The worse thing about the whole process is staying in a county jail while the case creeps through the court system. County jails are ten times worse than prisons, so even if a defendant takes his case to trial and wins, he he's already been punished.

My charge of armed robbery of a vehicle in Jackson County, Mississippi, was dropped. Then two federal marshals came a couple of days later to take me one county and one state over to the Mobile County, Alabama, Metro Jail. I was beginning to get the hang of being booked into this particular county jail. The creature comforts here left little to be desired, even if it was better than the place I'd just left. My rating of this fine facility dropped a few stars since the last time I'd visited it, when it was a mere shit hole. My first couple of nights this time, my bed consisted of a blanket and sheet on a cement floor with a roll of toilet paper for a pillow. I woke up well rested every morning to a wonderful continental breakfast of weenies and grits delivered by room service. It was so good, I requested the same meal every morning, and to my surprise, my wish was granted.

I was back in Mobile to face the federal charge of bank robbery. If I hadn't run the day the police tried to arrest me, this would have been the only charge I'd have faced. I didn't know at the time that the typical sentence for robbing a bank with a note is only three or four years. Such is the influence of hard-core drugs on the thinking process.

Christmas, 2001, came and went painfully. The TV in the cellblock was blaring constantly, and the Christmas music in the commercials had me covering my ears and humming to avoid hearing them. I had been locked up for more than a year now and was slowly getting used to it, if that is at all possible. I wasn't experiencing the immobilizing depression that I'd endured for the first six months. It was just a dull constant ache that I tried to relieve by fantasizing about escaping. I had my life on the lam all planned out. I spent hours thinking about how I would actually escape. I'd go over the fence, steal a car, rob a bank, rob a drug store, change my identity, and maybe leave the country. Of course, if I'd been able to actually go through with this so-called plan, I would just be making my problems worse. Thank God, I wasn't stupid enough to try it. Or smart enough to succeed. But these reveries were the only way I could cope with the situation I was in. They were just a defense mechanism, because at the time my only other option was suicide, which also received plenty of contemplation.

While I was dreaming about escaping, I received a court summons in the mail. Rhonda was taking me to court because I hadn't signed the divorce documents yet. I went straight to the phone and tried to call her. She picked up the phone and then hung up. I tried again. She didn't answer. I tried again. "TALK TO ME GODDAMMIT." I was frothing at the mouth.

The next day a guard called me outside the cellblock and told me not to call my wife again. She had called the jail and asked them to stop me from calling her. The guard had a stupid, smug, shit-eating grin on his face as he opened the door for me to return to the cellblock.

My heart was in my throat. Now I felt like a stalker. Was this what I'd been reduced to? I was becoming psychotic. Or maybe I already was. My state of affairs was breaking me down, making me think irrationally. Well, the environment of a county jail doesn't exactly foster mental health. Every minute I was in there seemed like a lifetime. Every breath I took, I was fully aware of the pain I was feeling, as if the very act of inhaling was causing my distress.

My depression and self-pity was beginning to petrify, hardening into intense hatred for Rhonda, for myself, for everyone. There were no more tears to shed. My tear ducts were parched. I was experiencing a metamorphosis from my weak, pathetic, self-pitying, former self into a self that realizes life can be hard and cruel and hardly ever fair. In a sense, I was becoming stronger, tougher, and harder. I was learning not to sweat the small stuff. This was my trial by fire.

It was obvious by now that Rhonda wasn't going to give in to my condition that she come and visit me once before I signed the divorce papers. When my mom sent me a letter explaining what she and the rest of my family had been going through since this tragedy of my design began, I decided to go ahead and get it over with and signed the papers. My mom sent the letter to me after I got into an argument with her about sending me some money for the commissary. Up to this point, I had been assuming that the only person I had harmed was me! I finally began to realize how bad I had hurt the other people in my life. I was a real-life Tasmanian devil. Whirling and spinning out of control, destroying everything within my sight and reach. My mom's letter to me was like a mirror that reflected my ugly self-centeredness back to me.

The divorce contract I signed stated that Rhonda was to keep all the material items in her possession and I kept the items in my possession. All I had was a toothbrush and a comb. She had everything else we'd bought. But now I don't care about any of that. It's amazing to me, how attached I was to my material possessions before I lost my freedom. They don't mean a thing now. He who dies with the most toys leads one hell of an empty life. The things I value most now cannot be bought with any amount of money.

While I was awaiting sentencing after pleading guilty again, I was transferred one more county over, this time to the Baldwin County, Alabama, Jail. I'd seen the insides of way too many county jails by this time, and this one wasn't much different. Again, I was placed in the most violent cellblock in the jail, D block. The racial tension was intense. A lot of the weaker white guys were intimidated and harassed incessantly.

That's when I started forcing myself to use my left arm in spite of the pain. I wasn't about to go through what I'd gone through in the jail in Mississippi. The muscles in my arm, from my elbow to my fingers were atrophied. I hadn't been using my arm for the last sixteen months because the pain was too intense. So I started doing push-ups regularly. We also made weights with plastic garbage bags filled with water to do arm curls with. My weight increased to more than two hundred pounds, and I clipped my hair down to nothing and grew a goatee. I no longer looked like someone to mess with. Such superficial appearances are what these animals pay attention to, so they never tried to play their brutish games with me. I sat back and watched them fight, most often with each other.

An inmate came in from Florida and somehow managed to smuggle in an ounce of weed. The whole block was high for three days. Even some of the so-called born-again Christians, who were trying to repent of their former sins, were toking it up. As long as the pot lasted, all the racial tension, hatred, and bullying dissipated and everyone got along. I could smoke pot and lead a normal life if I weren't such a hard-core dope fiend. The reason marijuana is bad for me is that it feeds the beast inside me, keeping him alive and making him stronger. Other than that, and the fact that it is against the law (for impractical reasons); marijuana is a harmless drug, certainly not as harmful as alcohol. But that is an argument best left to other people. I can only express how it affected my life.

That wasn't the only time I got my hands on dope in the Baldwin County Jail. An inmate in the next block over came in with pot and crystal meth. When I heard about that, all the commissary items I had in my possession went under the door that separated the two blocks. I snorted a couple of lines of the meth and stayed up all night long playing chess with my cellie. The next day, every time I closed my eyes, all I could see was the visual echo of a chessboard. When I walked around in the day room, I experienced the delusion that everyone was a chess piece and I was trying to figure out the best way to move them. I couldn't be beaten off the board that day as guys kept coming up and saying, "Let me play the winner." My focus was so intense that I never made a mistake all day and into the night. Thus we see the short-term benefits of such a drug. That is how so many people get hooked when they try it. You feel like Superman, you're capable of superhuman feats. But then the evil imp of addiction pulls the old bait and switch on you. It takes away the euphoria, bliss, and nirvana, and leaves you with obsession, compulsion, and insanity. By the time you realize what's happened, you find yourself in rehab, an emergency room, or a jail cell.

I went to court again for my sentencing hearing. The sentencing guideline for my charge was forty-eight months. The big question in my mind was whether the judge was going to agree with my Texas judge and run the four years concurrent with the thirteen years I already had, or run it consecutively, thereby giving me seventeen years.

The prosecutor wanted to stick it to me. She railed on and on about how I was a menace to society, putting citizens' lives at risk by running from the police. This was true. But when she said I was running around robbing convenience stores, my jaw dropped. I told my public pretender that I'd never robbed a convenience store. He just stood there like a bump on a log and didn't say a word. The crimes I'd committed and admitted to were bad enough, but I didn't need this prosecutor trying to make me look worse than I already was. I'm sure my attorney believed I should be punished for my crimes, but his job was to make sure I was treated fairly.

Maybe it was a psychological ploy by the prosecutor to get me riled up when she accused me of a crack-head crime. She probably wanted me to say, "But judge, I didn't rob any convenience stores, just banks, drug stores, and a car dealership." It was a moot point, anyway. I think the judge had already decided what sentence he was going to give me, because he knew Judge Lake in Texas. He sentenced me to forty-six months to run partially concurrent with my Texas sentence. Twenty-eight months of the forty-six months were to run concurrently, and the remaining eighteen months were to run consecutively. That gave me a total of fourteen and a half years. I was relieved. I was sure he was going to hit me hard after the prosecutor finished her rant.

I received quite a few visitors while I was in Baldwin County. My mom, dad, brother, and even Rhonda's mom, sister, and aunt came to visit me. A list of prisoners who would receive visits was always posted in the block the day before so we could be ready. The Tuesday after my weekend of getting high on meth, I was called to visitation when my name had not appeared on the list. My feet and hands were cuffed, as usual, because I was considered a violent inmate. As the rest of the inmates and I shuffled down the corridors from our cellblocks to visitation, I was trying to figure out who was coming to see me. Could it be Rhonda finally? My heart sped up in anticipation. More than once I was called to a visit without knowing who it was, and each time I had the same thought, that it might be Rhonda. Each time I was disappointed that it wasn't her, but someone else that I was still glad to see was always there.

I was in the middle of the queue when we reached the end of the hallway. Then the guard said, "Reeves, you're gonna be in here," and he opened a door off to the side. Now I knew this wasn't going to be a regular visit, or I would have gone through the door at the end that led to the visitation booths.

The room I was led into looked as if it served as a classroom and a chapel. The cold fluorescent lights buzzed overhead as I sat in one of many plastic chairs in front of the lectern. There was a blackboard on the wall behind it. When my mother walked in through a different door, one look at her red, puffy eyes told me something was horribly wrong. Even though she wasn't crying at the moment, I could tell she had been crying for a long time.

My limbs went icy cold and my heart pounded painfully as I heard the familiar sound of blood rushing in my ears. (But what good is the fight or flight response when you're in foot and handcuffs?) I stood up. I knew someone had had an accident, or worse, but who? Who? Who? "What's wrong?" I asked.

"Wait until your dad and Chris get here," she said.

And right then I knew it was Brian, and I knew he was dead. "It's Brian, isn't it?"

"He had an overdose."

"He's dead?"

She nodded her head, yes. I buried my face in my hands. The hot tears I thought I could shed no more came immediately.

Then my dad and my brother, Chris, came in. My mom and dad sat on both sides of me rubbing my back and trying to comfort me. The only sounds in the room were the buzzing fluorescent lights and the clinking of my cuffs as I shook with sobs. The thought crossed my mind that Brian might have committed suicide. It was something I'd always thought he was capable of doing. I had to ask.

"Did he do it on purpose?"

"We don't think so. He was found in a motel room. Angie took his car and billfold and the police haven't been able to find her," Angie was his girl friend.

"When did this happen?"

"Friday night. We wanted to let you know sooner, but there were just too many things to do."

The same night my brother died, I was getting high on crystal meth.

"What was he doing?" I asked. "What drugs?"

"He was on Oxycontin," Chris said, "but we won't know for sure until the toxicology tests come back. Mom, Dad, and Renny had to go to Pensacola to identify him because his billfold was gone."

This was when I fully realized what kind of hell my parents were going through. This was when I saw that they were suffering a hell of a lot more than I was. They must seriously be asking themselves what they did wrong as parents, to have one son going to prison for a long time and have another one die. It was a double blow to them, tragedies less than two years apart. They didn't deserve this, especially at this time in their lives.

"You going to be alright?" my dad asked.

"Yeah, I'll make it. What about y'all?"

"We'll be okay."

We hugged each other, or rather they hugged me, since my hands were in cuffs, and then we said our goodbyes.

What goes through one's mind immediately after hearing the news of a loved one's death? Up to this point, I'd wanted to escape so I could continue my self-destructive dealings with the devil. With Brian's death, that was out of the question. Shuffling back to my cell that afternoon, I made a vow to not do anything else to hurt my parents ever again. The ghastly thought of their having to identify Brian's body still horrifies me. I found out later that it was my older brother, Renny, who had actually performed that dreadful chore, but at the time I thought it was my dad who'd done it. I had never really considered that what I had been doing could be just as distressing to him and my mom. Other than these thoughts, I was pretty much numb with shock.

When I got back to my block, I told my cellmates that I had to use the toilet. I put a sheet up over the door like we do when we need privacy and just cried my eyes out, squeezing out all of the pain that was left in me. And that was it. The well had run dry. I was anesthetized now. Callousness replaced what little warmhearted sensitivity was left in me. I was in a daze for the rest of the day.

I once read a magazine article titled, "How stressed are you?" It had a list of life's top twenty stressors. If you experienced just one of the top five, you were supposed to be pretty frazzled out. Well, here I was in jail, enduring the entire top five—the death of a loved one, a prison sentence (if long term, add more points), divorce, the loss of a job, and a major illness (gunshot wounds). Four of the five are due to my own actions, and every time I have felt stressed since then, I ask myself if I am responsible for the tension. Invariably, the answer is yes.

The night I learned about my brother's overdose and death, I prayed like I have never prayed before or since. I stayed on my knees at my bunk for at least an hour. During that time, I had a vision, or maybe God was really talking to me. You can call it what you want. I don't care because the description of what happened is just words. It was as if God were there looking down on my self-induced suffering. He was shaking his head, but he had a smile on his face because my problems were really nothing and the answer was so simple.

All you have to do is live your life the way I want you to live it. Seek ye the kingdom first. Everything else will fall into place. You don't have to worry about a thing. Is that really so hard?

It was an epiphany that would set me on a spiritual marathon that I couldn't endure.

Chapter 10
Lenny Bruce said It Would Be like Kissing God

How fast has brother followed brother.

WILLIAM WOODSWORTH

My first memories of Brian are a little hazy, as are all my primary recollections. They're tied to my oldest brother, Renny, because the two of them were inseparable when I was very young. I have vague memories of watching them play baseball in our neighbor's yard. One day I was accidentally hit in the head with the bat and knocked out. I also remember going trick or treating with them one Halloween. They yelled, "Bigfoot's coming!" and took off running, leaving me crying in the street. I was terrified of Bigfoot, and they never lost an opportunity to torment me because of that childish fear.

Even as a kid, Brian was always getting into a lot of mischief. If he was told not to do something, that usually meant he was going to do it. And I always tried to tag along. Sometimes he would let me, sometimes not. I looked up to him and idolized him. He often took advantage of this and could make me do just about anything, including his chores, just by promising me that I could do this or that with him.

He loved to hunt and fish. We all did. It's what males in south Alabama enjoy the most. When he got old enough to drive, he bought a Jeep and used to love to take it into the woods. More than once, I was with him when he got stuck in a mud hole miles from the nearest house, which we would have to walk to while covered from head to toe with mud. His first job, when he was a teenager, was at a bait and tackle shop. Something happened at that job. I never knew the whole story, but supposedly my parents caught him with a lot more money than he was supposed to have in his wallet. He told them some story about someone approaching him and paying him to deliver a package while he was at work. It was just the sort of thing he was always getting into, and a lot of it rubbed off on me. He never really got in trouble with the law when he was a teenager, but he was always right on the edge.

As a kid, I was a guinea pig for Renny and Brian's experimental ventures. One time they built a huge tree house and tied a rope from it to a tree about thirty yards away. They wanted to be able to slide down to the ground using a pulley they had affixed to the rope. But of course they were too afraid to try it out first, so they asked me to do it. If I'd said no, they wouldn't have let me play with them anymore, so after they kicked me in the butt a few times, I did it. I don't remember being scared. I just did what they told me to do. Halfway down the rope broke and I plummeted ten feet to the ground and landed on my back. It knocked the breath out of me, and then I started crying. When Renny ran to see if I was all right, he told me it was the rope's fault and told me to kick it. So I did. "Stupid rope! You hurt me."

Another time, I was walking across our backyard alone, or so I thought until I heard the *pphhhtt* of a pellet gun and felt a sting on my arm. I looked down to see a purple blood blister already rising on my skin. Then Brian came running out from behind a tree. "Did I hit you? It must have ricocheted off of the house." Yeah. Right.

Throughout his high school years, Brian was either a real asshole or excessively nice to me, the former more than the latter. The first time I ever got drunk was the Saturday afternoon he took me cruising with him. I drank three and a half beers and puked out the window, all down the side of his car, as we were driving down the road. When we pulled over to talk to one of his buddies in a parking lot, the guy said to Brian, "Dude, you got puke all over your car."

Brian moved to Birmingham after he graduated from high school. He was mechanically minded and always loved to work on cars, so he went to an electronics school for a while, and then he was employed at a succession of car dealerships. He was much friendlier to me after he moved out of the house and would let me spend a weekend with him every once in a while. This was when we started smoking pot together. When it was fun to smoke pot. I always had such a good time that going back home gave me the blue devils. Birmingham was a booming metropolis compared to Jackson it made me hate my hometown that much more.

When I was fourteen and fresh into puberty, Brian started dating a girl named Christy, who was still a senior in high school. Christy was the most beautiful girl I had every laid my eyes on. I thought my brother was one lucky dude. I think he was thoroughly in love with her and wanted to get married. While Brian was at work, she and her friends came over and hung out, or they took me to the mall or the zoo or we went to Christy's house. I was in heaven. Then she went to Florida over spring break with her friends, and when she came back, she decided that she didn't want to settle down, so she broke up with Brian. She broke his heart. I don't think he ever recovered. That was the end of the Brian who was fun loving and mischievous.

It wasn't long after this that a friend who lived in the same apartment complex introduced him to Dilaudid and the needle. This became a demon he would battle for seventeen long years. He was twenty years old then, and this was the beginning of the end of his life.

It was shortly after this that he just disappeared. He moved and he didn't tell anyone where he was going. I know from what he told me later that he got hooked on shooting cocaine, but he never told me exactly what happened. He told me afterwards that if I was ever around anyone shooting coke, I should get away from them. I suspect he was with someone who overdosed and died, and he was afraid he might be charged with a crime.

A year and a half later, when I was a senior in high school, he showed up at our house one day. His appearance was wholly changed, as if he were disguising himself. His hair was longer and peroxide blonde and he had grown a mustache and lost a lot of weight. He was scruffy and shaggy now, where he had looked very preppy before.

He said he had moved to Pensacola, Florida, where he lived for the rest of his life. He met another girl; her name was Teri, whom he later married. She knew about his drug use, but probably not the extent of it. She even did a few drugs herself. The first time I met her, we all did ecstasy. After they got married, she quit and probably thought she could get him to do the same. I know she tried, but it proved to be a lost cause. He went into rehab a couple of times, but he never achieved any lasting sobriety. She eventually gave up, and they got divorced.

My relationship with Brian around this time was often contentious. The only reason we got together anymore was to get high, and we always suspected each other of not sharing. Every time we saw each other, I would scrutinize his eyes and behavior for clues to whether he was high and what he was on, and I am sure he was doing the same to me. We were two stingy, greedy brothers, but when it came to dope, it reached a level of rabid mania. After Teri left him, Brian sank deeper into drug use. Once or twice when I visited him, he forged a prescription and I took it to the drug store. One time, I saw him get so high that he would be laid back on his couch, nodding, smoking an imaginary cigarette, and even thumping the ashes in an imaginary ashtray. Another time, I saw him do a shot of Demerol, while already loaded up on methadone and whatever else, and try to walk through a wall. He bumped his head, backed up, and tried again until I yelled, "Brian! Sit down, man."

He snapped out of it for a moment. "Huh?" he mumbled, and he finally sat down.

He eventually ended up in rehab again and actually made some progress. He was clear-eyed, full of energy, and somewhat more caring and outgoing. That's when he helped get me into rehab. When I got out, I stayed with him one weekend. It was the last and only time the two of us had been clean together in more than ten years, and I was bored out of my skull.

He stayed clean a lot longer than I did. I don't know exactly how long he stayed clean, because I don't know when he started back. If I had to guess, I would say it was about a year. When he relapsed, he was worse than ever, as all addicts are after a period of not using, no matter how long that is. From that point on, either he was in prison or I was, so I didn't see him very often during the last few years of his life.

If I could use his death as a motivation to never use again, then I could give some meaning to his life, and his death would not be for nothing. He died alone in a motel room. He'd been battling his demons for many years. I always followed in his footsteps, but now I have to choose a different course.

I don't want to live like that.

I don't want to die like that.

In the Baldwin County Jail, there were about five or six inmates who had formed a Bible study group. They met in a cell every night, read a few Bible verses, and then discussed them and how they related to their lives. I joined them the night after I found out about Brian's death. I had laughed at them before, especially after a couple of them got stoned when the weed came in and after two others got in a fight with each other after disagreeing about the meaning of a Bible verse.

For me, it all amounted to nothing more than foxhole prayers, anyway: "God, please get me out of this mess I made and I'll give my life to you." I believed that if I quit cursing, shared everything I had (which wasn't much), prayed, fasted, and studied the Bible, and then God would see how obedient I was and solve all of my problems. I really got into Bible study. A minister from the street visited me and gave me Bible study courses to complete. When I had a visit or a phone call, Bible study was all I could talk about. I went overboard. I took it to the extreme, just like I do with everything. Of course I couldn't keep it up. God just wasn't working fast enough for me.

In the years since I was arrested, I've seen several people go through this kind of compulsion. It's almost a rite of passage for some convicts, and it's amusing to observe. They look and act as if they are mentally ill, and every one of them is convinced that they can keep up this charade for the rest of their lives. (As with every rule, there are exceptions, but they are rare.) You can't just go from living, thinking, and acting like a demon to acting like an angel in a matter of months.

So I kept it up for a little while, but my patience eventually ran out. It had been more than six months since my sentencing, almost two years since I'd been arrested. I was tired of this county jail tour I was on, and prison was beginning to seem like a paradise that I couldn't wait to get to. I was beginning to see guys who had been sentenced after I was leave for prison. Why was I still sitting here in purgatory? I still had another serious charge to face in Gulfport, Mississippi, for the drug store robbery, but my lawyer didn't know anything about it, so I assumed I was heading to prison as soon as I left Baldwin County.

I was praying to God to send me to prison. Surely he could answer a prayer like this, right? How many people pray to go to prison? It didn't seem like too much to ask. Maybe you're supposed to pray to the devil with a petition like this, but I just wanted the lesser of the two evils.

One day I was playing cards to pass the time and kill my everlasting boredom when I felt a burning itch on the top of my foot. I thought a fire ant had bitten me. The itch was persistent and wouldn't go away. The next day, there was a welt the size of a quarter with a white head on my foot, and the burning was a deeper ache. It continued to get worse for a couple of days until I finally got some medical attention. Thinking it might be a brown recluse spider bite, they lanced it and tried to squeeze the pus out, and then they prescribed antibiotics. None of this helped. Soon my whole foot was swollen, and every day it got worse. I went to medical again and screamed bloody murder when they squeezed it again. This was beginning to be more painful than my gunshot wounds.

It continued to worsen. Within a few days, I could hardly stand up anymore. When I did, my whole leg throbbed with pain as the blood drained down. It was swollen all the way to my knee now. To get medical attention in Baldwin County Jail, we had to fill out a request slip and send it out with our mail and wait a couple of days for them to retrieve it. I had already done this twice, but by now my foot and leg were so bad that I didn't have a couple of days to wait. I started banging on the cell door to get the guard's attention. He came, took a look at my foot and leg, and said he would call medical. An hour later, nothing had happened, so I pounded some more. I thought my foot was going to rot off before they realized that this was something serious. I pummeled the door until both my fists were sore.

They finally came with a wheel chair and took me to medical. They wanted to lance and squeeze again, but I said, "No way! I want to see a doctor. A *real* doctor." I was adamant.

They gave me some Darvocet (which I couldn't believe) for the pain and sent me to the medical block. A few hours later, they came and cuffed me up and loaded me in a van and took me to a doctor's office in Bay Minnette. The doctor gave me a local anesthetic to deaden the pain, then lanced and squeezed it. Nothing but blood came out. He had me admitted to the hospital and put on the strongest IV antibiotics they had.

I spent three wonderful days in paradise. After almost two years in county jails, there was nothing like having my own TV with my own remote control. On top of that, I also had pretty young nurses bringing me coffee and making sure I was comfortable. I was also getting fairly decent meals. Even if I was handcuffed to the bed with Jethro, the guard, watching me, I enjoyed every minute of my hospital stay. I needed a respite from all the din and chaos of the jail. I was experiencing sensory overload, because in a jail, what a person sees, hears, smells, tastes, and feels is all within a very small spectrum, and it goes on every monotonous day after monotonous day after monotonous day. The fact that I enjoyed staying in a hospital is proof of how upside down my world was.

The only good thing about being returned to the jail was that I got to stay in the medical block, which was a lot more laid-back than the rest of the jail. Plus there were no cells, just rooms partitioned off, with six bunks to a cubicle. But I was still languishing in jail, and by now I was mad at God because he was letting me go through so much pain and misery at a time when I was trying to live by his will.

So I gave up. What good was God when he continued to let me suffer like this? When he left me stuck in this hellhole? I was finished with my little spiritual endurance race. I couldn't see the light at the end of the tunnel, so I quit running.

Chapter 11
Society's Trash Bin

In the middle of the journey of our life, I came to myself within a dark wood where the straight way was lost.

-DANTE ALIGHIERI
DIVINA COMMEDIA

Two weeks later, when they told me to pack my stuff and step out of the block, I didn't know if I was being sent back to the gladiator dome or actually leaving this abode of the damned. I found out as soon as I stepped out into the corridor. There was another inmate from the next block over also waiting outside. He was expecting to be sent to a federal prison too, so that had to be where I was going. We were taken back to the Mobile County Jail for two more nights in that shit hole of the lowest order, and then we caught a flight on "con-air," bound for the federal transfer center in Oklahoma City.

Even though I had done time in Alabama, I had never been to prison, not a real prison, anyway. Ventress and Red Eagle were like summer camp compared to the facility I was about to enter. Part of the prison experience is the feeling of despair at knowing you will not be free again for a long time. An inmate with only a couple of years to do is enduring a different prison than one with ten years, even though they may be in the same institution. In other words, prison is as much (if not more) mental and emotional than it is physical. There aren't many things in the human experience that can change a person's outlook, attitude, belief system, values, and personality more than a long-term prison sentence. More often than not, the change is negative. After spending three weeks in Oklahoma City, this was my challenge. I knew I was going through some major changes and was about to undergo a lot more.

About a hundred or so of us inmates were shackled up and loaded onto another "con-air" flight. These plane rides were about the only excitement any of us had experienced, and would experience, for years. Alexandria, Louisiana, was our first stop. That's where I got off. I had already been told that I was going to Pollock, a high-security penitentiary that some inmates referred to a USP (United States Penitentiary). I had been warned about the drugs, gangs, and stabbings that go on in these places, but I didn't care because I knew it had to be better than the county jails I just spent two whole years in.

Two days before Thanksgiving, 2002, twenty of us got off of the plane and stepped into a cold, gray, November drizzle. We were bussed to the prison, about twenty miles away. The exterior of the prison matched the day—cold and gray. We drove through a series of gates in the perimeter fence, through the wall then were led off the bus and into holding cells.

There are no words to adequately describe the apprehension and dread we felt. There were a couple of guys on the bus who had been here before and were coming back from court. Their stories about gang fights and stabbings were not doing anything to alleviate my fear and trembling. All of the new guys were inquisitive about everything, but the number one topic of interest was the commissary.

"What kind of shoes do they sell, dog?" asked one of the Mexicans, who, from the looks of his tattoos, was probably a gang member.

"They got high tops and jogging shoes, a couple of Reeboks. They got four or five to choose from," said a skinny redheaded dude with a smug expression that suggested he was an experienced convict.

"What kind of meats they got?"

"They got summer sausage, oysters, pepperoni, shrimp, and crab meat. They got a lot of cheese, too."

I just sat back and listened, and eventually the conversation came back around to the gangs and the stabbings.

"There was one dude got strung out on heroin and in debt to the Texas Syndicate for five hundred dollars," one of the inmates told us. "They shoulda known he couldn't pay that much, but they just kept feeding him, and he kept telling them the money was coming, but it never did. Then one day they caught him in the stairwell outside my unit when we were coming out for chow. Man, they almost cut that dude's head off. When everyone saw what was happening, they turned around and went back in the unit. Nobody wants to walk by and see that shit. The cameras see you; they'll snatch you up for investigation and put you in the SHU for three months." The SHU was the special housing unit, also known as the hole, which is where we ended up that night so SIS could make sure it was safe to put us on the compound. The SIS is the investigative department that keeps track of the gangs and looks into all the crimes committed in the prison. They stay pretty busy.

That night I slept in a cell with two Mexicans and a short, gray-haired Cuban. Two of us slept on the floor. Every time I saw the Cuban on the compound after that night, he always stopped and asked me how I was doing, even though he could barely speak English.

My first morning in the prison, I was awakened by a Muslim muezzin's call to prayer. The first words in Arabic mean, "God [Allah] is supreme. I witness that there is no God but God. I witness that Muhammad is the messenger of God. Hasten to prayer."

But the dissonance of the call startled me from my sleep before the sun came up. To me, it sounded like Tarzan screaming in the jungle.

SIS interviewed each of us before they would release us. When it was my turn, I was put in a chair facing the desk. The office looked like a holding cell. There was nothing on the white cinder block walls and there were bars over the window.

"Who are you affiliated with?" asked the investigator, who looked like a Marine with his buzz cut and a shirt that was stretched to its limit over his biceps.

"Who am I affiliated with?" I had no idea what he was talking about.

"Who do you run with? What gangs are you in?" he asked with a deadpan expression.

"Nobody."

"Do you have any enemies here? Anyone you have testified against?"

"No."

"Are you homosexual?"

"No." I was starting to find these questions humorous and cracked a smile, but he remained dead serious.

"Is there any reason you know of why we shouldn't let you on the compound?"

"Not that I know of," I said, "but I've never been to a federal penitentiary before."

"Okay. Not if, but *when* you're on the yard and a fight breaks out and you hear a warning from the guard tower, get on the ground immediately. We're trained to shoot center mass. There are no warning shots."

I chuckled. "Yeah." I thought for sure he was joking now, but he maintained the same stone-faced expression. He wasn't joking.

All of us who were deemed safe were rounded up like lambs to be led to the slaughter. We were all green and never been to a penitentiary before. Some of the guys had to stay in the hole to be investigated a little further because of gang affiliations or because they'd made a lot of enemies in the federal prison system. Some of them were being sent to Pollock for disciplinary action and still had time to serve in the SHU.

I didn't know whether to feel lucky or dammed. I was intimidated by all the stories I had heard, and the whole place just had a foreboding vibe. The COs regarded us with a *you poor sons of bitches* demeanor as they released us to the compound. Yeah. *Go like sheep among wolves.*

Hollywood does get a few things right about prison. When the eight of us stepped out the door and stepped on the sidewalk that leads to the center of the yard, convicts came streaming from all directions to line both sides and watch us. I've never felt more intimidated in my life. Hundreds of pairs of evil eyes scrutinized every one of us, up and down. I kept my focus straight ahead, my sights on the housing unit that was to be my new home. I found out later that the convicts weren't doing this to intimidate us. They were mostly looking for someone they might know, either from the streets or another prison. They were also looking for anyone they might have had a beef with at some other penitentiary. And of course, any known child molesters or snitches were going to be dealt with on the spot with a good, steel-toed boot stomping.

There were three of us "new boots" from Alabama. We had never been to a federal prison before so we stuck together. One was Mack, who had robbed a bank and was serving only a five-year sentence. He was older than me by a few years and had a laid-back, whatever-happens personality. At the moment, however, he was a little uptight, and you could see the fear on his face. The second guy, Rodney, was the same age as Mack, and had been in and out of prison all of his life. He was serving nineteen years for using a firearm during a crime of violence. He liked to rob grocery stores, and the police had pulled up while he was still in one. He took hostages and had a twelve-hour standoff before he finally gave up. He had already served five years in state prison in Alabama before being transferred to Pollock.

After we had run the gauntlet, several white dudes walked up to us.

"Where'd y'all come from?" asked one of them. I could tell he was obviously a white supremacist by the shaved head and Nazi swastika tattoos all over his neck and arms. He was a big, imposing dude with a deep, authoritative voice and a handle bar mustache. Just the sort of character you would expect to see in a prison.

"County jail," Mack and I answered simultaneously. "He came from state prison in Alabama," Mack said, nodding toward Rodney.

"Oh. So ya'll fresh in the system. All ya'll from Alabama?"

"Yeah," Mack said.

"My name is Rooster. If ya'll need anything, let me know." The three of us introduced ourselves and shook hands with Rooster. The other convicts just nodded to us, and they all turned and walked away.

Then we walked on to our units. Rodney and I were put in the same one, which I am glad of. At least I wasn't the only new guy there. Every inmate along the way stopped what he was doing and stared at us. I was relieved to be on the opposite end of this scenario a few months later.

I went to the cell I was assigned to and placed all my meager belongings on the top bunk. My new cellmate was nowhere to be seen. When it comes to cell assignment in the penitentiary, they don't mix the races, so I knew my new cellie was white.

Pretty soon, an inmate walked up to the door. He was fiftyish, with a cap and sunglasses on and a gray ponytail.

"You just got here, huh?"

"Yeah." I looked at him with suspicion. I already knew that anyone who acts too familiar when you first meet them has a hidden agenda. Besides this, the guy was wearing sunglasses inside.

He stuck out his hand. "My name's Knutson." He was wearing weight lifting gloves with the fingers cut out.

"David." I reached out and shook his hand.

"Where'd you come from?"

I would be asked this question one hundred times before the day was over.

"County jail in Alabama. I spent the last two years in five different county jails. I had a lot of charges." I had to throw the last part in there so he wouldn't think I was too green.

"Your cellie's name is Brooks," Knutson said. "I think he's at work. He's an AB [Aryan Brotherhood]. You look like you might be acceptable to him."

I would get to know Knutson all too well in the next few years. He was an anti-government militia-type gun-nut from Montana. He had a forty-year sentence, which at his age, amounted to a life sentence.

He nodded at me. "If you need anything, I'm just a few doors down. The guy that came in with you, Rodney, I think he said his name was, moved in my cell."

"Alright," I said, but I was thinking, *there is no way in hell I'm accepting, anything, un-requested, from anyone in here. I'm not that naïve.*

About five minutes after Knutson left, while I was folding my prison issue khakis, my new cellie, Brooks, walked in. My first thought was - *oh, shit. This is one hard-ass looking motherfucker.*

His hair was greased straight back and he had a handlebar mustache. There were Nazi tattoos all over his arms and neck, even under his left eye, where he had the two letters, NS, which I found out later, stood for North Side.

"You're my new cellie, huh? My name's Brooks."

"David." We shook hands.

"My other cellie's gone to court, but you can stay here till he gets back. It'll probably be a few months."

"Alright." I didn't feel like I had much choice.

"I see you got a 079 number. You from Houston?" He read the register number off my shirt. The last three digits signify the court district an inmate is sentenced in.

"No. I was just arrested there. I'm from Alabama."

"Well, I'm from Houston, so I guess you're alright with me since you got that number."

We talked some more as I made my bed and put my prison issued belongings in my locker. Brooks was serving seven years for being a felon in possession of a firearm. He had served a lot of time in the state of Texas, most of it in segregation because he was a gang member. Everything about him said he was a convict—the way he walked, the way he talked, the way he dressed. He even had a tattoo on the back of his neck that was just the word *Crime*. He was deep into the politics of the prison and started telling me which groups to avoid and which gangs were beefing with each other.

I'm sure he took one look at me and saw someone who was green and scared. This was all too surreal for me. It was nothing like prison in Alabama. This was the real deal and I wouldn't have been surprised if a riot broke out at any minute. All I could see was hatred and hostility on all the tattooed faces and callousness in the dead eyes. It would take me a long time to get used to this.

One of the things that overwhelmed me at first was the racism. The racial tension in some of the county jails was intense, but it was one sided. Here, it was different: it was a power struggle. I was constantly told, "We can't let 'em get control of this TV," or "We can't let 'em get that cell." The cafeteria was split down the middle. One side was black and the other races split up the other side with still more blacks. The Native Americans had their tables, the Mexican gangs had their tables, and the white section was broken down into even smaller subgroups. The skinheads and the AB and their associates had their tables. The squares, lames, and bugs were relegated to the worst places and sometimes had to stand with their trays in their hands until they could find a spot to sit down. This was one situation where I was lucky to have Brooks for a cellie.

There was always trouble in the cafeteria because someone had sat at the wrong table and wouldn't move until he was finished with his meal. Nobody wanted to lose face. A problem like this wasn't dealt with on the spot. Say a white guy sat at a Mexican Mafia table because he had nowhere else to sit. The shot caller for the Eme, as the Mexican Mafia is called, goes to the shot caller for the AB and says, "One of your *compañeros* sat at our table today. You need to straighten that up or there's gonna be a war." The AB goes to the transgressor and tells him he needs to check into the SHU or pay the consequences, which usually involves getting beat down when he least expects it by two or three guys looking to "put in some work."

I tried to settle into my new life in the penitentiary. It was hard, but I had no choice. I was going to be here for a while. Pretty soon, I started attending church services in the chapel. I have to admit it was mostly out of boredom. Every time they had a Bible study or a special guest, I was there, and I spent more time reading the Bible. There was a pattern developing here. Every time things became unbearable for me, I went crying to God, trying to find some comfort in his word.

My mom and dad sent me two hundred dollars to buy what I needed from the commissary. I purchased sweat pants and a sweatshirt, a Sony Walkman radio, a Timex Iron man watch, and a pair of Nike running shoes.

I also discovered that I could go to the recreation center and check out a guitar. I used to play a little before I lost my freedom, but I was never very good. I knew I was going to have plenty of time now to learn whatever I wanted to. The neurological wiring in my left arm and hand was still pretty screwed up. My fingers were still numb, the last joint in my index finger wouldn't bend, and my thumb wouldn't open up enough for me to grab something like a cup. Somehow, though, I could just barely make my fingers fret the strings on the neck of the guitar, enough that, with plenty of hard work and practice, I might finally learn how to do what I've wanted to be able to do my entire life.

After two long years of being cloistered in county jails, I could finally pursue another one of my passions, running. The first day I went out, I ran six miles. When I finished, my feet had blood blisters all over them, partly because I had worn nothing but shower shoes for two years. My hips, knees, ankles, and toes, and every muscle in both legs were throbbing with pain, but so much distress had never felt so good. I was beginning to feel alive again.

About the second month I was there, things began to get pretty violent. Each night for four nights in a row, there was a stabbing. On the fourth night, I was on b-yard beside the handball courts, walking back to my unit from the chow hall. I heard keys jangling as officers started running in the direction of the cafeteria. Everyone stopped what they were doing to look. Then I heard the warning from the tower in the center of the yard. THERE IS AN INSTITUTIONAL EMERGENCY. ALL INMATES GET ON THE GROUND OR YOU MAY BE SHOT. I was standing still, like everyone else, looking at the chow hall, when, suddenly, there's a bowel shaking, BOOOOMMM overhead. Without consciously making a decision to move, I found myself lying flat on the sidewalk with my fingers in my ringing ears as sparks rained down all around me. It was quiet for a few seconds, and then I heard the sounds of jangling keys again. The officers were running back in my direction now. I looked at the faces of the other inmates scattered on the ground around me. They looked as startled as I felt.

Then, out of the corner of my eye, I caught a flurry of movement about thirty yards behind me. There was a body on the ground, bouncing up and down in the dust with four or five Mexicans circling around him, kicking and stabbing him at the same time. Warning shots were fired from the tower, contradicting the warning I had been given during my SIS interview.

As the COs arrived, panting and out of breath, the attackers peeled off one by one and were thrown on the ground and handcuffed. The ominous calm returned as the officers attended to the poor bastard lying in the dust. The ambulance squad came running with a stretcher. They worked on him for a few minutes, then, put him on the litter. As they sped past me, the guy's arm bounced off the side of the stretcher. I discovered later that he was one of the Mexicans that I spent the first night in the SHU with. The Texas Syndicate had discovered that he was a snitch. They'd created a diversion by randomly ambushing someone coming out of the cafeteria, and when the officers responded to the first assault, they attacked their intended target on the other side of the compound. I've seen them communicate with each other across the yard using whistles and birdcalls. Of all the prison gangs at Pollock, the Texas Syndicate was the most militaristic. They're highly organized and disciplined, and when they attack they mean to kill.

We were locked down for a week after this incident. Getting locked down was something I would have to get used to. Who wants to be locked in a room the size of a bathroom with another man for a whole week or more? I got to know several guys way more intimately than I cared to. Every personality quirk, every character defect, every obnoxious habit would reveal itself in a matter of days. During lockdown, I spent all this time lying on my bunk reading. It only took a couple of days for me to begin staying up all night and sleeping all day. My body seems to naturally prefer these hours when given the choice. By the time they unlocked the doors, I had become so accustomed to the tranquility of having nothing to do but read, that I didn't want to come out. I felt drugged.

Things returned to normal after the lockdown, and I began getting used to life in the pen. I started following a daily routine. I used to get up every morning and go eat breakfast, then go back to sleep until about ten o' clock. That was a bad habit that I had to break. Everyone kept telling me that you don't sleep in the daytime in a penitentiary because you never know when a riot might break out. Or you might wake up with a knife in your back because you looked at someone wrong in the chow line or failed to say, "Excuse me," when someone thought you should have. I usually read, drink coffee, and listen to radio until lunch. Then I go out to the recreation yard to work out. I jog in the afternoon. After chow in the evening, I go to the band room to practice my guitar.

One evening, I was walking back to my unit with a guitar when I was approached by a guy that looked to be in his late forties, with salt and pepper hair in a buzz cut and a mustache. He spoke with a Latin American accent, but I could tell he was not from Mexico like most of the Latinos here.

"You play guitar, no?" he asked.

"I'm just learning. I used to play bass. A little." I was still very leery of anyone just walking up to me and starting a conversation.

"That is even better. I need someone to play bass in my band."

"I don't know. It's been a few years since I've played, plus I've got nerve damage in my left arm."

"But you can still play, no?" He was persistent.

"A little. It's gonna take some time."

"How you get damage of the nerve?"

"I was shot when I was arrested. It's a long story." I didn't want to get into that with someone I'd just met because everyone has a ton of questions when I tell them I was shot by the police.

"I look at you and know you can play," he said. "You come to the band room tomorrow night."

"I'll come to listen, but I know I can't play right now."

"Alright, I see you then. My name is Panama."

Guess that explained where he's from. "David," I said as we shook hands.

I didn't think anything else about it until I saw him again the next day. I had forgotten I'd told him I would come to the band room. I'd planned on practicing some more by myself.

"You come tonight, no?"

"Yeah, but I can't play, I really need to practice for about a month before I play with anyone."

"Okay, I see you tonight."

Man, this guy was persistent and couldn't take a hint. Maybe it was the language barrier. I decided to go.

When I showed up at the band room, there were Panama and two other guys with guitars and a drummer, but no bass player. Three guitarists and none of them want to play bass. That's bullshit. If you can play a guitar, you should be able to play bass, too.

Panama asked me to have a seat, the seat right next to the bass guitar. Nobody introduced themselves and they all looked pissed off.

"You know 'Black Magic Woman' by Santana?" Panama asked.

"I know the song, but I don't know how to play it." I was already asking myself what I'd gotten into.

"It goes like this," and he started showing me the bass line. It looked relatively easy, so I reluctantly picked up the bass guitar. We played the song and I did all right until my left hand started cramping and I had to stop.

I looked at Panama. "Like I told you, I'm not ready. I need to practice some more."

"Man," said one of the guitarists, "I thought you said this kid could play." He was a short, stocky, Polynesian-looking dude with a knit cap pulled down halfway over his eyes.

Panama just sat there with a stupid expression on his face and shrugged his shoulders. I wanted to leave, but then one of the other guitarists suggested we play "Free bird."

Now I really wanted to leave. Even if I could play it, I didn't like this song and didn't care to play it. But they showed me how it goes, and when we played it, it sounded like a train wreck, and not entirely because of me. These guys weren't exactly professional studio musicians themselves, but of course I was the scapegoat. So I said it one more time: "I'm not ready to play yet. Give me a month or so and I'll try again." Then I excused myself and left.

Panama continued to pester me about playing every time I saw him. "I hear you when we play 'Black Magic Woman.' You got timing. Is very important. Nobody else here got timing on the bass."

He gave me the tablature, which is the sheet music for bass and guitar, for some of the songs he wanted me to play. I kept putting him off because I thought I wasn't good enough to play yet, even if my hand wasn't screwed up.

I got to know Panama very well over the next five years. He was of French ancestry and was born and lived on the islands of Tahiti until he was nine years old. His mother and father divorced at this time, and his father took him to live in Panama. He was well educated and his father was wealthy, but this did not stop him from getting involved in cocaine smuggling. He said he was somehow associated with Noriega in the early eighties, but I have no way of knowing whether or not this is true. He revealed this to me only after we'd known each other for several years, and I have no reason to think he was lying. He was not one to boast or brag. He was supposedly the next in line to head

Noriega's smuggling operation when he was arrested, and he also had dealings with Pablo Escobar, head of the Medellin cartel at the time. Noriega essentially used Panama as a pawn. He was arrested by Panamanian authorities and then released through the back door of the jail where DEA agents were waiting for him.

While he was awaiting trial in Texas, he was involved in a plot to escape from the jail where he was being held. He had a gun smuggled in and was set for the jailbreak. They were going to take the warden hostage, and there would only be one opportunity to do so. When the time came, however, Panama was called for a lawyer's visit. His partner had the gun and proceeded with the plan without him. To make a long story short, the plan failed, his partner killed a guard and got the death penalty, and Panama got life without parole, added to the twenty years the feds eventually gave him.

When I met Panama, he had been locked up for fifteen years. At first, he continued to sell drugs in prison. But by the time I had met him; he had changed his ways and was repenting of his former sins. He said he never realized what drugs did to people until he saw it with his own eyes in prison. He grew up in a culture where drug smuggling was an acceptable occupation, where even the leader of his country was involved in it. He was far removed from the streets of the U.S., where his product was doing its damage.

I felt sorry for him. I know he was responsible for the death of one person and maybe more, but I saw a man who was truly remorseful for what he had done, even if it did take more than ten years in prison for him to reach that state of contrition. He was in his early twenties when he committed these crimes, and now he was almost fifty. The judicial system has no way of knowing exactly when a person in prison has been punished sufficiently enough to change who they were. Sometimes it doesn't happen, in fact, and the criminal is released back into society worse than when he went in, but sometimes it does happen and the person is never released. I know without a shadow of a doubt that if Panama were released today, he would never commit another crime. I may be naïve and not the greatest judge of character, but if there is one person I can help when I get out of prison, it will be Panama.

I got to know some good people at Pollock, and I also got to know some bad ones. My cellie, Brooks, was in the latter group, but I still got along with him all right. He tried to teach me the ways of the penitentiary, as he saw them, and he was always busting my chops for being so green. Every time someone left our cell after coming by for a visit, Brooks would say, "He's a homo," or, "He's a degenerate gambler," or "He's a scandalous dope fiend, watch out for him." Pretty soon, I was looking sideways at everyone in our unit. Maybe they actually were all these things, but the way Brooks put it, they were all snakes that I should avoid at all cost. It took a while for me to figure out that he was just fucking with me.

Brooks never put any pressure on me to join the Aryan Brotherhood, but when one of the skinheads tried to recruit me, he nudged me in that direction. They asked me to play football with them a couple of times.

"Go play with them," he told me. "They're good dudes."

"I don't know," I said. "I just wanna do my own thing."

"You need to hang with the guys more often. Don't be such a lame."

Part of me wanted to. I was beginning to feel like a loner. I pathetically wanted to be accepted by a group of guys. So I played football with them. I still have scars on my knees from that one game on a cold, January Sunday night.

The day after the game, Panama and several other guys whose acquaintance I had made came up to me and said, "What the fuck are you doing, hanging around those guys? If they get into it with the blacks, you'll be a target. I've seen it too many times. If they get locked up for anything, you'll get locked up just for associating with them." That was as far as my prison gang recruitment went.

I began practicing in the band room regularly. As soon as it started conflicting with my church attendance, I gave church up. Things were getting easier for me, so I didn't need God anymore.

It had been almost a year since I'd used any drugs. One night Brooks asked me if I wanted to smoke a joint. The angel said, "No." The demon said, "Yes!" The angel yelled, "NO!" The demon screamed, "YEESS!" A brawl ensued. The demon bit off one of the angel's wings, the angel kicked the demon in the balls, and the demon, infuriated beyond reason, summoned all the rage of hell and lashed out like a tornado against the angel. When the dust settled, feathers floated down, landing on the broken halo.

I stood behind Brooks, looking over his shoulder as he unfolded the small piece of paper that contained the green ganja, but the ganja wasn't green, nor was it even ganja. It was a tan powder. Heroin. The demon was disappointed and salivating at the same time. Brooks immediately took it to some other dope fiend to get rid of it. He didn't do heroin. He'd tried to buy weed, but the dealer gave him the wrong "paper."

I began hanging around with a couple of other guys in my unit, Curly and Carl, who were musicians. They liked to drink the hooch that was made from fermented tomatoes and sugar, so it didn't take me long to join in. I had nothing against old Mr. Bacchus. The tomato wine didn't taste too bad once you got used to it.

It cost five dollars for a quart, also known as a "neck," and was sold in small plastic garbage bags. The guys would cook up five gallons at a time, usually in a footlocker in their cell. Without exception, they were eventually caught and sent to the SHU. They also lost privileges, such as commissary, phone calls, and visiting rights, for a certain amount of time. They would also lose a certain amount of the little bit of good time we are given. If an inmate stays out of trouble, which is almost impossible at a federal penitentiary, he gets fifteen percent off of his sentence. To the majority of inmates, this is not enough of an incentive to play nice. For most of these guys, a trip to the SHU is a vacation. It's not like what you see in the movies, where an inmate is placed in solitary confinement in a dark cell with no clothes and only bread and water. To a true convict, the outside world doesn't exist anymore, so phone and visitation rights don't mean a thing, and you don't have to shop in the commissary if you know how to hustle up stamps. In other words, when the federal government abolished the parole system because "get tough on crime" politicians were looking for a vote, they took away the Bureau of Prisons' ability to punish criminals once they're on the inside. The inmates have nothing to lose.

Excuse me for going off on a rant here, but when a criminal starts his so called career with a little minor mistake or crime, the public acts like its proof of his inherent badness when he graduates to more violent crimes after spending a little time in prison. Did these assholes ever consider that the prison system might be incubating baby lawbreakers into more sophisticated, more violent criminals? The members of the Irish Republic Army used to call time in an English prison "going to university." And so it is with the penal system in the United States. For drug dealers, it's nothing more than an extended business convention. If I wanted to start selling drugs myself, I could now have contacts in Columbia, Mexico, and just about every other South American country, as well as a whole distribution network set up in every major U.S. city. I've also met hundreds of bank robbers who've all shared with me the mistakes they made. If I went out to rob a bank now, I'd do it right. I've also met just as many meth cooks, who, as a group, seem to be the most committed to their criminal occupation, and you can bet they're sharing and refining their recipes.

I don't have a solution to the criminal problem, but there has got to be a better way than our current system. The cure shouldn't be worse than the disease. Or at least the cure shouldn't make the disease worse.

Excuse me for getting off the story, but I had to get these thoughts down on paper while they were at the surface. Now where was I? Oh, yeah. I got drunk on tomato wine and liked it so I got drunk some more, so I started making my own wine. In no time, I was smoking pot when it was available and buying Klonopin from a couple of guys that got them at pill call. Klonopin is like a long lasting Valium, so I kept as much of it as I could in my bloodstream.

When I first got to Pollock, everyone pegged me as a Christian because I was always going to the chapel. They were quick to put labels on people—Christian, Muslim, dope fiend, bug, homo, snitch, killer, or lame. Once one of these jackets got put on someone, it was hard to shake it off. But I made such a quick about-face that the Christian tag didn't stick for long.

Brooks' cellie eventually came back from court, so I had to find another cell to move to. There was an older guy in the unit named Bobby, who was from Oklahoma and needed a cellmate, so I moved in with him. He was sixty years old, of medium height, and slim with gray hair and eyeglasses. He was also missing several teeth, and while I was living with him he had all his teeth pulled so he could get dentures. Bobby was an old school convict. He had been in and out of prisons since the sixties, mostly for robbing drug stores. He was a real drug store cowboy. He loved to shoot Dilaudid. You could see him getting all excited, rubbing his hands together, just talking about it. He didn't think his drug addiction had anything to do with his spending half of his life in prison. Like most addicts, he had this delusion that he could control his addiction, that he could stop any time he wanted to. The only problem was he never wanted to stop.

At the time I moved in with him, I had already given in to the desire to get high several times, even though part of me still wanted to stop. Drugs are like kryptonite. I was powerless and weak against them. On reflection, it was a bad idea for me to move in with Bobby, but he did give me a little proper guidance on how to do my time.

Eventually it happened. I was chilling out in the cell, reading a book when Bobby walked in with his homeboy, another old-school convict named Ron. Ron only cared about one thing—getting high. It was how he did his time. He had someone from home sending him plenty of money to help him achieve his life's ambition. He spent half of his time in the SHU, because he failed drug test after drug test. He was on the so-called hot list, so he was tested at least once a month.

Like I said, I was lying on my bunk reading a book when Bobby came in and sat on his bunk below mine. Ron sat in a small chair at the metal desk. He pulled out several pieces of foil from his sock. The foil was actually little squares cut from a potato chip bag and folded into flat rectangles about the size of the tip of a shoe lace. This little rectangle is called a "paper." A paper of heroin sells for twenty-five dollars, though it's probably worth only about ten dollars on the street. Ron unfolded two papers and emptied the contents into a plastic spoon. Then he added a little hot water and a small piece of cotton. The syringe was half a pen barrel that had a rusty needle melted into the end. On the other end, a black piece of rubber was tied on with a rubber band so that it could be squeezed to push the air out. When the needle is stuck in the cotton and the rubber is released, the drug is drawn up into the pen barrel and is ready for injecting.

There is a physical reaction that takes place in the body of a drug addict when he is exposed to a drug like this. Adrenaline starts flowing, the heart starts beating faster, the bowels loosen up, and the hands start to shake. This is the thing non-drug addicts don't understand.

They think it's all in the head. When my body has a reaction like this, my will power goes out the window. Yeah, it's the kryptonite effect. I was experiencing it as I watched this familiar ritual take place.

When Ron and Bobby finished fixing, they took one look at me and they could tell I wanted to get high, too.

"Go get five books and you can have some of this, too," Bobby said as he scratched himself.

A "book" is five dollars' worth of stamps. After watching Ron and Bobby shoot up, I was desperate. It's like there's an on/off switch in my head. When the switch is on, I want to get high, and it's almost impossible to turn the switch off. I become a man on a mission that won't be completed until I'm blitzed, obliterated, wasted.

So I went to the store man and borrowed five books. My credit was good. I got the stamps, and then got my paper. That should have been the hard part, but it wasn't hard at all.

I had made it this far in my career without catching any diseases. I knew that Bobby and Ron both had hepatitis C, a chronic liver disease, which I didn't know much about at that time. We didn't have any bleach to clean the needle, but I didn't care. I didn't care whether I lived or died, anyway. I felt my life was fucked up beyond repair, so I wasn't worried about catching hepatitis C. Like I said before, the switch was on, and I couldn't turn it off. The switch also seemed to affect the part of my brain that links actions to consequences. I was unwilling, or unable, to look at any long-term effects of my actions. I was going downhill in a car with no brakes, and I didn't care whether I crashed or not.

Back in my cell, I proceeded with shaking hands with the process of converting the powder in the foil to liquid in a syringe. Now for the hard part. The needle was so dull that I couldn't hit any of the remaining veins (the ones that hadn't yet collapsed from the years of mainlining) in my arms. My veins kept rolling to the side after the needle punctured the skin. But I kept trying. I wasn't about to give up that easy. I poked so many holes in my skin that I had blood running down my arms. I finally gave up on the arms and tried my thighs with the same results. I was beginning to feel nauseated and frustrated. Blood was coagulating in the needle, so I had to keep stopping to make sure it was clear, which caused me to lose a small amount of the drug each time. I must have poked myself about forty times. I finally hit pay dirt on the inside of my left thigh. I had to randomly jab the needle in hard and fast, trying to hit my target. When the barrel filled with blood, I knew I had hit bull's eye. My hands were shaking as I squeezed the rubber tip. The bloody elixir went into my vein, thence to my heart and into my brain.

My whole body was engulfed in orgasmic euphoria that expanded and swelled and eventually peaked as my head went back and my face contorted in an expression of rapture. As the rush slowly ebbed, a glowing, warmth filled my entire body. For the next eight hours, I was oblivious to the cares of this world. If I'd hated myself before, I loved myself now. If I'd thought I was stupid before, I was the smartest man alive now. If I'd felt sorry for myself before, I was devoid of self-pity now. All my negative thoughts and feelings were positive now.

Addiction to drugs in prison is more than being in prison inside a prison. There is a synergistic effect. It's hell in a whole new dimension. Now I was about to pay the price for shooting heroin in prison. I knew I probably had hepatitis C, if not something worse. The biggest consequence was that now I really, really wanted to get high. To get high, I needed money, or some sort of tradable commodity. The only way I could get money was to call home and come up with some sort of bullshit lie about why I needed the money. "I need a hundred dollars for shoes." "I need one hundred and fifty dollars for art supplies for my painting class." "I need seventy five dollars to pay on my fine, or they are gonna put me in the hole and take away my privileges." I tried to find ways to make money myself. My orderly job only paid me twenty dollars a month. That definitely was not going to support a drug habit. It wouldn't even support my coffee habit.

I had gotten high a few times when I was in the county jails during the previous two years, but it was nothing like this. It was never enough to achieve the state of well being that I was feeling now. I had spent many, many hours fantasizing about getting high, and I had plenty of drug dreams. This is what a lot of drug addicts experience when they abstain from using. Every night I had dreams that I was trying to get high. I woke up plenty of nights holding my breath because in my dream, I was smoking crack and would inhale and try to hold my breath as long as possible so I could get as much as I could into my system. Or I had dreams where I kept shooting up but couldn't seem to get high. I'm never able to get high in these dreams, so I keep trying over and over again. Even now as I write this, I've been clean for almost four years, and I still have drug dreams occasionally. The only difference is now in the dream, I realize that I had been clean all this time and now I will have to start all over again. I wake up relieved that these dreams aren't true, relieved that I am not in *that* prison, *that* nightmarish, hollow existence.

But back then, I wanted more heroin. I had to find a way to hustle. But I wasn't very good at hustling. I tried to put my artistic talents to use by drawing portraits for money. Inmates will always pay for this type of service. They'll pay for homemade birthday and holiday cards and picture frames made from potato chip bags. They'll pay someone to clean their cell, do their laundry, and work on their radios. Some guys even buy old shoes, stitch them up and clean them, and sell them for profit. There's a hundred ways to make money in prison. Inmates have their own little economy where the price of a stamp can even fluctuate, depending on how flooded the compound is with stamps at the time.

My portrait drawing didn't last too long. Sometimes they came out good, sometimes they didn't, and some customers were easy to deal with. Some weren't. It soon became apparent that this wasn't going to support a drug habit. Eventually the Texas Syndicate member I was buying dope from asked me if I wanted to sell some papers for him. He would give me one for every five I sold. I said yes.

That was the stupidest decision I could have made. For one thing, I was too naïve. I was fresh into the system. I was green. This was out of my league. Second, I didn't have the type of personality that is required in a drug dealer. I lacked the shrewdness and ruthlessness a drug dealer needs. Third, I was a dope fiend, and you can't be a successful dealer and user, too. At the time, though, I didn't see any of this. All I could see was that I had found a way to get high. I knew several guys that were junkies, so I didn't have any problems selling a few papers here and there.

It lasted a month. Then the connection ran dry and my supply ran out. This was either divine intervention, or I was just damn lucky. The stress level of trying to live like this was unbearable, and I was at the breaking point. I stayed in my cell for a week and went through withdrawal. I was afraid to step outside of my cell door because I knew the devil was out there waiting for me. He wanted me—mind, body, and soul. I realized that I would do anything to get high, and there are plenty of people in prison that will take advantage of such a person.

This it, I told myself. *This is the last crossroad I will come to. If I choose the wrong path, there will be no turning back*. I had lost everything—mentally, physically, and spiritually. I was still sinking, wallowing at the bottom of this human garbage can. What was it going to take for me to stop?

Narcotics Anonymous and Alcoholics Anonymous meetings were held in the chapel once a week. Mack, my homeboy from Alabama who arrived here with me, talked me into going to a meeting. I was reluctant. I didn't see how sitting in a circle with a bunch of other losers whining about their problems was going to help me with mine. I had been in and out of NA and AA meetings for the last ten years, been to rehab on the street and in prison, so I doubted I was going to hear anything new. But I went anyway. I said I wanted to quit.

Shortly after I returned to my cell after the meeting, Knutson knocked on my door.

"I got five dollars I owe you for that portrait," he said.

"It's about time. That was, what, a month ago?"

"Times are hard. Here. I figured you'd rather have this." He pulled a neck of wine from the inside of his jacket.

Kryptonite.

"Fuck."

"You want it or not?" he asked.

"Yeah, but don't bring this shit around me anymore."

"Well, excuse me. I thought you liked it."

"It's a love/hate thing." I took it and poked a hole in the plastic and poured it into my cup. I guzzle it down as fast as possible for a stronger effect, and then flushed the bag down the toilet.

What the fuck is wrong with me? Do I have a split personality or something? Am I Dr. Jekyll and Mr. Hyde? I'm a walking contradiction, that's what I am. I'm strong and I'm weak. I'm smart, but I act stupid. I want to quit and I want to use. I have a demon and an angel on my shoulders, and they take turns controlling my thoughts and actions. So much for the AA meetings.

Every time I turned around, Carl and Curly or someone else who knew I liked to get high was in my face with some mind-altering chemical. In my current state of mind, it was impossible for me to turn anything down. I was too weak and powerless. I couldn't say no to anything that would help me escape for a second from my reality. If I used to run from the everyday problems of life before I got locked up, how was I supposed to stop now that these problems were amplified and magnified a thousand times?

Seething in the midst of my own inner turmoil, I found myself in the midst of outer turmoil on the recreation yard one Saturday. One of the skinheads, who was just released from the SHU stabbed another dude in retaliation for some previous altercation the two had had. All hell broke loose. It was right after lunch, when there could not have been more people on the yard. The riot started on C-yard. From the fence where I was standing on B-yard, I could see about thirty skinheads and blacks fighting, stabbing and beating each other with padlocks. The guard in tower eight fired warning shot after warning shot, to no avail. The recorded exhortation from the tower to get on the ground sounded out. Skinheads were running from all directions toward the fight. One of them came out of the door of the education department, running across the softball field, dust flying from his feet where the warning shots slammed into the parched earth. He never slowed down until a guard tackled him and two more piled on top. Suddenly, everything became silent. Hundreds of inmates were kneeling in the yard, not saying a word. All their eyes were focused in one direction, toward something that was happening just out of my sight, beyond the corner of the C-unit building. Brooks, Rooster, and a couple of other Aryans were standing at the fence, watching.

Shane, a big, twenty-something white dude who used to get drunk and stand outside his cell block yelling racial slurs, was now yelling at Brooks and Rooster. "Do something! Why are ya'll just standing there? Fucking *do something*."

Rooster held out his hand, palm forward, to try to quiet Shane, who continued yelling as he paced back and forth along the fence.

I should point out that the AB members on the yard here at Pollock were mostly from Texas. I've been told that they would be run off any other compound by the Brotherhood, and I was now seeing why. The skinheads were going hard. This was what they had been waiting and preparing themselves for, but these Aryan posers just stood by and watched, afraid now that Shane was drawing attention to them.

The situation on C-yard must have been brought somewhat under control, because the PA system announced that all B-unit inmates should return to their cellblocks. Realizing that I might be in danger, I picked up my pace a little. I finally reached my cell, which was four floors up, and went straight to my window. There I had a good view of all of B-yard and some of A and C as well. Inmates and guards were running in all directions. Some of the guards had beanbag guns and tear gas launchers. I grabbed my belt and the padlock from my locker to make a weapon in case someone wanted to try me.

Back at the window, the next thing I saw was Shane on the ground up against the fence, getting his face stomped in by a couple of black dudes. His whole head was covered in blood. Surprisingly, Rooster walked up, and the black dudes ceased their assault on Shane. They put up their fists, as if they were ready to box, when Rooster held his open palms out toward them. One of them backed up and the other put his fist down for a second, but then brought them back up as if he couldn't decide what to do. He finally backed off.

Rooster was very charismatic. He was well respected by all of the inmates. He looked like Wyatt Earp on steroids with a shaved head, so it didn't surprise me that the assailants retreated. Its too bad Rooster was murdered less than a year after being released from prison a couple of years later.

Eventually the Special Operations Response Team (SORT) came in with their padded suits, shields, and helmets, looking like the Teenage Mutant Ninja Turtles. Pretty soon, the riot was under control. A few white guys had been randomly attacked and stabbed. They'd had the misfortune of being separated and caught alone by groups of four or five blacks.

We were locked down for two weeks. All of the white gangs were removed from the yard. The skinheads were shipped immediately to other prisons; the AB and the Dirty White Boys were locked up in the SHU for several months. The advice I was given about hanging out with the skinheads turned out to be true.

The tension was still high after we were released from lockdown. Violence creates fear, and fear creates more violence. In the SHU, two of the DWBs managed to get out of their cell and attack one of the black orderlies serving chow in the corridor. They stabbed him in the eyeball. The rumor on the yard was that one of the guards let the two DWBs out of their cell to let them do their dirty work. This story only exacerbated the tension and fear on the compound. The place was a powder keg, but it had the effect of keeping everyone on their toes and minding their manners. For me, there definitely wasn't anymore sleeping in the daytime.

As things slowly returned to normal, I eased back into my former routine. I started practicing the guitar up to eight hours a day and began playing in a heavy metal band with Carl and Curly. This is where I met Bruce who was to become one of my closest friends over the next few years. We would write our own songs and Bruce would sing (or maybe "scream" is more appropriate) the lyrics he had written. It probably sounded like crap to most people, but we had fun doing it, and it was a tremendous release of our anger and frustration. No matter how bad a mood I might be in before band practice, I always left feeling renewed and energized.

I was still drinking occasionally and making my own. One day, I returned to my cell after band practice to find my cell door locked. I had been cooking a gallon of wine and had it hidden in my locker, so I knew this was why my door was locked. I went to the CO's office.

"Why is my door locked?"

"What's your name?"

"Reeves."

"I shook down your cell and found wine in your cellie's locker."

"It wasn't my cellie's," I said reluctantly. "It was mine."

"Then you need to report to the lieutenant's office."

When I got to the lieutenant's office, I was placed in a holding cell for four hours. I had to sit there, staring at the wall, trying to figure out what kind of punishment I was going to receive. I didn't care about having to go to the SHU. I just wanted to be able to keep my commissary and telephone privileges. I had to decide if this was how I was going to do my time. If I wanted to turn my time in prison to my advantage and make it count for something, I could look at this time as wasted years or use it as a gift to learn things I've always wanted to learn. I could be like Bill Murray in *Ground Hog Day*, where he continues to wake up on the same day over and over. Instead of continuing to make the same mistakes, he decides to use the time to his advantage.

As it turned out, even though this was my first write-up, I was punished pretty severely. The warden wanted to crack down on all the drinking, so he was enforcing a zero-tolerance policy. I lost twenty-seven days of good time, plus I lost my telephone, commissary, and visitation privileges for ninety days. I was also put on the hot list and breathalyzed randomly for the next year. The only mercy I was given was no time in the SHU, but that was the least of the punishments they could have given me. I didn't mind lying on my bunk all day, escaping from this hellhole with a good book and nothing else to do. I love nonfiction, biography, history, and true adventure. The books I've read have taken me all over the world. I've been to Italy, Spain, Russia, Argentina, Chile, the French Marquesas, Japan, China, India, Morocco, and Tanzania. I've explored the Amazon, the jungles of Borneo, and climbed Mt. Everest several times. I've traveled across this country and through Death Valley on my way to the gold mines in California in 1849. I've sailed the Caribbean to the Bahamas. I've been to Paris more times than I can count, and I've also been to the Soviet gulags in Siberia and to the French prison on Devil's Island. I've been a hostage of terrorists in Beirut, and I've escaped from a Turkish prison.

After everything I'd been though—or more correctly, put myself through—it was this one minor incident that made me stop destroying myself. I drank one more time. I'd started working at the UNICOR factory and came back to my cell after work one day. My cellie (I had a different cellie by this time) had a gallon of wine in a cooler on the desk. I was still too weak to handle an ambush like this, so, one last time, I guzzled down my half. The date was October 15, 2004.

It was around this time that I read a book by Viktor Frankl called *Man's Search for Meaning.* Frankl says that we can find meaning in life when confronted with a hopeless situation, a situation that cannot be changed. What matters then is to bear witness to human potential at its best, to turn tragedy into triumph, to take a predicament and turn it into an accomplishment. When we cannot change a situation, we must change ourselves. Frankl was a Nazi concentration camp survivor who found meaning in his suffering. I am in no way trying to make my own plight similar to his. His suffering was much more horrific, and not of his own design, whereas my own misery was created by a twenty-year series of bad choices.

After reading Frankl, I read every book I could get my hands on that was about people surviving predicaments worse than my own. I soon realized how lucky I was that

I hadn't committed my crimes in some other time or place; that I am in America in 2000 instead of, say, France in the late nineteenth century. I am lucky to be fed three decent meals a day, to have air-conditioning, television, telephones, a paying job, clean water, and a chance to make myself a better person. My suffering comes from being physically removed from my family and friends. I have missed out on a lot of birthdays, holidays, and vacations. I couldn't be there when my brother died or when my grandmother passed away in 2004. I missed the birth of my niece and seeing my other niece and nephew grow up.

I have come to see that my situation is not totally hopeless. I will have one more shot at liberty. However faint the light is, I am beginning to see a few rays at the end of the tunnel, but if I continue to drink and get high, there will be only darkness ahead. I am tired of this beast inside me, controlling me, driving me to self-destruction. I had to stop feeding him. As much as I would like to, I can't kill the beast. He's still a part of me. *But I can put him to sleep.* I can put him in a coma. But one drink, one toke, one hit will wake him up. He'll be stronger than ever, and I don't have the strength to wrestle him anymore. Besides, I've been there, done that. There's nothing left for me to experience in that dark, enigmatic world but pure hell.

It's time to move on to new things.

I started attending a yoga class taught by one of my acquaintances. I am convinced that yoga helped me get through those first months of sobriety when, for the first time in my life, I had to say no to getting high. Yoga is so much more than stretching. It strengthens and calms the mind, which is what I needed more than anything else. It taught me that I could control my thoughts, that I was not at the mercy of those images, feelings, and beliefs that kept flashing through my head and telling me to get high. Thanks to yoga, I learned discipline and self-control and gained peace of mind. The war was finally over.

I had to make a few other changes, too. I had to get out of the unit I was living in, where there were too many bad influences that had a knack of finding me at my weakest times. So I moved to A-1, the behavior modification unit, which houses the inmates participating in the CODE program. The population is small because the regular convicts avoid such programs, so the majority of us had single man cells. Panama lived there too, so he helped me get moved in. The inmates on the compound that had mental problems also lived there. So the unit was fairly quiet. This was completely different from the zoo I had just left.

Chapter 12
Serial Escapists, Psychopaths, and Unexpected Inspiration

We live in a fantasy world, a world of illusion. The great task in life is to find reality.
-IRIS MURDOCH

I got a job at the prison factory, which is called UNICOR, sewing shorts for the Army. That way, I wouldn't have to call home and beg for money anymore. I started out at forty-six cents an hour, which comes to about seventy-five dollars a month. It wasn't a lot, but it was enough to buy what I needed from the commissary. The meals in the chow hall get old after a while, so it's nice to have some money to eat something different every once in a while. My job kept me busy, kept me off of the yard where trouble was always brewing, and made my time speed along a little faster.

I also decided to give AA and NA another shot. For the first time in a long time, I felt at peace with myself, and I wanted to keep it, so I started attending a couple of meetings every week. Before, I'd always judged the program negatively, telling others and myself that it is a bunch of bullshit that just doesn't work. That it was just a bunch of people whining and crying about their problems, but they were going to use anyway. I never did everything that was asked of me, only half measures. But that's like judging a book after reading only a few pages. This time, I decided to go to any lengths, to use any means necessary to get clean. What did I have to lose? Nothing.

Quitting is always the easy part. *Staying quit* is what I always had trouble with. I made my own hell out of using drugs. It was my death style. So now I was going to have to make a life style. I had to make a life out of staying clean. I would have to change everything about myself. I'd put a lot of energy into being a drug addict. Now I was going to have to put that same energy into staying clean.

The next couple of years at Pollock were relatively peaceful. There were still occasional fights and stabbings, but they were usually isolated incidents not involving gangs. My time was spent working, playing music, running, and doing yoga. Before I knew it, in fact, I had a year of clean time, real clean time. I still had acquaintances that did dope and drank occasionally, and they would sometimes try to get me to join them. The thing that stopped me from saying yes was that I didn't want to lose the peace of mind I'd found. I knew it would evaporate the second I gave in. It might feel good for a couple of hours, but the opposite feeling would last for days, and possibly forever.

My sponsor in AA told me to ask myself if there was a point in any of my days where I felt better than if I was high. At first, the answer every day was no, but as I started paying attention, I realized there were several times when I did feel better than I would if I were getting high. When the guys I work with crack me up until tears are streaming down my face and my laughing muscles cramp. When I finish my yoga routine and meditate in the corpse pose. When I'm in the band room playing and everyone else is also in the groove. When I'm running and my mind leaves these walls and the razor wire and the miles click off without my knowing it.

Every Saturday evening, I ran as far as I could. I eventually started running from the time the yard was opened at five o'clock until it closed at eight-thirty. On several occasions, in the summer months when the afternoon and early evening showers would come in, then dissipate; I'd see the rainbow stretching all the way across the prison. Sometimes as I ran I saw double rainbows.

When most people would use rainy weather as an excuse to stay indoors, I came to love running in the rain. As long as there was no lightning, the prison staff would leave the compound open. One January Saturday night, a warm rainstorm blew in. I was the only one in the yard that night, the only one who enjoyed playing in the rain. It was like I was still a kid. The rain came down in heavy sheets. At times, the deluge was so thick I could hardly see the buildings of the prison around me. It was a spiritual experience like I have never had before. Here we were, just God and me, and He was washing away all the dirt and filth that had accumulated in my soul. I felt his presence more than ever in the rain that night. I felt a peace that is worth more than anything this world has to offer.

In the summer of 2005, I received a letter from the prison records department. The letter said that I had been indicted in Gulfport, Mississippi, for the drug store robbery I had committed. Good-bye, peace of mind. It had been almost five years since I'd committed that crime. Why did they wait until now to prosecute me?

The light I was beginning to see at the end of the tunnel faded, and that old feeling of impending doom returned. I had been telling myself and everyone else how lucky

I was that I hadn't gotten more time. Now it looked like I spoke too soon. After I got that letter, I was in a daze for the rest of the day. I could think of nothing else. Luckily, no one offered me any kind of mind-altering substance, because I would have indulged. I had no peace of mind to hang on to. More luckily, I was able to analyze the situation clearly. I saw how I sought to use to escape negative emotional states. That's why I liked to get high. It's why I liked the feeling so much. It felt better than the alternative. I had been too weak to deal with even the slightest adverse sensation. It was way past time for me to man up and quit being such a wimp.

In the penitentiary, physical and mental weakness is despised. Weakness of any kind is sought out and either stamped out or used against the weakling. I came to despise weakness, too, but more so in myself. I had wallowed in self-pity my whole life, even though I had every chance and every opportunity to become successful at whatever path I chose to take. Self-pity may be excusable, or at least expected, when someone has a hard life because of things outside of their control, but mine was inexcusable and pathetic.

I didn't know what was going to happen to me. I didn't know if they were going to come and tell me to pack my belongings tomorrow and transport me to another county jail or what. Besides the fear that I might get more time, possibly even life, my second fear was to stay in a county jail again. I had seen too many county jails already, and they're all the same—purgatory.

What I found out was that the charge would be on me until I was released from federal prison, at which time I would be picked up by Harrison County Sheriff's Department, unless I chose to voluntarily go back and get it over with. I figured time was on my side. I had done five years and had eight more to do with the feds. I could wait a year or two, when there would be more time between the actual commission of the crime and the present. That might give me an advantage, because by then, so much time would have passed that maybe the prosecutor would give me a break just to get it over with.

It happened that Hurricane Katrina struck the very next month and almost destroyed Gulfport, Mississippi. What impact would this have on my case? I heard reports about courts in New Orleans having to throw out tons of cases because evidence was lost or destroyed. But I wasn't that lucky, so I just put the whole thing on the back burner, and decided to worry about it later.

In the spring of 2006, things started to get violent again. The gangs started fighting again, there were several assaults on correctional officers, and then someone escaped. Richard McNair had arrived in Pollock in 2005. He was serving at least one life sentence that I know of, maybe two. I do know that it was for murder and attempted murder, back in the eighties, so he had been locked up for a while. I used to see him out on the track whenever I ran because he liked to run, too. He had been in the Air Force and liked to stay in shape. I developed a rapport with him, especially after he started working in the UNICOR factory. He worked in the section that repaired mailbags for the U.S. Postal Service. Sometimes my foreman left for a few days and I had nothing to do, so I helped McNair with the mailbags. He was fairly intelligent, was a nice guy, and carried himself real well, not like the typical convict. He was upbeat and had a positive demeanor, the kind of person I chose to associate with.

In 2006, I was in the Challenge program (which replaced the CODE program) and had to attend classes in the morning, so I went to work after lunch. One week, my foreman was gone on vacation, or something, so when I got to work, I went to the mailbag section and helped McNair. That is what happened on Monday and Tuesday of that week. On Wednesday, when I came in, he was nowhere to be seen. It was no big deal. I thought maybe he'd gone to the dentist or something. About fifteen minutes after everyone had returned to work, however, we were called back to our housing units and locked down. A fight had broken out during lunch, so everyone assumed that this was why we were being locked down.

The next morning, I was listening to the local radio station. Here's what I heard: *Richard Allen McNair has escaped from the federal penitentiary in Pollock.* At first it didn't even register with me. I'd always assumed it would be impossible to escape from this high-tech fortress. Then I thought they were talking about the prison camp next door to the penitentiary. But then … wait a minute—that name sounds familiar. I knew him as Rick, so it took me a minute to realize whom the radio was talking about. Jesus Christ! Rick had escaped!

We were still locked down when one of the counselors came around to interview us.

"Do you know why you're locked down?" he asked me.

"Yeah, there was an escape."

"How do you know that?"

"I heard it on the radio this morning."

"Do you know who it was?"

I nodded. "Richard McNair."

"Did you know him?"

"Yeah, I worked with him."

"Does it surprise you that he escaped?"

"It doesn't surprise me that he tried. He's got two life sentences, I think. It surprises me that he actually succeeded."

"Did you know that he was trying to escape?"

"No. I had no idea." That's when I said, *Uh, oh*, to myself. *I've already said too much. They're going to think that I know more than I actually do.*

That was the end of the interview. We were released from lockdown later in the day. I had several people come up to me and say they thought I was the one who had escaped. As one guy said, "When they said it was a tall, white dude that runs all the time, I thought it was you."

This is supposedly how it happened. Part of McNair's job was to stack mailbags that needed repairs on pallets, then shrink-wrap them. These pallets were then taken to the warehouse outside the prison. For security reasons, nothing is supposed to leave the back docks of the factory until all inmates are returned to their units and counted at four o'clock every afternoon. But our factory manager was always rushing things, always pushing and pushing. *Get this shit outta here today!* Pretty soon, McNair noticed that the pallets he was turning out were going straight to the warehouse instead of sitting on the docks as they're supposed to.

So he made a pallet with a hollow center and somehow managed to find just the right idiot to shrink-wrap it after he'd crawled inside. The same idiot took it to the back dock. This was all supposedly caught on camera, and the rumor floating around the compound later was that the two actually hugged each other before Rick got in.

The forklift driver from the warehouse picked up the pallet and took it right out through the back gate. That's where there was another security lapse. McNair should have been discovered here by the officer, whose job is to inspect every vehicle leaving the prison. The pallet reached its destination at the warehouse, where McNair burst out of the shrink-wrap and out of the warehouse without having been seen by anyone. A warehouse employee eventually discovered the suspicious looking hole in the pallet and alerted the prison.

A few hours later, after the prison authorities had figured out that it was McNair and notified the local law enforcement agencies, a police officer detained a man fitting McNair's description who was jogging on the railroad tracks that happen to run right beside the prison. The cop questioned him. It was all caught on the camera in his patrol car. We got to watch it the next night on the local news.

"You fit the description of this guy that just escaped from the prison nearby," the cop says.

"I assure you, I didn't just escape from a prison." McNair is wearing a prison issue T-shirt and shorts bought from the commissary. He's even got on one of the Walkman radios we can buy along with a bottle of water.

The cop continues to question him and McNair plays it off, calm and cool, not showing a bit of nervousness. The cop eventually lets him go, which simultaneously saves his life and makes him look like an idiot. McNair wouldn't have given up without a fight, and like I said before, he was in real good shape and knew a lot of martial arts.

The cop wasn't very experienced. He didn't know it at the time, but he was dealing with a criminal genius. This was McNair's third escape from prison. But obviously he didn't know how to stay out, because eighteen months later he was caught in Canada.

Everyone at the prison cheered him on. They were glad to see someone outsmart the prison authorities. But the fallout from his escape was no small deal. I, for one, was called to the lieutenant's office the following Saturday morning. I was handcuffed and led to a conference room that probably not too many inmates ever see. Seated around the table were the head of SIS, a lieutenant from SIS, and a United States Marshall, who did most of the questioning.

I was on camera the two days prior to the escape, working with and talking to McNair for hours at a time. If I refused to talk with my interrogators, I would go straight to the SHU for at least ninety days, plus lose my job and my single-man cell. So I told them what I knew, which was nothing. They wanted to know what we talked about, every subject of our conversations, but all of our discourses were just small talk, bullshit to pass the time. Two or three times, they asked me, "If you knew anything, would you tell us?" Again, an answer in the negative would send me straight to the SHU, do not pass go; do not collect two hundred dollars. Every time we're locked down because of some violent disturbance or occurrence, every inmate in the compound is interviewed and asked the same question. This is when the majority of these knuckleheads, who have lied, cheated, and stolen their whole lives and have no intention of ever changing, suddenly become righteous and honest. They can't wait to tell the interviewer, "I wouldn't tell you shit." They consider the prison authorities to be the enemy, who they lie to everyday, but all of a sudden they want to spit in their face with the truth. They would do well to remember the saying, "Keep your friends close, but keep your enemies closer."

Later that day, the lieutenant sent an officer to my cell to confiscate my running shoes. They wouldn't tell me why, so I was beside myself with worry. They must really think I had something to do with the escape, but McNair had never spoken that word to me. It had never crossed my mind that he was thinking of escaping.

About an hour after they took my shoes, I was called to the lieutenant's office again. When I got there, I was placed in the holding tank. Now I was sure they're taking me to the SHU. They were somehow going to charge me with helping him escape. After thirty minutes of fingernail biting and heavy sighing, I was taken out of the cell and to the lieutenant's office. The lieutenant was kicked back and relaxed in the chair behind his desk.

"What kind of running shoes did McNair wear?" he asked.

My relief was audible. I realized this is why they'd called me up here. "Uh, I … I don't know."

"Come on," he said. "I see you out there running every day. I know when you run, how far you run, and what direction you run. If you are half as smart as I think you are, you know what kind of shoes he wears." I didn't realize this until later, but he was using a psychological tactic to boost my ego after I'd been softened up in the holding tank. What he said caused me to unconsciously want to cooperate with him.

"I think he wore New Balances. I'm not sure."

"Was he a pronator?"

"I think so. You must run, too."

"Yeah, I like to run triathlons."

It was my turn to ask some questions. "What do my shoes have to do with this?"

"We just wanted to see the pattern on the soles of the running shoes sold here."

"Oh, do I need to quit running so y'all won't think I'm trying to escape?"

"No. Just keep doing what you've been doing." He sat forward and put his elbows on the desk. "That's all for now. We may have some questions for you later on. You can come back and get your shoes tomorrow."

"Alright." I turned around and walked out. From then on, every time I saw this lieutenant, he called me Running Man.

We didn't go back to work for a week, during which the FBI and the high ranking Bureau of Prison officials conducted their investigation of McNair's escape. Several guys who worked with him or were acquainted with him were locked up in the SHU. They locked up one of my former cellies for telling them during his interview that he didn't know McNair, when they had him on camera talking to him. The UNICOR factory manager lost his job because of his security violations.

During most of the time that I was in the CODE program, I had a single-man cell, but occasionally, I voluntarily let someone move in with me if they were coming from another unit to start the program and I was already acquainted with them. But you never know what someone is really like until you live in a room the size of a broom closet with them.

Clay was in one of my bands, so he was no stranger to me. He had been in Desert Storm in Iraq. Then he came home and murdered his wife and threw her off a cliff (his words). He was Jewish and the same age as me. I never judged anyone negatively for the crimes they had committed because I believe people can change; otherwise, there is no hope for me. But as I got to know Clay, I found I was unable to dismiss my knowledge of his crime. I'm not a psychiatrist, but I've read a lot about psychopathic personalities, and he definitely fit the description. According to him, psychopathology was his diagnosis when he was on trial, but in this sick environment, that's something worth bragging about, because it meant *don't fuck with me. I'm crazy and might do anything.*

Even though he acted arrogant and condescending to just about everyone else, he never did anything to me to make me dislike him so much. He had a smugness that irked the hell out of me. Maybe I saw something in him that I didn't like about myself. I certainly did a lot of soul searching while I was living with him. Sometimes I would go days without saying a word to him because I didn't want to get in a conversation with him about anything.

We had to live through a couple of weeklong lockdowns and one that lasted almost a month. After the first one, I couldn't stand the sight of him. His voice went straight to my spine, where it rattled every nerve in my body. It boiled over one night when I was in the cell preparing something to eat. Clay just walked through the cell door after taking a shower and just stood there. It's a common courtesy to give your cellie space for a few minutes after they take a shower, but I hadn't realized he was taking a shower when I started my cooking. Now I could feel his eyes burning a hole in the back of my head, so I hurled my spoon, food and all, at the wall and walked out.

After a few minutes, he walked up to me. "What did you do that for?" he asked. "I didn't do anything to you."

I didn't know what to say. I knew I had overreacted, so I made an asinine comment. "You get on my nerves. That's just how I am."

"That's bullshit."

I was starting to get mad now. I didn't want to have an argument with my cellie in front of the whole unit, so I walked back to the cell. He was right behind me. I turned on him.

"Dude, I can't stand the sight of you or the sound of your voice."

He looked at me, and then said, "I don't understand why you act like this when I dig you, man."

"Aw, fuckin' Christ. Please tell me I'm not havin' this conversation"

I grabbed my food and walked out. I felt bad about how I had blown up, so I apologized later on just to try to clean up my side of the street. But I also immediately started trying to get him moved out of my cell so I could have some peace. I didn't know if there was something wrong with me or was it him. I've had much worse cellmates before and since, but never one that I disliked more. I couldn't seem to reconcile his crime with his personality.

It was around this time that I decided to go ahead and arrange to go back to court in Gulfport, Mississippi, for the drug store robbery. Another year had passed, and I was nearing the halfway point of my federal sentence, so now was as good a time as any to get it over with. Even though I set the procedures in motion, I prayed they would just drop the charges. The crime was now almost six years old.

I was going through some major transformations in 2006. Part of it, was brought about by a female correctional officer that started working in my unit at that time. There were plenty of female staff, but I never paid any attention to them and they never paid any attention to me. What would be the point, anyway?

Marilyn worked at night in my unit a couple of times. She would come to my door, which was right beside the CO's office, and talk to me when we were locked down at ten o'clock. It was good to have a normal conversation with a member of the opposite sex. I assumed she was just being nice.

But one day I was walking with Panama to return a guitar to the recreation department and we came across her in the corridor. She said, "Hi," and smiled as I walked in, but on the way back out she stopped me.

"Where are you going?" she asked.

"Back to my unit."

"Come back," she whispered. "I gotta tell you something."

"Alright, I'll come back on the next move." This blew my mind. Now she was being more than nice to me – or so I thought.

I'd been locked up too long for this kind of attention. It was making my head spin. She looked pretty good. She had straight, raven black, shoulder length hair and a nice figure. She was a couple of years younger than me, but she looked like she was in her twenties.

When I went back, I walked down the corridor with her.

"I just wanted to tell you I think you're special," she told me. "You're different from the other inmates here. I want you to stay out of trouble."

"I will stay out of trouble. I have no intention of screwing up my life anymore."

"How much longer do you have?"

"About six years."

"Do you think you'll stay here or go someplace else?"

"I don't know. Right now, it looks like I will be here for a while." My mind was spinning in overdrive by now. I asked a stupid question. "Is there something happening here, between us?"

"Yeah, if you weren't in here." She said.

Ouch. That hurt. Why did I have to ask such an idiotic question? The move was about to close, so I had to go into recreation, the chapel, or education. I chose to go to the chapel, since there was an AA meeting going on.

She walked with me and unlocked the door. "I'll talk to you later," she said.

"OK," I said.

I went into the meeting and sat down. My head was spinning like a tilt-o-whirl and adrenaline was coursing through my body.

This is the cruelest punishment incarceration gives us. Sex is a natural, biological need. Humans, like all other creatures on the planet, are compelled to obey this instinct. It's a physiological, psychological necessity on par with our requirement for food, water, and oxygen. Well, maybe a smidgen below them, since I've never known anyone who died from sex deprivation. But the drive is nonetheless extremely powerful, and to deprive a man in the prime of his life of this vital need for years on end is cruel and unusual punishment in my book.

So, about thirty minutes into the meeting, I looked up and here she was coming. She walked in and asked if she could have some of our coffee. For the next few weeks, she kept turning up wherever I was. She came to my band practices a couple of times, she came to my unit, and she came to the classroom where I practiced my guitar. She was supposed to be working elsewhere in the compound.

One day when I went back to my unit after lunch, I found her working there.

"Don't go back to work," she said. "Tell them you're sick, or something, and come back and talk to me."

That's what I did. I sat in her office the rest of the day. I was under her spell. It was just too much for me. I'd been locked up for six years and had six more years to go, and what I wanted as much as freedom itself was in my face, but I couldn't touch it. It was pure torture. I felt physically sick for a couple of weeks. A chemical reaction was taking place in my brain and manifesting itself in my body. I did a lot of heavy sighing, trying to expel this ache in my chest.

I had to force myself to see nothing could come of this. If something did, it would only get us both in trouble, and that wasn't something I wanted to risk. I tried to tell her this and explain what she was doing to me.

"You know you're driving me crazy," I said. "I've been locked up too long to deal with you rationally."

She just smiled coyly, twisting her hair around her fingers.

"But I want to thank you for giving me some hope in myself," I added. "I haven't felt too good about myself for a long time."

"You have a lot to be proud of," she said as if she were surprised at what I'd said. "I was just telling Pam (another CO) the other day that you're the only one here that I would help if I could." She paused. "If ya'll could get parole or something…"

"Yeah." What could I say? "But I have no idea what I'm gonna do when I get out. What would you do if you had six more years to do in a place like this? What would you do with your time?"

"You should write a book," she said. "You've got a good story to tell."

"I've thought about that," I admitted. "Maybe I will."

Chapter 13
To Hellenbach Again

I don't like people who have never fallen or stumbled. Their virtue is lifeless and it isn't of much value. Life hasn't revealed its beauty to them.

-BORIS PASTERNAK
DOCTOR ZHIVAGO

One day I was called to the records department. I was told that I had a court date in Gulfport, Mississippi, and the Harrison County Sheriff's Department would be picking me up in a month or so. It was horrible news tempered only by the fact that I finally got my single cell back on the same day. I had gotten rid of one problem (Clay) only to have a bigger one take its place. Now I had to mentally prepare myself to return to another county jail. Compared to where I was about to go, I was living in paradise.

I've never run as much as I ran during the next few weeks. I ran every morning and evening, averaging eighty miles a week. I was trying to kill the dread I felt, but I wasn't about to do it with drugs and alcohol again. If I became addicted to running to deal with my feelings, at least that was better than the alternative. Running is such a meditative act that I feel like I can face anything life throws at me when I have that endorphin afterglow at the end of a run.

Even though I thought I was ready, I was still caught off guard when my boss told me I needed to pack my property and report to receiving and discharge (R and D). That old familiar feeling of blood draining out of the bottoms of my feet came back. My hands turned cold and my face went pale.

My patience and endurance had been tested in several different ways since I began my incarceration. My feet and hands were shackled up and attached to a belly chain around my waist, and then I was stuffed into the back of a sheriff's car on a plastic seat with no legroom. We were in the dog days of summer and the car was not air-conditioned. The drive took six, long excruciating hours (they got lost at one point). Six long hours that I had to breathe their stinking second hand smoke. When we arrived in Gulfport, my clothes were completely soaked and I was one sip of water away from dehydration. But I never opened my mouth in complaint. I accepted all such treatment as punishment for my crimes.

When a criminal is sentenced to prison, what exactly does that mean? First, it obviously means a loss of personal freedom. But does it automatically include the other things I've had to endure? Was I sentenced to a loss of dignity? Was I sentenced to extreme physical discomfort for hours and days at a time? Where does it say in the law books that I was sentenced to have wannabe-cop correctional officers treat me with disrespect and hatred and put my health in jeopardy?

After I was booked into Harrison County Jail (there was that awful smell again), they put me in solitary confinement for thirty-six hours. At first I thought this was a good thing. It was what I wanted, to be alone, not to have to deal with the animals that inhabited this place. The violence in a penitentiary like Pollock has one good side effect: the men are respectful and courteous to one another to an extreme. Uttering two words—"Excuse me" —can save your life. But in a county jail, there is no such respect. They bump into you, they scream and yell when you're on the phone, and they cut in line when chow is served. Just put me in solitary. I didn't expect to be here that long, anyway.

The solitary cell was so cold I wouldn't have been surprised to see icicles hanging from the ceiling. The first night, I hardly slept at all, not with one thin sheet, a blanket with holes in it, and no pillow. The next morning, depression hit me so hard, it was as if I had put it in a syringe and injected it. Maybe, I thought, I should have waited another year to take care of this. I could be looking at a life sentence here. With all of the uncertainty and fear, I felt like I was being arrested all over again. I had forgotten how painful a county jail could be. I felt it to the marrow of my bones. I was actually missing Pollock.

I am not going to lie. I cried like an abandoned baby. I couldn't console myself. If only I had a book to read, I could get my mind outside of these walls, but it was just my thoughts and me. Except for the bone numbing cold, I was sensory deprived. I got down on the floor and did a few hundred push-ups just to get warm and boost my endorphin count. That worked for a while, but I was whimpering and shivering within an hour. *Please, God—do something! Anything. Put me in the zoo. Anything would be better than this.*

I made it through another long, cold night, curled up in a tight fetal position with the blanket over my head. The next day, I was taken to the most violent cellblock there. When I walked through the door, the other inmates were literally swinging from the bars, braiding each others hair, and strutting around, competing for the alpha male spot. *God help me.*

I was an experienced con by that time. I knew how to carry myself in these situations and that's what they were paying attention to. They were looking for any sign of weakness in me. The guard just says, "Find a cell," then he closes and locks the block door. It was like the sound of a needle being scraped across a record. The music stops. All of the swinging, braiding and bouncing stopped for about ten seconds. All eyes were on me. I walked in with my head up. I'd learned that a quiet confidence gets the most respect. Everyone went back to whatever inane activity they were in the middle of, and pretty soon one friendly cat came up to me.

"You can cell with Dallas," he said. "His cellie just went to the hole. Two oh nine." He pointed at the cell.

Well at least that ended my depression. It was just replaced by an uncomfortable anxiety.

The next day I got a visit from my court appointed attorney.

"Well, Mr. Reeves, the prosecutor wants to give you twenty years, day for day. No parole. No good time."

My jaw dropped. "I'm already doing fourteen and a half years in federal prison."

"When is your federal sentence over?"

"Two thousand thirteen. When the judge sentenced me in Texas, he sentenced me to the high end of the guidelines. He recommended that the judge and prosecutor in this case drop this charge or give me a concurrent sentence."

"He can only recommend it," the attorney said. "He has no jurisdiction here."

"I know that," I replied, "but wouldn't it help if this judge and prosecutor were aware of it? I have my sentencing transcripts at home."

"Yeah, if you can get that to me, that might help. But I can't promise anything."

"I just don't want to have to do any extra time. I'll take a fourteen year concurrent sentence if I have to."

"I'll see what I can do. Your trial is set for March."

"Six months away?" I asked. I don't believe it.

He managed a smile. "That's fast, compared to everyone else. They're still backed up from Hurricane Katrina. Just sit tight. I'll get back in touch with you after you get me that transcript. Here's my card with my phone number and address."

"Alright. Thanks."

I don't know which is worse—six more months in a county jail or the possibility of twenty more years in prison. Well, no, it is really a no-brainer. But I was expecting to get this over with a little quicker.

But out of all of my sojourns in county jails, this turned out to be the easiest one. Maybe it was because I had learned how to do time. Doing time is something to be learned if you want to keep your sanity and stay out of trouble. Maybe it was because the inmates were just easier to get along with. We were allowed to go outside to a walled off recreation yard for about an hour every day, which was something I rarely got to do at the other county jails. A little sun on the face every day does a lot to improve the mood and attitude. It's not something you notice unless you've been deprived of sunlight for months at a time.

In Gulfport, I turned to the Bible again to try to find a little consolation. I had spiritually matured somewhat by this time. For two years, I had been completely clean and sober. I had no desire to use. I had been abstinent for long periods before, but never free of the desire, so this was terra incognita for me, unexplored territory. This freedom allowed me to grow in several ways. When I turned to the Bible this time, I was just looking to grow a little more. Whether you believe in the Bible or not, it's still a huge, wonderful story, full of everything man will ever experience. Whether it's true or not is beside the point to me. Either way, there is still a huge amount of wisdom in this book, more than you could ever learn in a lifetime.

God had already done the greatest thing he could do for me. He had removed my desire to use drugs. It's as if he looked down on me and said, "Son, you've had enough," and for that I was grateful. Even if I did get twenty more years in prison, I said to myself, then that was his plan for me, and I'd look for the good to come from it.

Something else that helped me grow spiritually was learning how to deal with the other criminals in a place like Harrison County Jail. There was one twenty-something-year-old kid here who was charged with capitol murder for killing and raping his grandmother. How do you deal with this? I was living in the same small space with this guy, so interaction was unavoidable. Some of the other inmates taunted him, some completely shunned him, and some dealt with him the same way they did with everyone else. But I was full of curiosity about him more than anything else. This was a bona fide, living, breathing monster. Is there a more heinous crime, a more outrageously evil act?

His name was Jerry. He was nerdy and obese, with straight black hair that fell over his eyes. He thought he was so much smarter than everyone else, but he acted passive and seemed starved for attention. Except for his passivity, he reminded me a lot of my former cellie, Clay, who was actually much smarter than most people I've met in prison. Both Jerry and Clay had committed abominable acts of murder against a family member.

But who am I to judge? Society has seen fit to put them in the same place it put me. Was I any different? Any better? I've tried to look for the good in everyone I've met in prison since then. I believe there is no such thing as a good person or a bad person. It's not white or black. We all fall somewhere along the spectrum and move back and forth throughout our lives. Some of us fall far down, but that doesn't mean that we can't rise back up, stronger because of our experiences.

It turned out that Hurricane Katrina did help me out. The courts in Harrison County were extremely backlogged, thanks to the storm, and the jail was severely overcrowded. The judicial system was under a lot of pressure to clear out the oldest cases. Since my case was more than six years old, I could have not picked a better time to come back and face my charges.

When it was time to go to trial, therefore, I had three things going for me: the time that had passed since my offence, my federal judge's recommendation, and the backlog and overcrowding. The prosecutor offered me seven years to run concurrent with my Texas federal sentence that had begun in 2001. The judge went along with it. So, basically, I was given time served plus one year to end in June 2008. It turned out better than I'd hoped.

With this two-ton weight lifted off my shoulders, I could breathe easy again. Even though I couldn't wait to get back to Pollock, where I could run, play music, and see my old, goofy comrades, the two cellmates I had at Harrison were plenty of entertainment. One was a short, stocky, Vietnamese cat named Li, the other, a tall, gangly dude about my age named Patrick. They kept me in tears of laughter the entire time I was there. Sometimes it seems like the worse the situation is, the harder I laugh. There was a lot of horseplay and goofing around, and if we made Li mad, he would say in his Asian accent, "Kiss my yellow ass."

Two weeks after my sentencing, the same two deputies who had brought me here finally took me back to Pollock. This time, the car had air conditioning and the ride was quicker because they didn't get lost. Only a person who has been through the ordeal can understand how happy I was to return to this gray, violent prison. Sure, I would rather be returning home, but it's best not to even entertain such thoughts.

I was gone for only six months, but the changes that had taken place in the compound during my absence were incredible. There were a lot of new angry faces. A few of my former associates had gotten in fights and been shipped away. There had been another suicide, bringing the total to four since I'd arrived in 2002. There were also a lot more skinhead and AB gang bangers who weren't here when I left. The tension in the air was palpable.

My buddies, Bruce and Panama, were still here. I was happy to see them, as well as Patrick El, one of my coworkers who always made me laugh. There was also a good news/bad news situation: Clay was living in my old cell, which was a handicap cell and prized by everyone because it was a larger than regular cells. The flip side was that he was waiting to be transferred, so I gritted my teeth and moved in with him, hoping the situation wouldn't be as bad or as long as last time.

Who did I see at breakfast my first morning back? Marilyn was working in the chow hall, scanning ID cards for the meal.

"I haven't seen you in a while," she said.

"I just got back from court."

"That's what someone told me. Did everything work out all right?"

"Yeah," I said. "Better than I thought it would."

"I'm working in B3 tomorrow," she whispered so the other people in line wouldn't hear. "You better come by and see me."

I just smiled and kept moving. I hated talking to her when other inmates were around. Any time any female was in sight, they just stared like the lecherous profligates they were.

I had only been back two weeks when the powder keg exploded again. I was walking back to my unit after breakfast, and was right under tower 8 in the middle of the compound when the "institutional emergency" alarm sounded. I knelt down and stuck my fingers in my ears, but that wasn't necessary, judging by the direction all the officers were running. YARD RECALL was announced over the PA system five minutes later, so I headed back to my unit, unaware that a black DC inmate had just stabbed a white inmate to death. The white guy's cellie, who was an AB, grabbed two knives and stabbed the DC inmate to death.

The rest of the compound was unaware that two racially motivated killings had just occurred until the two stretchers were wheeled past the chow hall while breakfast was still being served. Pandemonium ensued, and it spread to a couple of housing units. A lot of violence could have been avoided if they had taken the stretchers through the corridors and not past the chow hall. It would have been just as quick.

We were locked down for a month. The worst thing about that was that I was locked in the cell with Clay, whose transfer was put on hold because of the lockdown. There was nothing I could do but grin and bear it.

I survived with my sanity intact, and when Clay was transferred a couple of weeks later; I didn't even say good-bye to him. I was just relieved that I would never have to deal with him again. I feel horrible about having such animosity for another human being, but something about him was just repulsive to me, and this was at a time when I was trying to live a more spiritual life. Looking back, I think he was lacking one character trait that would have been more appropriate for someone in his shoes—humility, a trait that cannot be feigned.

A new era of violence began at Pollock with these two killings. A football game that summer erupted into a knife fight in which one of the players was disemboweled. There were stabbings almost every day. Every morning on our way to breakfast, we would see a new trail of blood on the sidewalks. One night after band practice, I was walking back to my unit with my guitar and had to enter the bottleneck created by the fences that intersect at the center of the compound. Violence erupted. The target of the fury ran into me as he was trying to escape from his attackers. Although I was slammed into the fence, I continued walking as if nothing had happened. The reaction of the other witnesses was to plug their ears with their fingers, but the officers never saw a thing.

By this time, ninety-five percent of the inmates carried or had knives stashed somewhere. The sound of knives being sharpened was ubiquitous. I heard it when I jogged around the track. I heard it coming from the cells above mine at night, and I heard it in the UNICOR factory. The knife manufacturing business was a lucrative enterprise. Parts of the drum kit started going missing. Exit signs and metal light covers were removed and sharpened. They would take the stainless steel backs of the watches sold in the commissary and use them to cut knives from the bleachers around the softball field and basketball courts. Everything that wasn't tied down, and even things that were, were fashioned into weapons. The SHU was so full that the guys getting caught with knives weren't even locked up. The saying was, "I'd rather get caught with it than get caught without it."

I had decided when I was in Gulfport that I would start attending Catholic mass when I returned to Pollock. Panama used to beg me to go, but I didn't want to hear it, especially when I was still using. I told him that if I did go to church, I wasn't going to a Catholic service.

"The Protestants are like Burger King. 'Have it your way.' But with the Catholics, there is only one way, the original way, the true way," he would say.

So I finally gave it a shot.

Father Keith was the same age as I. He was short and a little chubby, with unruly, curly brown hair and glasses. He was very talented, smart, and full of contagious energy, wonderful characteristics for a spiritual leader.

The first day I went with Panama, Father Keith was playing a Celtic song on an acoustic guitar. It looked like some complicated shit and sounded really good. So of course he had me right there.

I was baptized and confirmed on All Saint's Day after several months of instruction. We had mass every Saturday and I truly looked forward to going. It was the first time that I didn't have to force myself to go to church..... or cringe after I got there.

We were locked down again in the fall of 2007, and no one knew why until we were interviewed the next day. Two more deaths, and again, it was one black and one white, but supposedly they weren't related. The white guy allegedly committed suicide by stabbing himself in the neck while in the shower. The black inmate was stabbed in the heart for the crime of snitching.

The Bureau of Prisons uses a point system to determine a prisoner's security level. From highest security to lowest, federal prisons are rated as one of the following: supermax, penitentiary, medium, low, and camp. For inmates, the criteria include percentage of time served, history of violence, drug use, on detainer from other law enforcement agencies, and other factors. These determine what type of prison an inmate is housed in. I'd already spent five years at Pollock. Finally my points were low enough for me to transfer to a medium security prison.

There was no better time to leave than now. I'd been lucky to spend this much time in a penitentiary without getting into serious trouble, but now I felt like my luck was running out. There had been too many close calls lately. A Christian acquaintance, whom I attended AA with, was singled out as a snitch and stabbed. He wasn't a snitch, though. He was just hated for being a stand-up Christian who had values different from the immoral majority. My friend and homeboy, Billy, had been put in for a transfer to the Marianna Federal Correctional Institute in Florida. Now that my AA friend had been stabbed, Billy and I were the only two left attending the AA meetings every Saturday morning in the education building. Out of fifteen hundred inmates, I would guess that at least eighty-five percent had problems with alcohol and drug use … and only two of us were trying to find an answer to our predicament. There was no end to the needling and ridicule we got from the other inmates, who thought they didn't have any problems nor had their own answers.

"Dave," one of the guys said to me, "where are you going?"

"AA. C'mon and go with me."

"Naw, I don't need that shit. The government's got you brainwashed."

"Some of us need our brains washed."

I decided to go ahead and try to get transferred to Marianna myself. It was closer to home, and I would be transferred somewhere eventually, anyway. I'd already been at Pollock for five years, locked up for seven, and had little more than five to go. The violence at Pollock was extreme and frequent, but never once did I have to fight or back down from a fight. I did my own thing and was respected for it.

It had been months since I'd seen Marilyn. The day after the last time I saw her, someone was found in one of the cells in the unit she was working in, stabbed pretty bad. I know she was afraid of the increasing violence and wanted to get a job working in one of the guard towers or outside the walls. I believe she finally achieved that goal after the stabbing. A male prison is no place for a woman to work, anyway, unless she's tough as nails. I'm glad she found a better place to work.

Billy and I were called to receiving and discharge at the same time to pack our property, but I was scratched off of the list at the last second. I had to wait two more weeks, until the week before Christmas, 2007, to catch a flight on "con air" to the Oklahoma City Federal Transfer Center.

Nothing had changed since I'd been there five years earlier. There was nothing to do but watch TV, play cards, work out, and read. Everyday was the same. I got stuck there for two months.

I made two good friends. Eric was a big biker dude from Des Moines, Iowa. He had pled guilty to selling methamphetamine for a life sentence so his wife wouldn't receive the same sentence, even though he said she had absolutely nothing to do with the crime. The feds gave her ten years, anyway. They had a three-year-old son who had to be put up for adoption. Man, I felt sorry for him. Sure, he should have known better, but what the feds did to this family was by no means protecting society. For every Eric they lock up for life, two or three more will spring up to take his place. There has got to be a better way.

Eric was a huge bear of a man, with a big, bushy beard, but he wouldn't hurt a flea, from what I could tell. He was being sent to a penitentiary for the first time, so I tried to give him all the advice I could.

My other new friend was Abdullah, an Egyptian from New York City. He was also a big guy with a beard, plus a shaved head, Malcolm X glasses, and a small tattoo of a flower in the middle of his forehead. When I first saw him, the impression he made on me was not good. He also had a life sentence, but had been down for a while.

As I got to know Abdullah, I learned my first impression could not have been more wrong. He looked like a very serious Muslim, appeared to be full of hatred, but, actually, he was hilarious and kept me in fits of laughter. I, a Catholic convert, joked with him about the Crusades or about him possibly being a failed suicide bomber, and of course he came back with jokes about pedophile priests or the Spanish Inquisition.

Eric, Abdullah, and I made an unlikely trio. A Midwestern, meth-addicted biker, an Egyptian Muslim from New York City and a drug-addicted white boy from Alabama. We didn't fit the stereotypes. While in prison, I made friends with guys like this, guys that didn't fit some stereotype, who thought outside the box. Panama, Bruce, and Patrick

El, who were not afraid to be themselves in a place where the pressure to conform is overwhelming and they didn't conform to anyone else's standards but their own,

Starting when I was a little kid who wasn't picked for the Little League team, every time I've ever made an effort to fit in or conform to the status quo, the results were disastrous for me, usually resulting in rejection. My talents have always been artistic, but those talents aren't exactly nurtured in south Alabama. My own history explains why I have respect for people who aren't afraid to be different, who aren't afraid to be themselves.

A camaraderie forms in places like prison, camaraderie not unlike the sort I've read about that forms in the military. When you're confined in close quarters with other guys for long periods of time, you can't help but get to know them better than you would under normal circumstances. Abdullah and I had Eric horrified by all the tales we told each other (and him) about the violence and lunacy we'd seen in penitentiaries. The sight of this huge man feeling afraid of his future was humorous, but it was also understandable. His size alone would ensure that he wouldn't have any problems from the other inmates. His problem was that the rest of his life had been stripped from him. He'd been buried alive.

The strength of my recovery was tested while I was at the transfer center. An older guy came in with a walker and was placed in the handicap cell. I'd gotten a job as an orderly for four dollars a week to sweep, mop, and serve dinner trays. It took up a little of my time and killed some of the boredom, and it also allowed me to buy coffee and get any food trays that were left over. (There is no commissary for the inmates in transfer; only for the orderlies, who can spend the four dollars they make.)

This older guy with the walker saw that I had access to the extra food and coffee. He had somehow smuggled in an Oxycontin tablet. (I assume he hid it in his walker.) What he wanted for it was some coffee and a few extra trays of food.

Oxycontin! After my long history of seeking drugs, the reward centers of my brain lit up. Hell, yes, I wanted it. But I was able to stop and analyze the situation. If I said yes, all my hope for the future would be shot to hell. Even so, the sleeping demon inside me looked up and murmured, "C'mon. Just this one time. No one here will know about it. You won't have to worry about it because you'll be gone any day now."

After three and a half years, the angel had gained a lot of strength, and the demon's pleadings were weak and pathetic. The angel said, "Three and a half years. We've done good! Betcha never thought you'd see the day. Sure, if you take this pill, you might, *might*, mind you, feel good for a few hours. Then what? Eventually, it will be offered again. Then what? And again. Then what?"

So I told the old man that I would see if anyone else wanted the pill. I wanted him to get rid of it as quick as possible so that it wouldn't still be there, tempting me. Old Beelzebub can be pretty persuasive. I wasn't going to snitch on him, not because I don't believe in snitching (what he was doing was more dangerous to me than to anyone else), but because I don't agree with the Bureau of Prison's or the federal government's punitive practices. Yeah, he should be punished, but taking away more of his life would only delay and exacerbate the inevitable. As far as I know, he never sold it. Eventually he left for his destination.

I had survived a major test. Saying no to the heroin, weed and alcohol at Pollock had become easy for me. But saying no to this pill had been a lot harder. It was cheap, I would have known exactly what I was getting, and no one here knew my history. I might have a future, after all.

I was awakened at three o'clock one morning soon after for another flight on "con air." Before I left Pollock, I'd been told that Billy had been transferred to Talladega instead of Marianna, so he was the last person I expected to see walking through the door of the holding cell that morning. There haven't been many other times that I've been so happy to see a familiar face. He was my homeboy and fellow AA comrade, and we were flying to Marianna together.

Chapter 14
The Last Leg

If you ever get a second chance in life for something, you've got to go all the way.
-LANCE ARMSTRONG
IT'S NOT ABOUT THE BIKE

I arrived at the Marianna Federal Correctional Institute in February 2008. Compared to Pollock, this place is not even a prison. There are no fights, no politics, and no gangs, except for a few wannabes. It took me a couple of months to realize that I don't have to constantly scan my surroundings and watching my back. (The sound of jangling keys, however, still puts me in a state of hyperawareness.) Inmates finish their sentences here, and just about every day someone goes home. Almost everyone has a release date in the not so distant future, so everyone behaves themselves for the most part. Of course, there are a few knuckleheads and crash test dummies.

Marianna has a drug treatment program and, regrettably, also a sex offender program, mostly for child molesters caught in Internet stings. That's the only thing about Marianna I don't like. Those guys disgust me, but society has seen fit to put them in the same garbage can as me, so I have no choice but to deal with it.

My release date is June 2013. If I get six months in a halfway house, I'll taste freedom by Christmas of 2012. Where I sit now, that's not too far away. I'll stay as busy as I can, and the time will fly by. When I get there, I'll be able to look back and say I achieved a lot. I've completed a Microsoft computer course and am also now a COMP TIA A+ certified computer technician (certified to tear some shit up. *Just a little humor*). At least I'll have picked up another job skill during my incarceration. I also got the payroll clerk position at UNICOR – the same job I had at Pollock.

I wish I could write a happy ending here and now, but the happy ending to this story can only come at the end of my life, when I'll be able to look back and say that I haven't used drugs or alcohol since October 15, 2004. I could continue writing this book for the next four and a half years that I'll be locked up, then write a happy ending that has me walking out of prison, a free man for the first time in twelve and a half years. While that will be a great day for me, it will probably be more nerve wrecking than anything else. And it won't be the end of the story; it will be the end of one chapter and the beginning of a new one.

Even though I've been clean for more than four years, I am by no means patting myself on the back. The real test will come when I walk through the prison gates. It's easier to say no to drugs in prison than it is on the street. I've seen a lot of drug addicts come into the prison system and stay clean the whole time they're in, but as soon as they step back outside these walls, they pick right up where they left off. Of course, these guys didn't see any reason to work on their recovery while they were in prison and couldn't wait to get back out and get high again.

For myself, I have to find some sort of higher meaning for my life. My question is not *what is the meaning of life?* It is *what does my life mean?* For most of my existence, my life has felt empty and meaningless—*what am I supposed to do? Where am I headed? What's the point?* I always tried to do what I thought was expected of me because I didn't know of any other way to act. Now I know that I have to, and want to, work in the field of addiction treatment.

It's almost a cliché for a drug addict to want to become a counselor when he or she gets clean. It's also stressed in AA and NA that if we want to keep what we have, we have to give it away. That's the twelfth step. We can give it away by telling our stories at meetings, bringing others to meetings, helping another addict work the steps ... there are plenty of ways. This is my purpose for writing this book. Here's another cliché, but it's true: if my story helps just one person, then I'll be satisfied that I achieved my goal. What higher calling could I possibly have than perhaps saving someone's life? And what could give my life more meaning?

I've wrestled with God over and over during my incarceration. I've reached out to him when all hope was gone, shunned him when he didn't answer right away and also shunned him when things were going a little better for me. I've learned that I will always need his presence in my life and that he's always there even when I can't see or feel him. I pray for his will and guidance, and the answer I've gotten back is that it is his will for me to help other addicts. Helping others will help keep me clean and give meaning to my life, and I will be doing his will. I need three things like the desert needs water: sobriety, meaning, and God's will.

I feel an affinity for other addicts, especially the ones who have suffered and are trying to find a better way to live their lives. I feel their pain as if it were my own. I wouldn't wish my worst enemy to endure the mental and physical pain I endured those first six months in 2000 after I was shot and arrested. There can be no worse suffering than trying to take your own life and not succeeding when you have only a small sliver of hope to hang onto to prevent another attempt.

That small sliver of hope has grown into a volcano of joy, and if I can rebound from the pit of hell I was in, I believe anyone can. My addiction to drugs was as strong as I believe an addiction can be. Saying I was hooked is inadequate; I was impaled and could not get loose without becoming self-destructive. The only way out I could see was to risk my own life and eventually try to take it.

I remember the self-pity I felt those first few months as clear as if it happened yesterday. I kept asking myself, *why? Why did I have to have this body and mind that craved drugs so strongly?* I felt like it wasn't my fault that I was sitting in a jail cell, facing years of my life in prison. I felt like it was a chain of events set in motion when I was fourteen and smoked that first joint, a chain of events that I was powerless to stop.

When I'm talking with other addicts about the prospect of future use, my response is, "Been there, done that." Drugs and alcohol have nothing left to offer me, but more pain, misery and self-doubts. More loss, more tears, more self-hatred, more depression, more suicidal thoughts, and no peace of mind. There are other things I want to experience with the time I have left in this world. I want to go mountain climbing, sailing, and kayaking; I want to go fishing with my dad. I want to go to an Alabama Crimson Tide football game. I want to run more marathons and make more music. And I want to help other addicts find a way out of their self-imposed prisons. I want my brother's life and death to have served a purpose. I don't want him to have died for nothing. The way I see it, if I use again, he will have died in vain. I keep him in my thoughts and prayers every day. Anytime I'm offered dope, his face should pop into my mind's eye. How could I ever use again? I want his life to have meaning, which is something it didn't have when he was alive and using.

Another thing that should keep me clean is knowing that I have hepatitis C. It would surely be a death sentence if I got hooked again and used like I did before. There is a treatment for this disease. Interferon is a chemotherapy-like treatment that kills the virus in a large percentage of carriers. It's something I dread, but I must endure it if I am to return to a normal healthy state of being. For now, I can't even tell I have the disease, but that could change any time. Illness is just another heavy price that I'm paying for my years of self-destruction.

Over and over again, I return to the same question—*Why?* Why did I become such a dope fiend? Almost all addicts I've met in rehab, NA, and prison had some kind of trauma, abuse, or other horrible experience when they were growing up. Physical abuse, sexual abuse, witnessing violence every day, abandonment, neglect, divorce … the list is long. But I have no such excuse. I could blame genetics. There are addicts on both sides of my family, but even scientists can't fully explain how this works, so any attempt I make to claim heredity as the source of my addiction can only be seen as groping for answers.

Since I am not a psychologist, a psychiatrist, or a geneticist, I can only examine the facts that are apparent to me after much, much soul searching. Thanks to a few failures and childhood slights, I developed an inferiority complex early in life. My weak personality wasn't strong enough to overcome the result of being compared to my peers, who seemed to be better than I was. I was so starved for attention that I became the life of the party after I got drunk at a school dance at fourteen. I saw that I could change myself from the person I didn't like to someone everyone was talking about and laughing at his crazy antics the next day at school. And so began my long perilous journey to my present predicament.

I will continue to seek the answer to *Why?* because I want to be able to help other addicts. It's true that addicts have to have the desire to quit before they can make any progress. You would have better luck taking a bone from a bulldog than convincing an addict who doesn't want to quit, to stop using. Most of us are in major denial that we even have a problem. But even after there is a desire to quit, staying quit can still be extremely hard. As I've said before, it's easy to quit, but hard staying quit. It has been the hardest thing I've ever had to do and will probably continue be the hardest thing I will ever have to do. And I won't ever be able to call myself a success in this regard because, God willing, I should have plenty of life left to live. And no one knows what the future holds. God forbid I should ever have some kind of accident and wake up in a hospital … attached to a morphine pump again. It would take a lot less to awaken the demon sleeping inside me.

I can never sit back and say that I've completely recovered from my addiction. It has been with me for so long that it now defines who I am. I've been blessed with (or cursed with) a large amount of energy, and, unfortunately, I funneled all that energy into my substance abuse. I guess the end result (robbing drug dealers, pharmacies, and banks) is what happens when this level of energy is combined with an obsession with mood-altering chemicals.

Now I have to put this same level of energy into my recovery. Recovery has to be maintained on a daily basis and be top priority in my life, the same place the drugs were when I was using. I went to great lengths to use. I drove long distances, used when I was sick, used when I was broke, and broke the law to get drugs. When the drugs took everything from me, I was still heavily devoted to them. Getting out from under all that is a tall order for my recovery, but at least I know I have the energy to go for it.

It was twenty years from my first toke on a joint to my last drink of alcohol. Twenty years that I gave my life to this devil of an affliction. For the first ten years, I managed to control my use, but for the second ten years, it controlled me. For the first ten years, I didn't think I had a problem and saw no reason to quit. For the second ten years, I knew I had a problem. But even after several attempts to quit, I couldn't do it. For the first ten years, drug use was fun and exciting. For the second ten years it was pure hell on earth. For the first ten years, I could have quit if I wanted to. For the second ten years, it was too late.

Several times, I reached what I thought was the bottom and said to myself, *It can't get any worse than this.* But each time, I crashed through the floor and found myself in a deeper hole. The pain I had endured upon my arrival at my last "bottom" permeated every cell in my being. That was it. I thought I'd hit bottom before, but this one was the real deal. But that time I knew it could get worse. And today I know there is still another bottom waiting for me. I've seen it in the eyes of my condemned comrades. I've heard it in their stories. I've felt it when they've bared their souls to me, and it has scared the hell out of me. Literally, I hope.

Even though I know tomorrow is not promised to us, I still believe the best days of my life lie ahead. I can hardly wait until my present mental and spiritual freedom is intertwined with physical freedom. I am expecting an explosion of joy unlike anything I've experienced before. But maybe I shouldn't allow my hopes and expectations to reach such an altitude. You've really got to be careful about what you wish for. Anyway, if it is really the darkest before dawn, then the sun must be about ready to come up.

My Top Ten Reasons Not to Use

10. I don't want to disappoint my family and friends.
9. I have other things in life I want to experience.
8. I will be a hypocrite. I despise hypocrites.
7. My liver cannot take any more damage
6. I've worked hard to achieve several years of sobriety. Let the sleeping demon stay asleep.
5. I should love life enough to not wish to escape from it.
4. I will become hooked, lose control, and commit more crimes.
3. I will lose my peace of mind.
2. Drugs killed my brother and will kill me.
1. I am tired of being a loser.

After word by David's Mother

I would like to start by expressing my tremendous love for David. Just like my love for all of my children. It is so hard when your child is hurting physically and mentally and there is not a thing you can do to help. David started journaling when he went to prison as a way to sort out his feelings. I encouraged him to do this, feeling that writing his story, along with all of his feelings and the things he is dealing with in this process of living with the situation he created for his life would help him more than a thousand hours of psychotherapy. I have the greatest admiration for David, for his courage to write his story for the public to read and to honestly bare his soul, as he has in this book. If this book helps one person, it will be worth it.

Seeing his total honesty, I have to be totally honest myself.

Writing this book has been difficult for David, because he did not have access to a computer. He had to write each page out by hand, then go to the prison library and type it on a typewriter. When he had fifty or so pages, he put them in the mail to me. I believe the actual writing of this book took between two and three years. When he finally had written everything down and brought his story up to the present, he gave me the order in which to arrange the pages, so I could begin keying them in on my computer in order to get them in a format a publisher could work with. As we worked through this process, we corresponded by telephone twice a month, exchanged regular e-mails, and worked with his editor, Barbara Ardinger, in Long Beach, California and his cover designer Sundara Fawn from Ashville, North Carolina. Working on this book had challenges, it as I read and typed it, I have had to relive David's many challenges and the things he did. I know I would have come completely unglued if I'd had any idea the true extent of David's drug use and the lengths he went to obtaining drugs before he was arrested.

When my children were small, we talked about drugs and alcohol, but in our small town, we didn't think there was a drug problem. After all "*my*" children were "too smart" to use drugs, at least that is what I thought. A teen experimenting with alcohol was just a "normal" part of the process of growing up, so that was considered no big deal. *Wrong.* According to David, he was every parent's worst nightmare.

When David went on his crime spree, it was absolutely the most horrific, heart-breaking experience that has ever happened in my life. During the ten days he was missing, I was sure he would not come back alive. We were heartbroken and devastated. Although I tried to keep up my normal schedule as a realtor in Mobile, Alabama, I cried as I drove home every night. If my husband was home, I wiped my eyes and put a half smile on my face so I wouldn't bring him down, too. I remember one night. When I went to bed, I was in a low mood. I kept crying and saying, "Why? Why? Why?" I just did not understand why this had to happen. During that night, this old hymn started running through my head over and over:

Farther along we'll know all about it,
Farther along we'll understand why;
Cheer up my brother, live in the sunshine,
We'll understand it all by and by.1

This was God's answer to me. Further along, down this road of life, we will understand it all. The words of this hymn gave me the peace of mind I needed to work through my pain, grief and disappointment.

I had previously thought that losing Brian to death from his drug use was the absolutely worst thing that could happen to our family. I was so numb when he died that I was in a daze. Yes, I functioned, but I walled myself off so I didn't feel the hurt. My coworkers could not understand how I could come to work and act normal, but thanks to my solid, emotional brick wall I could do it.

I myself had a very difficult childhood. I was the oldest child of five born to my artist mother and my career military father. My dad was twenty years older than my mother, and I think he probably treated her as one of the children. He was military all the way. While we lived on Long Island in New York, my mother gave birth to five children in a little over six and one half years and there was two and one half years between my brother Billy and I! After the fourth child, she had a nervous breakdown. (Today we would call it post-partum depression.) The doctor advised my father that they should not have any more children, that her health and mental state could not withstand another pregnancy. But my dad didn't believe the doctor. After all, his mother had borne ten children and it hadn't hurt her! So sixteen months after my younger sister was born, my

---

1 "Farther Along," Words and music by J.R. Baxter and W.B. Stevens. Copyright © 1937 *In Public Domain* by Stamps-Baxter Music.

youngest sister was born. And my mom had another nervous breakdown from which she never recovered.

My dad did not get along with my mother's parents. I suspect that he kept her isolated from her parents, as I have no memory of them visiting us or us going to see them. This means my mother had all these children with absolutely no help or support. When my mother had her last nervous breakdown (I don't remember the first one), I remember she went missing and the police, my father and all of the neighbors were out looking for her. I remember it getting dark and I was very scared and upset. My dad raised chickens and garden produce, which he sold, in addition to having an electrical contracting business. My aunt told me that my mom was supposed to take care of all of the chickens and the garden in addition to her children, while my dad was working all day. I remember trying to help by gathering the eggs, but the chickens would bite me when I tried to gather the eggs, so I was little help. My mom was found that night under some feed sacks in the chicken house.

My dad then hired a series of housekeepers, and I was supposed to help keep the other kids quiet and in line. I remember trying to get the other children to be quiet and behave, to no avail, after all I was only six. So when my youngest sister was nine months old, my dad sold everything and we moved to Alabama for my grandmother to take care of us. My grandmother was a harsh, mean, unhappy woman who beat my oldest brother and me with a belt or anything else she could get her hands on. We lived there for almost seven years, until one day my grandmother hit me over the head with a chair and I decided I just wasn't going to take it anymore. I told my brother, Billy,

"I am going to run away." My plan was to go to town, hop on a train, and get as far away as I could.

Billy said, "If you're leaving, I'm going with you."

I said, "No," we argued until he finally saw he was not getting anywhere with me.

Then he said, "I am going to tell on you if you don't let me go, too."

So I said, "Okay." We spent the night in the attic of a house my dad owned, where our housekeeper lived. Early the next morning we left. Just before we reached the railroad tracks, however, the police picked us up. They took us to the home of one of my favorite aunt and uncles, where we stayed while our dad made plans to board us in the Methodist Children's Home in Selma, Alabama. The children's home was almost like heaven to me. We were encouraged to study and received an allowance for doing chores and making good grades. I was encouraged to develop my artistic talent and I learned to sew, in fact I became quite good at it. We went swimming, to movies and roller-skating, things I was never allowed to do, except on the very rare time my dad took us. We lived there for one year. Then, my dad got married again to a woman who was so good to us, it was as close to a real home as we could get. My stepmother helped my father see that he needed to allow us to be children. I won't go into any more details about me, because this book is about David, not me. With all of the things that happened to me as a child, I learned early on to wall my emotions off, to avoid the tremendous emotional pain I felt. It seemed that every time I opened a crack in the wall, someone or something devastated me.

I now realize in the deepest part of my heart, that I was not there for my children emotionally. I can remember times when I reacted very differently than most people would have reacted, to many situations in my children's young lives. It was like my emotions were frozen. I realize that I am a product of my dad's upbringing, as he was a product of his parents' upbringing. I have inflicted my own emotional childhood pain onto my children. For that I am very sorry. My dad never told me he loved me until the very last year of his life, and, unfortunately, I had the same inability to express my love for my children in a verbal way until they were grown and the negative patterns had already taken hold. I had nothing in my memory bank to know what a normal, supportive parent would do. I felt that because I was able to break the cycle of physical abuse, I was doing well. Even though I did the best I could with the experience I had to work with, today I am deeply sorry for having hurt my children.

I am so very proud of David for his courage in baring the most intimate parts of his life and holding nothing back. I know his future is going to be bright and that the best is yet to come for him. He has discovered that the root of addiction is not the use of substances, but patterns deep in the developing brain of a young child. He is studying and looking for an answer to the root question, *Why?* The abuse of drugs alcohol, food, sex, gambling, overspending, and anything else that interferes with living your life to its fullest is only a symptom. You cannot cure a symptom. You must get to the root cause.

At this point in time, David is at the Marianna Federal Correctional Institution where he has been moved into the drug unit. He continues to study and learn more about addictions and the root cause. I feel he is ready to live his life as a clean, responsible member of society.

Contact Information

Contact Author: David.Allan.Reeves@gmail.com
Contact Publisher: www.Trafford.com
Author's web site: www.RunningAwayFromMe.com
Contact Author for volume information on discount to purchase more than five copies of "Running Away From Me."

Bionote

David Allan Reeves was born on November 12, 1969 in Mobile, Alabama. David graduated from Jackson Academy high school in 1988. He studied psychology and art at the University of South Alabama and Troy State University-Montgomery. He presently works in the prison industry UNICOR, as a payroll clerk, keeping track of pay for the other inmates.

He also completed twenty-eight days at the Bowling Green Institute for his drug addiction and graduated from the Substance Abuse Program in the Alabama Department of Corrections and the CODE and Challenge programs at the United States Penitentiary in Pollock, Louisiana. He currently resides at the Federal Correctional Facility in Marianna, Florida, where he expects to be released in 2012.

Printed in the United States
By Bookmasters